HEGEL'S WORLD REVOLUTIONS

Hegel's World Revolutions

RICHARD BOURKE

PRINCETON UNIVERSITY PRESS

PRINCETON & OXFORD

Published by Princeton University Press
41 William Street, Princeton, New Jersey 08540
99 Banbury Road, Oxford OX2 6JX

press.princeton.edu

All Rights Reserved

Library of Congress Cataloging-in-Publication Data

Names: Bourke, Richard, author.
Title: Hegel's world revolutions / Richard Bourke.
Description: Princeton, New Jersey : Princeton University Press, 2023. |
    Includes bibliographical references and index.
Identifiers: LCCN 2023019043 (print) | LCCN 2023019044 (ebook) |
    ISBN 9780691250182 (hardback) | ISBN 9780691253114 (ebook)
Subjects: LCSH: Hegel, Georg Wilhelm Friedrich, 1770–1831—Political
    and social views. | Revolutions. | France—History—Revolution,
    1789–1799—Influence. | BISAC: POLITICAL SCIENCE / History &
    Theory | HISTORY / Military / Revolutions & Wars of Independence
    (see also United States / Revolutionary Period (1775–1800))
Classification: LCC JC233.H46 B664 2023 (print) | LCC JC233.H46
    (ebook) | DDC 944.04—dc23/eng/20230511
LC record available at https://lccn.loc.gov/2023019043
LC ebook record available at https://lccn.loc.gov/2023019044

British Library Cataloging-in-Publication Data is available

Editorial: Ben Tate and Josh Drake
Production Editorial: Nathan Carr
Jacket/Cover Design: Isabel Kokko
Production: Lauren Reese
Publicity: William Pagdatoon and Charlotte Coyne

Jacket/Cover Credit: Jean-Léon Gérôme, *Bonaparte Before the Sphinx*,
1886, France

This book has been composed in Arno

10 9 8 7 6 5 4 3 2 1

CONTENTS

ACKNOWLEDGEMENTS

THIS BOOK WAS first conceived at Queen Mary University of London and written at the University of Cambridge, with a short stint in between at the Freie Universität in Berlin. I owe to my then London colleagues an accumulated debt of gratitude. I should like to mention in particular Martyn Frampton, Patrick Higgins, Julian Jackson, Colin Jones, Miri Rubin, Georgios Varouxakis and Emma Yates. I also had the pleasure of working closely with Quentin Skinner over a period of ten years in London and am pleased to have this opportunity to record my sincere thanks to him for his help and advice over that decade and beyond.

At the University of Cambridge, I have benefited from working with many scholars in the history of political thought, including Duncan Bell, Annabel Brett, Christopher Brooke, Tom Hopkins, Samuel James, Shruti Kapila, Duncan Kelly, Luke Ilott, Adam Lebovitz, Emma Mackinnon, Chris Meckstroth, Jessica Patterson, Max Skjönsberg, David Runciman, Magnus Ryan, Sylvana Tomaselli and Samuel Zeitlin. I have also greatly benefited from my immediate colleagues in the field at King's College, not least John Dunn, John Filling, Ross Harrison, Tejas Parasher, Mira Siegelberg, Michael Sonenscher and Gareth Stedman Jones.

I have also been able to draw on the knowledge of Germanists, at Cambridge and elsewhere. Special thanks are due to

Christopher Clark, Eckhart Hellmuth, Charlotte Johann, Avi Lifschitz, Isaac Nakhimovsky, Martin Ruehl, Emily Steinhauer and Joachim Whaley. Included in this category are also scholars focused on German Idealism and Hegel in particular. In this connection, I have been helped in various ways by Elias Buchetmann, Andrew Chignell, Fernanda Gallo, Olivier Higgins, Stephen Houlgate, Reidar Maliks, Douglas Moggach, Michael Morris, Brian O'Connor, Robert Pippin, Robert Stern and Allen Wood.

More generally, I have drawn support from colleagues in political theory and the history of political thought in Britain, Europe, and the United States, including from Bruce Ackerman, David Armitage, David Bromwich, Greg Conti, Jon Elster, Seamus Flaherty, Ultán Gillen, Dina Gusejnova, James Harris, Eva Marlene Hausteiner, Melissa Lane, Noel Malcolm, Karuna Mantena, Samuel Moyn, Julia Nicholls, Niall O'Flaherty, Jennifer Pitts, Lucia Rubinelli, Paul Sagar, William Selinger, James Stafford, Richard Tuck, Richard Whatmore, David Wootton and Lea Ypi.

Research for this book was funded by the Alexander von Humboldt Foundation as well as the Deutscher Akademischer Austauschdienst. I also benefited from a Fellowship at the Wissenschaftskolleg zu Berlin in 2014–15. The publication of the book was greatly assisted by the efforts of James Pullen at the Wiley Agency and Ben Tate at Princeton University Press. My thanks are also due to David Edmonds and Emer Nolan for advice, as well as to the anonymous readers of the manuscript for their constructive criticism, which I was happy to follow. I am also obliged to Josh Drake, Nathan Carr, Susan Clark, Francis Eaves, Isabel Kokko and Lauren Reese for their care and tenacity in preparing the final version of the work.

Finally, I am above all grateful to Beatrice Collier, not least for her engagement with this project from the beginning.

PREFACE

A KEY FEATURE of modernity is the advance it made on previous epochs of world history. Despite this forward movement, the achievement represented by the rise of the West is widely censured within our culture. Hard-won values are cast aside as instruments of coercion. Liberalism itself is denounced as a form of subtle bondage. Correspondingly, universalism is condemned and rights disparaged. The engine of improvement is likewise excoriated: reason is convicted of domineering arrogance and enlightenment dismissed as retrogressive. These assumptions enjoy a prominent place in academic commentary. While their roots lie deep in nineteenth-century forms of pessimism, they later became an intellectual fashion. What started as an eccentric tradition of historical reflection—beginning with Friedrich Nietzsche and culminating in Michel Foucault—now occupies a central place on university courses. As a result, whole generations have been coaxed into a posture of suspicion. Freedom is equated with domination; equality is exposed as a means of exclusion; and liberal democracy is taken to be complicit with imperialism. Yet notwithstanding the pervasiveness of these ideas, they are belied by careful historical analysis. This confirms that while liberal values have indeed been embroiled in power politics, they were not the cause of systematic oppression. The modern world is still replete with glaring cases of injustice, but nonetheless its history records a process of liberation.

This view was first articulated by G.W.F. Hegel. During a career that spanned the first third of the nineteenth century, he revolutionised the study of history and philosophy. This led to transformative insights into the character of modern politics. One aspect of Hegel's originality derives from the nature of his approach. He interpreted recent developments in the context of world history: his framework was both trans-temporal and inter-continental. As he once reminded his readership, he studied the results of human labour over the course of 'several thousand years'.[1] This led to a comparative mode of investigation. Hegel's subject was the rise of modern values, which he situated in a longer-term account of civilisations. He focused on the progress from ancient China, India, Persia and Egypt to the formation of modern European society. While Hegel was in awe of the accomplishments of earlier periods, pining over the ruins of Palmyra and Persepolis, he also believed that modern conditions represented a breakthrough. In recent times, this judgement has been regarded as partisan and self-regarding. Hegel's endorsement of modernity has been chided as Eurocentric—as a parochial perspective that should in turn be provincialised. Yet this assessment has been informed by an inadequate grasp of the facts. At the same time, the criticism was intended to serve an ideological agenda. For Hegel's adversaries, justice requires that politics be cleansed of its past. However, for Hegel himself, progress presupposes building on existing resources. True reform, it followed, was dialectical in nature: it had to preserve as well as abolish and transcend.

---

1. G.W.F. Hegel, *Elements of the Philosophy of Right* (1821), ed. Allen W. Wood, trans. H. B. Nisbet (Cambridge: Cambridge University Press, 1991), p. 16.

Hegel's embrace of values that first emerged in Europe was not the product of idle prejudice. He was not motivated by either cultural or geographical chauvinism. What he championed, specifically, was a set of norms. He prized above all else the modern constitutional state based on the ideal of universal freedom. It so happened that this ideal originally appeared in Europe. But its emergence was of wider, cosmopolitan significance. One does not have to be French, British or German to appreciate the fundamental value of humanity. The principle is applicable in America, India and China. Nonetheless, it so happens that the precept of universal equality has identifiable historical origins. It appeared with the demise of Greco-Roman society and the rise of Christianity. It taught one consequential lesson: namely, that 'the human being as human is free'.[2] Hegel viewed this doctrine as an epoch-making development that had eluded Greek philosophy and Roman jurisprudence. It constituted a final revolution in consciousness. Its significance was that it marked the beginning of the end of slavery. Modern history had been a struggle to figure out its consequences. Indenture, serfdom and subjection to despotism were acceptable in the past but today they rank as abominations. Hegel took the transition to have resulted from intellectual change. Servitude presupposed different categories of human being. But it was challenged by the idea that 'the human being *as such* is free'.[3]

There is a bold simplicity to Hegel's central insight. The achievement of modernity was the termination of servile status.

2. G.W.F. Hegel, 'Introduction, 1830–31', in *Lectures on the Philosophy of World History: Manuscripts of the Introduction and Lectures of 1822–3*, ed. and trans. Robert F. Brown and Peter C. Hodgson, with William G. Geuss (Oxford: Clarendon Press, 2011), p. 88.

3. Ibid., p. 110.

But there was nothing automatic about this transformation. On Hegel's telling, it was an arduous and protracted process. In fact, the implications of the struggle for freedom had yet to be resolved since, far from having come to an end, history still faced an ordeal ahead. It was already a painful irony in Hegel's day that the aspiration to liberty flowered in the era of the Atlantic slave trade.[4] Even in the final year of his life, Hegel maintained that the meaning of freedom remained indeterminate. Looking back over forty years since the advent of the French Revolution, he remarked that the idea of liberty had been subject to 'misunderstandings, confusions, and errors, including every possible aberration'.[5] As this claim shows, there was nothing complacent about Hegel's assessment of contemporary society. However, its radical imperfections did not invalidate its chief gain. Hegel believed that Roman law had lacked the concept of a human being as demonstrated by its distinction between person (*persona*) and slave (*servus*).[6] In contrast to this impoverished definition of subjectivity, the modern world had enriched the notion of the individual. In universalising the concept of humankind, it 'completed' the idea of freedom, notwithstanding the fact that this was neither a linear nor a cost-free process. Nonetheless, in Hegel's mind, there was no doubting the overarching dividend. For that reason, he traced its evolution in its moral, religious, aesthetic and political dimensions. This book reconstructs his account of its unfolding course. Its development was the product of a sequence of world revolutions. Yet these were

4. G.W.F. Hegel, 'Vorlesungsnachschrift, K. G. v. Griesheim, 1824–5', in *Vorlesungen über Rechtsphilosophie, 1818–1831*, ed. Karl-Heinz Ilting, 4 vols (Stuttgart: Frommann-Holzboog, 1973–74), 4, p. 89.

5. Hegel, 'Introduction, 1830–31', p. 89.

6. Hegel, *Philosophy of Right*, §2.

not a series of cumulative successes, but rather a string of consequential failures.

In examining Hegel's treatment of world revolutions, the book is an exercise in elucidation. In the first place it seeks to clarify his conception of revolution as such. Hegel began with the paradigmatic case of the Christian revolution, which had transformed the Judaic understanding of the relationship between virtue and happiness. In advancing his analysis, Hegel drew on the thought of Immanuel Kant. Like him, Hegel regarded Christianity as having ended in failure. For Kant this outcome was brought about by inadequate moral commitment on the part of human beings. In response, Hegel strove to work out a properly historical explanation. This set him on the trail of diagnosing a sequence of world-historical mishaps, including the Reformation and the French Revolution. Each of these adventures had misfired, Hegel contended, because they pitted an awakening of moral conscience against existing means of improving ethical life. It was above all the bankruptcy of the French Revolution that haunted Hegel's philosophical career. For while he acknowledged that it encapsulated the moral ambitions of the age, he also regarded its mode of proceeding as having ensured its own destruction. Its abstract principles heralded a new dawn. Yet in practice they promoted a blind assault on things as they stood. In Hegel's terms, the Revolution embodied a spirit of pure 'negation', thereby failing to ground its values in institutions that might facilitate constructive political change.

For Hegel, the Revolution was not an agent of progressive reform, but a wayward symptom of the wider culture of the age. A second principal objective of this book is to delineate Hegel's understanding of this larger historical domain. Whilst the Revolution saw an eruption of disembodied ideas of freedom, the revolt took place against a more conducive background. In the shadow of the Christian conception of value, and the aftermath of the decline of feudalism, the rigid structures of a rank-ordered society had been steadily dismantled. In its place, a system of rights based on free subjectivity was incrementally established, with widespread and transformative consequences.[7] Religious dogmatism declined and the rights of property were more securely entrenched. At the same time, marriage contracts were liberalised while professional vocations became a matter of choice. In global terms, the division of society into clear-cut castes had been undermined. More locally, the accident of birth no longer determined social or political roles. The processes of civil society had devoured hereditary stratification. Hegel himself was critical of many of the results: 'atomism' led to isolation and 'liberalism' to fragmentation.[8] Consequently, any defence of liberal modernity had to be qualified and hedged.

It is plain, then, that as he surveyed the landscape of modern Europe, Hegel's most enthusiastic hopes had not been realised. In Britain, Germany and France, public accountability was incomplete. The organs of government were poorly differentiated and inadequately reconciled. Just as perplexing, rich and poor in civil society were condemned to collide. In general, rights had improved, but they remained imperfect. Moreover, they often conflicted with social welfare. Yet even drastic misfortune was not a recipe for despair. Hegel accepted, along with Thomas

---

7. G.W.F. Hegel, *Die Philosophie des Rechts: Die Mitschriften Wannemann (Heidelberg 1817/18) und Homeyer (Berlin 1818/19)*, ed. Karl-Heinz Ilting (Stuttgart: Klett-Cotta, 1983), §26A.

8. On atomism—'das Prinzip der Atomistik'—see ibid., §121A. For criticism of liberalism, see, for example, G.W.F. Hegel, *Vorlesungen über die Philosophie der Weltgeschichte 3: Nachschriften zum Kolleg des Wintersemesters 1826/27*, ed. Walter Jaeschke (*Gesammelte Werke 27.3*) (Hamburg: Felix Meiner Verlag, 2019), p. 1146.

Hobbes, that the state had been a benefit to civilisation, as well as agreeing, with David Hume and Adam Smith, that modern social and economic refinements had alleviated forms of subordination. Finally, he recognised, with Jean-Jacques Rousseau and Kant, that the capacity for freedom had granted opportunities for moral and political progress. Even so, from Hegel's perspective, there could be no guarantees against squandering these acquisitions. Yet he equally believed there would be no merit in sacrificing accumulated assets in the name of empty moral criticism. History had arrived at the consummate realisation that each person by virtue of their humanity was free and, given this attainment, political judgement could best orientate itself by refusing to go backwards. This meant conceding that modern consciousness would never trade its emancipation for superannuated forms of enthralment.

Ironically, despite his reputation for premature optimism, Hegel's verdict was a product of profound scepticism. In fact, he argued that the human mind was driven by its inclination to doubt. His whole system of thought was likewise structured around the practice of critique. But he also contended that it was superstitious to assume that doubt could never deliver certainty. Hegelianism is nothing if not a form of speculative knowledge worked out through a process of sceptical inquiry. Its subject is the education of the human race. In relaying his findings, Hegel took his audience on a tour of the past covering the totality of civilisational developments. Modern interpreters have underplayed this wealth of empirical material in order to extract from his thought accessible moral lessons. Alexandre Kojève, one of Hegel's most influential twentieth-century readers, exemplified this tendency. In order to illustrate the downside to this approach, the third main topic covered by this book is the reception of Hegel's ideas. Given the constraints of the argument, my focus is on the renaissance in Hegel studies that began around the turn of the twentieth century. For that reason, no attempt is made to retell the story of 'Young Hegelianism' as it played out in the nineteenth century. Accordingly, Marx's appropriation of Hegel's thought, although obviously a decisive event, is not my concern in the pages that follow. Given the scale of scholarship on Marx, his Hegelianism is a subject which needs dedicated treatment.

My goal in outlining the main features of the Hegel renaissance is to prepare the ground for an appraisal of the turn against Hegelianism, which I associate with Martin Heidegger, Theodor Adorno and Karl Popper. The consequences of this revaluation have left an enduring mark on intellectual life since the Second World War. The initial turnaround then accelerated through the 1960s. Some of the impact of the new priorities was sketched at the beginning of this preface. These twists in Hegel's fortune raise further questions about the uses to which celebrated thinkers can fairly be put. My interest is in Hegel as a political philosopher, and therefore in the purpose served by studying venerated figures of the kind. Addressing this issue makes up the final objective of the book. In many ways, the study of past political ideas was transformed by historians in the late 1960s. Unwittingly they were building on an older hermeneutical tradition, of which Hegel was himself a leading representative. According to him, the philosopher-historian should accept the death of the past instead of trying to resuscitate outmoded forms of thought. I conclude by assessing rival approaches to past ideas. This involves comparing historicism with revivalism. We are forced to ask: if great thinkers are merely products of their historical circumstances, how can we reanimate their antiquated wisdom?

HEGEL'S WORLD REVOLUTIONS

Introduction

INFLUENTIAL ELEMENTS WITHIN postwar intellectual culture staged a sort of insurgency against Hegel. The impact of this opposition is most immediately apparent from Hegel's diminished standing in university curricula. This contrasts starkly with his preeminent stature during earlier periods. For the German émigré thinker Leo Strauss, Hegel was 'the outstanding philosopher of the nineteenth century'.[1] This verdict was hardly an eccentric one. For many, Hegel's genius dominated the thought of the age. To begin with, his writings transformed philosophy between 1807 and 1831. During that period, a series of towering works appeared—the *Phenomenology of Spirit*, the *Science of Logic* and the *Encyclopedia of the Philosophical Sciences*—which completely reoriented the discipline. In addition, after his death, his philosophy played a commanding role through the middle decades of the century. But even if Hegel is denied his dominant position, he remains a vital link in the traditions of German thought extending from Kant and Fichte to Nietzsche and Heidegger. Besides, his overwhelming importance

1. Leo Strauss, 'Political Philosophy and History' (1949), in *What is Political Philosophy? And Other Studies* (Chicago: Chicago University Press, 1988), p. 58.

was in any case guaranteed by his place within the history of Marxism. Yet, notwithstanding his profound significance, his prestige as a political thinker has declined. In the anglophone world over recent decades, the study of his epistemology and metaphysics have revived, driven by the work of Robert Pippin, Terry Pinkard, Robert Brandom and John McDowell.[2] There have also been major treatments of his moral philosophy.[3] Yet there has barely been a monograph devoted to his political ideas since the beginning of the 1970s.[4]

The slump in attention was partly determined by the demise of Marxism as a worldview connected to a major state. Down to 1989, the Hegelian tradition was an inescapable feature of international realpolitik, and so inevitably garnered ongoing consideration.[5] In the United States, Hegel also continued to be invoked

---

2. See Paul Redding, *Analytical Philosophy and the Return of Hegelian Thought* (Cambridge: Cambridge University Press, 2007).

3. Allen W. Wood, *Hegel's Ethical Theory* (Cambridge: Cambridge University Press, 1990); Michael Hardimon, *Hegel's Social Philosophy: The Project of Reconciliation* (Cambridge: Cambridge University Press, 1994); Alan Patten, *Hegel's Idea of Freedom* (Oxford: Oxford University Press, 1999); Frederick Neuhouser, *Foundations of Hegel's Social Theory: Actualizing Freedom* (Cambridge, MA: Harvard University Press, 2000); Robert Pippin, *Hegel's Practical Philosophy: Rational Agency as Ethical Life* (Cambridge: Cambridge University Press, 2008).

4. Shlomo Avineri, *Hegel's Theory of the Modern State* (Cambridge: Cambridge University Press, 1972). In the same decade, in Germany, Karl-Heinz Ilting transformed the study of the *Philosophy of Right* with his edition of (and 'Introduction' to) G.W.F. Hegel, *Vorlesungen über Rechtsphilosophie, 1818–1831*, ed. Karl-Heinz Ilting, 4 vols (Stuttgart: Frommann-Holzboog, 1973–74). But see now in addition the important study, Elias Buchetmann, *Hegel and the Representative Constitution* (Cambridge: Cambridge University Press, 2023).

5. As evidenced by Z. A. Pelczynski, ed., *Hegel's Political Philosophy: Problems and Perspectives* (Cambridge: Cambridge University Press, 1971); Pelczynski, ed., *The State and Civil Society: Studies in Hegel's Political Philosophy* (Cambridge: Cambridge University Press, 1984); Leszek Kolakowski, *Main Currents of Marxism*, vol. 1: *The Founders*, trans. P. S. Falla (Oxford: Clarendon Press, 1978).

in debates about communitarianism, largely through the work of Charles Taylor.[6] Even so, with the rise of John Rawls, his canonical status dropped. In truth, by that point his imposing presence had already seriously receded. To some extent this was a function of developments within political philosophy. A new departure can be dated to the first concerted attempts to discredit German thought during the First World War.[7] Within another generation Hegel's work was being marginalised, indeed ridiculed, by Karl Popper and Isaiah Berlin. Their efforts were reinforced by the literature on totalitarianism, with whose triumph they had associated Hegel.[8] If this equation was bizarre, it nevertheless persisted.[9] Yet there are further cultural reasons for the diminution of Hegel's status, connected to the rise of anti-humanist thought in France and its remarkable success in the American academy. The label 'anti-humanist' is a somewhat general term intended to capture the turn away from Jean-Paul Sartre and Simone de Beauvoir, who had dominated the French intellectual scene in the 1940s and 1950s.[10] The shift had already begun with the writings of Claude Lévi-Strauss, as exemplified by the polemical final chapter in his classic study *The Savage Mind*.[11] The move against Hegel began to stir at approximately the same time. Its

6. Charles Taylor, 'Hegel's Ambiguous Legacy for Modern Liberalism', *Cardozo Law Review*, 10: 5–6 (March-April 1989), pp. 857–70.

7. J. H. Muirhead, *German Philosophy in Relation to the War* (London: John Murray, 1915).

8. Walter Kaufman, 'The Hegel Myth and its Method', *The Philosophical Review*, 60: 4 (October 1951), pp. 459–86.

9. John Bowle, *Politics and Opinion in the Nineteenth Century: An Historical Introduction* (New York: Oxford University Press, 1954), p. 43.

10. Luc Ferry and Alain Renault, *French Philosophy of the Sixties: An Essay on Antihumanism* (Amherst, MA: University of Massachusetts Press, 1990).

11. Claude Lévi-Strauss, 'History and Dialectic', in *The Savage Mind* (1962) (London: Weidenfeld and Nicolson, 1966).

protagonists were personalities such as Jacques Derrida, Michel Foucault, Gilles Deleuze and Jean-François Lyotard.

These disparate critics arrived on the scene after the 'return' to Hegel in mid-century France, associated with Jean Wahl, Alexandre Kojève and Jean Hyppolite. Their classic studies, which appeared between 1929 and 1947, had influenced a generation of existentialists led by Sartre, Beauvoir and Maurice Merleau-Ponty. New translations of essential works consolidated this revival. Reflecting on Hyppolite's interpretation of Hegel in 1947, Merleau-Ponty regarded the *Phenomenology of Spirit* as the source of all 'the great philosophical ideas of the past century'.[12] Even his critics, such as Søren Kierkegaard and Marx, are unintelligible in their own terms. In fact, in Merleau-Ponty's eyes, his opponents were closer to their instructor than they cared to recognise. For his part, Merleau-Ponty found in Hegel intimations of a plausible system. He believed that, far from having attempted to subject the data of history to 'a framework of pre-established logic', as was often supposed, Hegel revealed the meaning of experience according to an immanent process of development.[13] So in the 1940s, at least in France, Hegel was a starting point for philosophical discussion, rather than an object of shallow criticism.

II

However, in the 1960s a new mindset took root, and with its appearance a distinct understanding of Hegel emerged. In an aphoristic statement collected in the *Will to Power*, Nietzsche

---

12. Maurice Merleau-Ponty, 'Hegel's Existentialism', in *Sense and Non-Sense*, trans. Hubert L. Dreyfus and Patricia Allen Dreyfus (Evanston, IL: Northwestern University Press, 1964), p. 63.

13. Ibid., p. 65.

had argued that Hegel, like all great German philosophers, embodied a species of 'romanticism' forever afflicted by 'homesickness'.[14] According to this rendition, the longing for meaning distorted the search for truth in German Idealism. Foucault's *History of Madness* sought to expose this very distortion. Hegel became the foil against which the unmasking was conducted. Having operated as a kind of model, he now became a target. But what was derided was in truth a parody of Hegel of the kind on display in Nietzsche's depiction. The caricature gained momentum through the 1950s, encouraged by Louis Althusser's attack on Hegelian mystification.[15] Foucault challenged the same doctrines though often without mentioning Hegel's name. At other times he was more explicit: 'our entire epoch', he stressed in his inaugural lecture of 1970, 'is trying to escape [*d'échapper*] from Hegel'.[16] Usually arguing indirectly, Foucault dismissed core idealist principles such as the 'synthetic activity of the subject' and the 'movement of totalization' as superstitious legends.[17] Whilst the influence of Hyppolite is acknowledged in the *History of Madness*, and Hegel's discussion of *Rameau's Nephew* is mentioned in the work, the dialectic is dismissed by Foucault as a mystical delusion. Instead of charting what he termed the

14. Friedrich Nietzsche, *The Will to Power* (c. 1885), ed. Walter Kaufmann, trans. Kaufman and R. J. Hollingdale (New York: Random House: 1967), §419.

15. Louis Althusser, 'The Return to Hegel: The Latest Word in Academic Revisionism' (1950), in *The Spectre of Hegel: Early Writings*, trans. G. M. Goshgarian (London: Verso, 1997).

16. Michel Foucault, *L'Ordre du discours* (Paris: Gallimard, 1971), p. 30. Cf. Michel Foucault, 'La Grande Colère des faits', *Le Nouvel Observateur*, 652 (9–15 May 1977), pp. 84–86.

17. Michel Foucault, *The Archaeology of Knowledge* (1969), trans. A. M. Sheridan Smith (London: Tavistock Publications, 1972), p. 14.

'becoming of Western reason', he analysed the 'repression' carried out in its name.[18]

Foucault's narrative of the rise of reason during what he billed as 'the Classical age' aimed to replace the 'dialectic of history' with an avowedly Nietzschean style of interpretation.[19] Throughout his career down to the 1980s, Foucault would refine but never abandon this commitment. At an earlier stage he was still indebted to the idea of constructing a phenomenology of experience. But its features were remote from the Hegelian original. Antithesis or 'division' (*partage*) remained central to the analysis, but the prospect of reconciliation was discounted. Nietzsche's *The Birth of Tragedy* provided inspiration: as Foucault summarised the argument, just as the Socratic worldview had succeeded a tragic vision of life by conquering and silencing what went before, so also the age of reason began with a 'constitutive' moment of division.[20] Division here essentially meant conflict. In retracing the onset of antagonism, when reason was created at the expense of madness, Foucault rejected standard versions of the 'history of knowledge' whose representative works recapitulated the accumulation of truth by tracing the 'concatenation of rational causes'.[21] Opposing this genre, he acknowledged the influence of Georges Canguilhem. For Canguilhem, the progress of knowledge is most accurately seen as a history of error appended to shifting perceptions of truth.

---

18. Michel Foucault, *History of Madness*, ed. Jean Khalfa, trans. Jonathan Murphy and Khalfa (London: Routledge, 2006), pp. xxxi, xxix. On Hyppolite, cf. Michel Foucault, *Dits et écrits*, vol. 1: *1954–1969*, ed. Daniel Defert and François Ewald (Paris: Gallimard, 1994), p. 781.

19. Foucault, *History of Madness*, p. xxx.

20. See Friedrich Nietzsche, *The Birth of Tragedy and Other Writings*, ed. Raymond Geuss, trans. Ronald Spiers (Cambridge: Cambridge University Press, 1999).

21. Foucault, *History of Madness*, p. xxix.

Built into this analysis was a doubt about the legitimacy of self-authenticating reason. As Foucault observed, the idea of sovereign rationality gave rise to what he dubbed a 'despotic enlightenment'.[22] This species of enlightenment presupposed that the norms of Western rationality had acquired some kind of universal validity. Foucault proposed directing a more 'critical' strand of enlightenment against this problematic assumption. This entailed recovering a form of scepticism about rational inquiry which he sometimes traced to Kant.[23]

In Foucault's mind, the claim to universality rested on a spurious teleology. His interventions on this theme were written against the background of the French defeat at Dien Bien Phu in Indochina, announcing the beginning of the end of the colonial era. As far as Foucault was concerned, the Western claim to represent the epitome of humanity was actually based on 'economic domination and political hegemony'.[24] In order to subvert this self-serving logic, Foucault turned to what he described as an archaeological method.[25] The approach was designed to bar the resort to teleological reasoning. Accordingly, the historian was instructed to dig down through the sediments of the past, through successive layers of historical forgetting, in order to uncover the formation of a discrete power structure. In the *History of Madness*, this structure comprised the confrontation between reason and insanity during

22. Michel Foucault, 'Introduction' (1978) to Georges Canguilhem, *The Normal and the Pathological*, trans. Carolyn R. Fawcett (New York: Zone Books, 1989), p. 12.

23. Michel Foucault, 'What is Enlightenment?' (1983), in *The Politics of Truth*, ed. Sylvère Lotringer, trans. Lysa Hochroth and Catherine Porter (Los Angeles: Semiotext(e), 2007).

24. Foucault, 'Introduction', p. 12.

25. Foucault, *History of Madness*, p. xxviii.

the period of 'the great confinement' in the middle of the seventeenth century. On Foucault's telling, the encounter was less a struggle than a spontaneous overthrow. Rationality debased and mastered what it branded as unreason. This degraded status was pinned onto the figure of the madman. According to Foucault, the fabrication of a devalued 'other' was the condition of the victorious party's flourishing.

Generalising this perspective, Foucault regarded history as a succession of usurpations. It muted and manipulated its victims as it advanced. Ironically, notwithstanding repeated strictures against teleology, the process presupposed a functionalist logic. Rationality *depended* on the concoction of unreason: 'in our culture, there can be no reason without madness'.[26] In this way, underlying Foucault's habitual invocation of contingency there lurked a fundamental 'necessity'.[27] This was the supposed need to replace reciprocity with domination. The pattern pointed to a framework of investigation which Foucault thought could explain any number of power relations. To illustrate the scale of the phenomenon, he drew attention to the collision between East and West, a battle which he characterised as a rout rather than a contest. Construed in this way, the 'Orient' was offered up to the 'colonising reason of the Occident'.[28] Proceeding on that basis, Foucault's conceptual scheme prejudged his empirical evidence. Despite the crudeness of the model, or perhaps because of its simplicity, this moralising strain of analysis has flourished in the humanities down to our own time.[29] It was also

26. Ibid., p. xxxii.
27. Ibid.
28. Ibid., p. xxx.
29. A classic of the genre is Edward Said, *Orientalism* (New York: Pantheon Books, 1978).

prone to having the tables turned on itself, as shown by Derrida's critique of Foucault's book, which charged the very attempt to recover the meaning of madness with the same vexatious intent that was originally directed against the insane.[30] Derrida added to Foucault's project a Heideggerian twist: namely, the insight that the impulse to understand is itself an attempt to classify and to fix—to overcome the threat of indeterminacy by the imposition of rational standards.[31] It seemed that 'colonising' reason was both ubiquitous and multifarious.

The debt to Heidegger encouraged Derrida to regard Western philosophy as a structure of metaphysical hubris, albeit one perpetually undermined by its own fragility. By degrees, among the chief exponents of postmodernism, Hegel was cast as the culmination of a totalising mission.[32] By a strange exercise in verbal association, Hegelian 'totality' was identified with totalitarianism. In accordance with this idiom more generally, all values were presented as vehicles for interests. Every relationship was assumed to be a means of exploitation. Correspondingly, any appeal to standards was condemned as ethnocentrism.[33] Justice therefore had to be regarded as a sham. Nonetheless, the judgements arrived at by this mode of thought were suffused with righteousness. Despite the implied impossibility of ethics, the

30. Jacques Derrida, 'Cogito and the History of Madness' (1967), in *Writing and Difference*, trans. Allan Bass (London: Routledge & Kegan Paul, 1978). For discussion, see Edward Baring, *The Young Derrida and French Philosophy, 1945–1968* (Cambridge: Cambridge University Press, 2011), pp. 194–97.

31. Jacques Derrida, *Of Grammatology* (1967), trans. Gayatri Spivak (Baltimore: Johns Hopkins University Press, 1976), pp. 101ff.

32. Jean-François Lyotard, *The Postmodern Condition: A Report on Knowledge* (1979), trans. Geoff Bennington and Brian Massumi (Manchester: Manchester University Press, 1984), pp. 33–34, 91. Cf. Gilles Deleuze, *Nietzsche and Philosophy* (1962), trans. Hugh Tomlinson (New York: Columbia University Press, 2006), p. 157.

33. Derrida, *Grammatology*, pp. 109–10.

world was deemed to lie in sin. The incidence of evil was seen as all-pervasive. Given this situation, there was no space for mitigation or exculpation. And because there was no concept of reciprocity, there was no way of explaining moral failure. In Foucault's mature vision of the world, all socialisation was seen as an expression of power, and all power was equally tainted. At the same time, power was depicted as distinct from force: it was continuous, all-encompassing, and often concealed, quietly structuring attitudes and values.[34] Norms themselves were nothing but externally imposed rules mobilised by an appetite for subjugation. As a consequence, basic elements of liberalism—such as the principle that authority should be constrained by obligations—were treated by Foucault as expressions of violence rather than as means of stemming conflict. Society is regarded as an edifice of suppression implementing a litany of exclusions. The past assumed the shape of a 'system of subjection [*asservissement*]', a perpetual advance 'from domination to domination'.[35] It followed that the present was only an extension of the same process.

III

This bleak conception of humanity has its roots in a pessimistic philosophy of history which regarded the fabric of Western morality as a species of imposture. The idea of a fallen world was disseminated by Heidegger on the basis of his critical

34. Michel Foucault, 'Truth and Power', in *Power/Knowledge: Selected Interviews and Other Writings, 1972–1977*, ed. Colin Gordon, trans. Gordon et al. (Brighton: The Harvester Press, 1980), pp. 121–22.

35. Michel Foucault, 'Nietzsche, la généalogie, l'histoire,', in *Hommage à Jean Hyppolite*, ed. Suzanne Bachelard et al. (Paris: PUF, 1971), pp. 155, 157.

engagement with Nietzsche. The view was pessimistic in the literal sense that it interpreted human existence as the worst of all possible worlds. At least, what could be worse than the systematic hypocrisy of preaching moral rigour on the basis of prior scepticism about the viability of morality altogether? The inevitable result of such a combination of attitudes is a code of behaviour that mixes suspicion with self-regard. Nietzsche developed various strategies for combating this unhappy state, although it is hard to see that his recent disciples have anything comparable to offer. In *Daybreak*, Nietzsche traced the modern expression of pessimism to the philosophy of Kant. Notwithstanding contemporary perceptions, Kant was, Nietzsche contended, a moral sceptic: he admitted that all experience seemed to contradict moral autonomy, making the possibility of virtue a matter of mere 'faith'.[36] Unsurprisingly, Kant's original system was more intricate and involved. As he presented his case in the *Groundwork for the Metaphysics of Morals*, although in practice moral action was arduous in the extreme, its principle was evident to common understanding.[37] The core tenet was that moral worth resided in the motive of duty. However, historically, this precept had been corrupted by assorted religious dogmas which subordinated virtue to external obedience. The world-historical achievement of Christianity, for Kant, was that it repudiated this slavish posture of submission.

36. Friedrich Nietzsche, *Daybreak: Thoughts on the Prejudices of Morality* (1881), ed. Maudemarie Clark and Brian Leiter, trans. R. J. Hollingdale (Cambridge: Cambridge University Press, 1997), pp. 3–4.

37. Immanuel Kant, *Groundwork of the Metaphysics of Morals* (1785), ed. and trans. Mary Gregor and Jens Timmerman (Cambridge: Cambridge University Press, 2012), AA 4: 391. (Page references for Kant are throughout, wherever appropriate, to the *Akademie-Ausgabe* [AA].)

From a Kantian perspective, the Christian ideal, which based the merit of an action on the purity of its intention, constituted a thoroughgoing mental revolution. Yet this radically new awareness failed to produce results. The real-world manifestation of moral awakening was an incessant tendency to backslide. As Kant realised, the Christian message evolved into an imperious institution. The Reformation and French Revolution were likewise disappointing, despite their original promise. The assurance of rationality produced irrational results. Kant had tried to amend the standard Christian theodicies by connecting his moral theory to a philosophy of history. Yet the historical record documented a sequence of defeats. Undeterred, Kant salvaged from the wreckage a residual hope in 'progress'.[38] Nietzsche's sense in the 1880s was that this enterprise had failed. This led him to conclude that the Kantian programme was a mistake. Instead of searching for how the relevant missteps might be corrected, Nietzsche opted to abandon the Christian heritage altogether. Yet there was something puritanical about this revolt against purity. It entailed a rebellion against the current condition of the world.[39] Hegel believed that turning away from history in this fashion involved its own reactive form of asceticism. Like Nietzsche, he detected in Kant a dissatisfaction with reality. He ascribed the feeling of discontent to the dichotomies that governed Kant's thought.[40] Hegel thus saw in Kant

38. Immanuel Kant, 'Idea for a Universal History with a Cosmopolitan Aim' (1784), in *Anthropology, History, and Education*, ed. and trans. Robert B. Louden and Günter Zöller (Cambridge: Cambridge University Press, 2007).

39. Friedrich Nietzsche, *Writings from the Late Notebooks* (1885–88), ed. Rüdiger Bittner, trans. Kate Sturge (Cambridge: Cambridge University Press, 2003), p. 139.

40. G.W.F. Hegel, *The Difference Between Fichte's and Schelling's System of Philosophy* (1801), ed. and trans. H. S. Harris and Walter Cerf (New York: State University of New York Press, 1977), p. 89.

an estrangement from natural drives, but he also believed there was something compulsive about this slide into alienation. For Hegel, in other words, the antinomies in Kantian thought were symptoms of the age.[41] They formed part of a protracted struggle between reason and faith that extended from the ancient Greeks to Hegel's own time. According to Hegel, in the Athens of Socrates, philosophy was directed against the institutions of civic religion. By comparison, in the modern era, internal division undermined philosophy itself. To begin with, in medieval Europe, philosophical activity saw itself as acting in support of faith. However, during the Enlightenment they found themselves at loggerheads with one another. In one sense, what Hegel later called enlightened 'insight' (*Einsicht*) was victorious.[42] In Kant himself, for instance, religion was made accountable to the dictates of the understanding.[43] However, understanding could not satisfy the full range of human desires. As a result, it called on faith to resolve its difficulties. Accordingly, ultimate values in Kant were located in a metaphysical 'beyond' that was inaccessible to our cognitive capacities.[44] For this reason, as Nietzsche would later notice, morality for Kant became a matter for belief (*Glaube*). Hegel observed that the same outcome afflicted Fichte and Jacobi: 'Philosophy has

41. G.W.F. Hegel, *Faith and Knowledge* (1802), ed. and trans. Walter Cerf and H. S. Harris (New York: State University of New York Press, 1977), pp. 55–56.

42. G.W.F. Hegel, *The Phenomenology of Spirit* (1807), ed. and trans. Michael Inwood (Oxford: Oxford University Press, 2018), §§529ff.; cf. G.W.F. Hegel, *Encyclopedia of the Philosophical Sciences in Basic Outline*, Part 1: *Science of Logic* (1817), trans. Klaus Brinkmann and Daniel O. Dahlstrom (Cambridge: Cambridge University Press, 2010), pp. 9ff.

43. Immanuel Kant, *Religion within the Boundaries of Mere Reason* [1793] *and Other Writings*, ed. and trans. Allen Wood and George di Giovanni (Cambridge: Cambridge University Press, 1998).

44. Hegel, *Faith and Knowledge*, p. 56.

made itself the handmaid of a faith once more.'[45] For post-Kantian thought in general, scepticism about reason had proved counterproductive. Dialectical analysis offered a solution to this conundrum. The pure 'negation' of religion could never succeed, as the travails of the Enlightenment had demonstrated.[46] Instead, in Hegelian terms, reason could only progress if it capitalised on religion. This involved preserving its value in the process of overcoming its deficiencies: in the language of the *Science of Logic*, 'That which is sublated [*aufgehoben*] [...] is at the same time preserved.'[47] Popular interpretations of Hegel notwithstanding, this resolution could not be entrusted to the decrees of absolute spirit. It was brought about without foresight by the groping efforts of desire (*Begierde*). The consequences of the struggle were unanticipated, but not pointless.

The point was only intelligible in the context of world history. Unlike the Four Kingdoms of the Book of Daniel, which he invoked, Hegel constructed his narrative around four principal ages—the Oriental, the Greek, the Roman and the German.[48] His account of the process concentrated on pivotal moments of transition. In themselves, none of these took the form of instant ruptures or abrupt conversions. Revolutions were not realised by a sudden change of heart. Change was incremental, tortuous and prolonged. Hegel's transitions embraced the demise of Egyptian civilisation and the passage from

45. Ibid.

46. For the moment of pure negativity in the dialectic, see Hegel, *Encyclopedia*, §§80–81.

47. G.W.F. Hegel, *The Science of Logic* (1812–16), ed. and trans. George di Giovanni (Cambridge: Cambridge University Press, 2010), p. 82.

48. G.W.F. Hegel, 'Natur- und Staatsrecht nach dem Vortrage des Professors Hegel in Winterhalbenjahr 1818/1819 von G. Homeyer', in *Vorlesungen über Rechtsphilosophie, 1818–1831*, 1, p. 344.

the Greek to the Roman world. This evolution included the crisis of Judaism which unfolded in the context of the rise of Christian values.[49] It also comprised the fate of assorted schools of thought from Stoicism and Epicureanism to Scepticism. These epochal shifts constituted the 'world revolutions' of my title. They formed the subject matter of the *Phenomenology* and the *Philosophy of World History*. In addition, they shaped the argument of the *Philosophy of Right* and undergirded both Hegel's aesthetics and his history of philosophy.

Hegel was sharply focused on the repercussions of these upheavals as they determined the character of the modern world. Feudalism, absolutism and enlightenment were among the principal stages in the process. Hegel's account of their trajectory was acute and sophisticated. European historiography still trades on his conclusions. However, while drawing on his notion of decisive turning-points, it has neglected his concern with more protracted developments.[50] Hegel's analysis was indebted to recent conjectural histories constructed by—among other figures—Rousseau, Hume and Kant. He also drew on the abundant research of Montesquieu, Smith and Gibbon. Despite the often synoptic character of his delivery, he subjected the dynamics of change to minute scrutiny. His presentation was

---

49. For the transition from Christianity itself, see now Michael Rosen, *The Shadow of God: Kant, Hegel, and the Passage from Heaven to History* (Cambridge, MA: Harvard University Press, 2022).

50. In the German literature see, for example, Reinhart Koselleck, 'Einleitung', in Otto Brunner, Werner Conze and Koselleck, eds, *Geschichtliche Grundbegriffe: Historisches Lexikon zur politisch-sozialen Sprache in Deutschland*, 8 vols (Stuttgart: Ernst Klett Verlag, 1972–97), 1, p. xv; Friedrich Meinecke, *The Age of German Liberation, 1795–1815* (Berkeley, CA: University of California Press, 1977), p. 2; Hans Rosenberg, *Bureaucracy, Aristocracy, and Autocracy: The Prussian Experience, 1660–1815* (Cambridge, MA: Harvard University Press, 1958), pp. 202–28.

often illustrative, but for all that attentive to the precise causal sequencing of events. In opposition to the assumptions of what he described as British 'empiricism', Hegel took the human will to be embroiled in the data of history. With his customary exegetical incisiveness, he recognised idealising dimensions to Locke and Hume.[51] Yet, for him, they both failed to show how history was made, rather than simply happening. Fundamentally, they lacked a coherent theory of freedom, and with that any hope of providing a credible account of political value. These points are linked, since while freedom, for Hegel, was the source of normativity in politics it was also the central object of contention in contemporary history.

IV

The main political controversy to occur in Hegel's lifetime concerned the meaning of the French Revolution. In one sense, according to Hegel, that episode was a climax in the sequence of world revolutions. In another, it was a token of a deeper process of adjustment. It shared certain features with the original Christian rebirth. To quote one verdict on yet another event, it seemed to present the chance of 'a new world being born in great suffering'.[52] Yet, like the Christian renewal, the French Revolution stalled. It spluttered forward into failure burdened by the baggage with which it had to travel. Therefore, in reality, it was neither a clean break nor a moment of deliverance. The appearance of a breach hid a more convoluted course.

---

51. Hegel, *Faith and Knowledge*, pp. 68–69, 78.

52. The expression is Eric Hobsbawm's, referring to the Russian Revolution in discussion with Michael Ignatieff on *The Late Show*, BBC, 14 October 1994.

Much of Hegel's political philosophy is dedicated to retracing the path to 1789 with a view to understanding its significance. This entailed both understanding and contextualising the Revolution. It is standardly assumed that Hegel was an enthusiast for the events in France.[53] This involves a basic misconception. It is true that Hegel applauded the triumphant expression of freedom. In this he welcomed the idea of a new era of statecraft in which power would be constrained by principles of justice. Nonetheless, what actually happened deviated from this optimistic prospect. There was the spark of a new dawn, but it quickly fizzled into darkness.[54] Crucially, disappointment long pre-dated the advent of the Jacobin Terror. For Hegel, derailment began in the summer of 1789. The lesson of this experience was not that good intentions met with defeat, but that idealistic projects were necessarily foiled. Programmes of pure virtue turned from the world as it existed. They were motivated by what Hegel termed an attitude of negation. Unlike some of his nominal disciples in the twentieth century, Hegel regarded this as a feckless form of antagonism. Revolutionaries sought to transcend the environment in which they operated, but they were inevitably devoured by the conditions they strove to surmount. From Hegel's perspective, the problem did not lie in the hope for a better world, but in the idea that moral rectitude was sufficient unto itself.

53. Joachim Ritter, *Hegel and the French Revolution: Essays on the Philosophy of Right* (Cambridge, MA: MIT Press, 1982). A more balanced view can be found in Norbert Waszek, '1789, 1830 und kein Ende: Hegel und die französische Revolution', in Ulrich Herrmann and Jürgen Oelkers, eds, *Französische Revolution und Pädagogik der Moderne* (Weinheim: Beltz Verlag, 1989).
54. G.W.F. Hegel, *Vorlesungen über die Philosophie der Geschichte* (1837), vol. 12 in *Werke*, ed. Eva Moldenhauer and Karl Markus Michel, 21 vols (Frankfurt: Suhrkamp, 1986), p. 529.

As Hegel saw things, modern Europe was a child of the Reformation. The age of Luther inaugurated a wistful sense of divergence between morality and the actual state of the world.[55] Feelings of torment, regret and remorse captivated consciousness. However, Protestantism could not resolve the discontent it unleashed. Hegel believed that its failure was inherited by the Enlightenment. Philosophy now challenged the tenets of tradition and, as a result, it was made to seem as though purity confronted boundless corruption. Hegel contended that the experience of depravity extended beyond the countries of the reformed faith, noting that even the Jesuits felt impelled to scrutinise the recesses of the soul.[56] Naturally they handed the authority to make judgements over to the church hierarchies. By extension, Hegel regarded Catholic states as withholding from individuals the right to exercise personal responsibility, which led in the eighteenth century to polarisation across the religious divide. On one side, Protestantism retreated to 'the moral point of view' whereby the feeling of righteousness was estranged from prevailing norms of conduct.[57] On the other side, Catholicism lacked a culture of public service, provoking popular fury against established regimes.

When the dam broke in France, the spectacle proved mesmerising. Before the deluge, across Europe, a prior transformation had occurred. Trust in the utility of social arrangements had given way to an emphasis on personal conviction rooted in self-governing volition. The autonomous self might either retreat into its own sanctuary or deploy its outrage as a force against the world. Hegel argued that the latter path was followed

55. Ibid., p. 505.
56. Ibid., p. 506.
57. Hegel, *Phenomenology*, §§599ff.

in France. In the section of the *Phenomenology* devoted to 'Culture', he traced its impetuous course. As Hegel described it, the impulse to 'absolute freedom' dismantled every obstacle in its way: hierarchies, associations and institutions fell.[58] As a consequence, power grew ferocious and undisciplined. At the same time, civil relations descended into acrimony and suspicion. Individuals were terrorised for attitudes they might hold. To implement this latter-day inquisition, politics was drawn into a cycle of revenge. Moreover, even after the incidence of vengeance had subsided, social atomism continued from the Directory to the July Monarchy. In the final months before his death in 1831, Hegel hankered after a resolution in which the spirit of dissent might coalesce with the existence of a reformed state. Earlier, in 1819, he wrote of his expectations since 1789 as having oscillated wildly between hope and despair.[59] That mood of apprehension persisted to the last. It seemed as though the age was trapped between the evidence of progress and a sense of the ongoing perversity of how society was constituted.

The feeling of perversity pre-dated the Revolution. According to Hegel, it was evident in the writings of Rousseau, Diderot, Kant and Goethe. It was most resonantly captured in Schiller's play *The Robbers*.[60] In the case of Kant, the revolt against perversity took the form of an assertion of autonomous freedom. However, on Hegel's analysis, the autonomous will in Kant proved both empty and ineffective. Under the influence of this style of reasoning, Hegel claimed, the characteristic reaction to moral

---

58. Ibid., §590.
59. Hegel to Creuzer, 30 October 1819, *Briefe von und an Hegel [Hegels Briefe]*, ed. Johannes Hoffmeister, 4 vols (Hamburg: Felix Meiner Verlag, 1952), 2, p. 219.
60. For Hegel's account, see the *Phenomenology*, §§367ff.

corruption in Germany was the cultivation of intellectual refinement. The craving for justice was confined to the formulation of principles. It followed that, with the Germans, the doctrine of right was restricted to 'quiet theory' (*ruhige Theorie*). By comparison, the French were determined that the call of duty should have a 'practical effect'.[61] This issued, as we have noted, in rage against the status quo. In Germany, on the other hand, the charge of quietism enjoyed an afterlife in commentaries beginning with Marx and lasting into the twentieth century.[62] On that basis, moral reformation in Germany was contrasted with revolutionary agitation in France. Heinrich Heine had been more subtle: for him, it had been necessary to work out a coherent philosophy before embarking on 'political revolution'.[63] Nonetheless, from Rudolf Haym to Jürgen Habermas, the comparison between Germany and France was used to castigate Hegel.[64] The intention was to devalue a presumed attitude of passive spiritualism in opposition to a commitment to political engagement. However, Hegel's aim had been to challenge this very antithesis.

In his 1822–23 lectures on world history, Hegel argued that without religious reform political change was impossible.[65] For

---

61. Hegel, *Philosophie der Geschichte*, p. 525.

62. Karl Marx, *The German Ideology* (1845), in Karl Marx and Friedrich Engels, *Collected Works*, 50 vols (London: Lawrence and Wishart, 1975–2004), 5, pp. 28–29.

63. Heinrich Heine, *On the History of Religion and Philosophy in Germany* (1835), ed. Terry Pinkard, trans. Howard Pollack-Milgate (Cambridge: Cambridge University Press, 2007), p. 115.

64. Rudolf Haym, *Hegel und seine Zeit: Vorlesungen über Entstehung und Entwicklung, Wesen und Werth der hegelschen Philosophie* (Berlin: Rudolph Gärtner, 1857), p. 359; Jürgen Habermas, *The Philosophical Discourse of Modernity*, trans. Frederick Lawrence (Cambridge: Polity Press, 1987), pp. 40–41.

65. G.W.F. Hegel, *Vorlesungen über die Philosophie der Weltgeschichte 1: Nachschriften zum Kolleg des Wintersemesters, 1822/23*, ed. Bernadette Collenberg-Plotnikov (*Gesammelte Werke* 27.1) (Hamburg: Felix Meiner Verlag, 2015), pp. 460–61, 461n.

him, ethics was the basic subject matter of religion, and so what he meant was that moral and political reform were mutually interdependent. A purely moral revolution was ultimately vacuous, while a frenzied assault on existing arrangements could only prove destructive. To make the point in Hegel's characteristic vocabulary, the one lacked actuality, while the other lacked rationality.[66] In Hegel's mind, the attempt to ignore these shortcomings was the cause of modern fanaticism. In the generations before the French Revolution, fanaticism was largely associated with forms of religious extremism. Comparable diagnoses appeared in Locke, Voltaire and Hume. Standardly, political turmoil was traced to religious causes. Most commonly, zeal was seen as a product of 'enthusiasm'.[67] That is, it was identified with the presumed influence of divine inspiration on conduct. However, Hegel provided a secular account of modern fanaticism, arguing that its sources should be sought in the rise of moral consciousness. With this shift in emphasis, he helped transform the understanding of political partisanship and, with that, the conception of the nature of civil conflict.

V

Because the French Revolution was a symptom of a larger phenomenon, it followed that it did not define the age in its entirety. From Hegel's perspective, events in France were a negative but local expression of an overarching positive purpose,

---

66. G.W.F. Hegel, *Elements of the Philosophy of Right* (1821), ed. Allen W. Wood, trans. H. B. Nisbet (Cambridge: Cambridge University Press, 1991), p. 20. Cf. Hegel to Niethammer, 29 April 1814, *Hegels Briefe*, 2, p. 28, on the 'unactuality' of purely moral consciousness.

67. J.G.A. Pocock, 'Enthusiasm: The Antiself of the Enlightenment', *Huntington Library Quarterly*, 60: 1/2 (1997), pp. 7–28

that of giving shape to the modern quest for freedom. Ultimately, Hegel supplied an audit of the prerequisites for the successful pursuit of that purpose. The starting point of the analysis was the rise of civil society. Its ascent presupposed the decline of trust as the governing precept of social relations. This transformative change was based on the break-up of sociopolitical orders and their replacement by anonymous market societies organised into classes. This marked the beginning of the end of the system of fixed privileges, the advance of wealth and education as determinants of social position and the appearance of talent as a principal cause of mobility. The fetters of a bygone world had been cast aside along with birth and heredity as defining features of society and politics. According to Hegel, these developments were propelled by the arrival of subjectivity as the organising principle of the modern world. Along with it came the requirement of qualification for public office, the demand for an accountable system of government, the importance of constitutional regulation and the need to balance welfare against rights.

Recent trends in political theory have treated these attainments as somehow complicit with oppression, or fundamentally compromised, or even as net losses by comparison with earlier times. These tendencies have assumed the form of hostility to liberalism, or just a longing to revive assorted aspects of the ancients. Hegel was himself an explicit critic of what he termed 'liberalism' (*Liberalismus*), yet he was also clear that little could be achieved without building on its foundations.[68] These included the existence of the modern state along with the resources of executive power and the mediating role of corporations. As far as Hegel was concerned, these accomplishments

68. Hegel, *Philosophie der Geschichte*, p. 534.

in the modern world brought dissatisfactions in tow. Partly because of this dual assessment, some of his arguments were eagerly rekindled in the first half of the last century. So, for example, whereas Friedrich Meinecke thought Hegel's relevance was to be found in his theory of the state, Georg Lukács believed it could be discovered in his concept of alienation. Between them, they raised the question of the uses of past thought in later periods. As I hope to have shown by the conclusion of this book, their question is still pertinent today.

The argument that follows has a number of objectives. First, it aims to interpret Hegel's thought in the context of his time. It pursues this goal with reference to his philosophy of history. After all, history provides the framework in terms of which he thought about society. As already noted, his overall analysis was encyclopedic in scope, embracing ancient civilisations as well as modern developments. The latter included the rise of religious freedom and the emergence civil society, respectively examined in Parts I and II of the book. Part III then recounts the reception of Hegel's political ideas, largely over the course of the twentieth century, extending from Wilhelm Dilthey to Karl Popper and beyond. Finally, in the last chapter of Part III, I consider the issue of the applicability of Hegel's ideas. This is to pose the question of how concepts formulated in one period might improve our grasp of problems in another. In general, the position advanced here is critical of attempts to transplant the norms of one age into another.

The question of transhistorical relevance naturally raises the issue of how we categorise different epochs. Part I of the book examines Hegel's method for differentiating between eras, which he thought of in terms of the progress from one 'shape of spirit' to another. As mentioned already, key transitions included the move from Judaism to Christianity and from the early church to the Lutheran Reformation. It is notable that he understood the revolutions he examined as enjoying world-historical significance. Each of them introduced a whole new temporal horizon. Part II of the book considers Hegel's account of more recent shifts, concentrating on the passage from feudal monarchy to the constitutional state. Since we are still living with the impact of this transition, our relationship to Hegel is in one sense immediate: he cultivated powerful tools for analysing how our societies have been formed. Even so, in no sense does this imply that Hegel is our contemporary. Important disparities divide the first third of the nineteenth century from our current situation. In Part III of the book, I show that assessing the nature of these discrepancies is a matter for historical judgement. My intention is to emphasise that this kind of judgement matters in both the history of political thought and political theory. Since this was one of the central themes in Hegel's philosophy, a reconstruction of his political ideas is the obvious place to start in order to tackle the problem.

PART I

The Kantian Revolution

Introduction

HEGEL'S INTEREST IN REVOLUTIONS developed in a revolutionary age. As a student at Tübingen in the 1790s, he closely followed affairs in France from the convening of the Estates General in May 1789 to the execution of Louis XVI in January 1793. Intense exposure to these events overlapped with Hegel's immersion in the thought of a revolutionary thinker. From his early twenties, he was drawn ever deeper into the philosophy of Kant. Above all, he examined Kant's analysis of the meaning of morality. He accepted the Kantian view that the purpose of religion was to enhance the moral faculties of human beings. As a consequence, he became interested in how these aptitudes had evolved historically. This partly grew out of a preoccupation with Kant's treatment of the impact of Christianity on our capacity for moral motivation. For Kant, the advent of the Christian faith entailed a sudden reorientation. It replaced a religion of service with a doctrine of moral purity. Yet, as Kant himself recognised, this renovation descended into a process of corruption, culminating in a new age of fetishistic devotion, and ultimately requiring a Reformation. However, in due course, even the

Lutheran Reformation failed. Since Kant could not account for this sequence of reversals, Hegel strove to construct an interpretation of his own. He was forced to develop a philosophy of history.

Whereas Kant believed that moral standards were inherent in human reason, Hegel argued that ethical norms had evolved over time. They were not so much the products of a fully rational consciousness as freely generated during the course of history as it advanced. The first part of this book charts Hegel's early account of that process of development. Freedom, for Hegel, was a precondition of moral behaviour. In fact, the aptitude for liberty was the source of value altogether. Since the trajectory of morality was bound up with the progress of freedom, Hegel set about recounting its history. This involved an examination of discrete civilisational moments as well as the links that connected them together. Hegel's choice of subject matter was determined by this central concern. He was interested in the shape of European freedom, which led him to examine formative episodes bridging the ancient and modern worlds: Judaism, Christianity, ancient Greece and Rome, the Reformation, the Enlightenment, and the French Revolution. Partly under the prodigious influence of Hegel, these events have played a defining role in Western historiography. Much like Kant, Hegel thought that each instalment had ended in disappointment. But, unlike Kant, he undertook to uncover the secular causes of failure. The next three chapters reconstruct his early attempts at diagnosis as he plotted his way towards figuring out a viable scheme of analysis. The centrepiece of his inquiries around the middle of the 1790s was the insufficiency of the Christian message. He thought that the promise of moral renewal had been stymied in point of practice. Benign intentions were thwarted by an inhospitable setting. Hegel drew the lesson that well-meaning dispositions needed to harmonise with the conditions on which they depended. This would later form the core of his indictment of the French Revolution. It would ultimately lead him to work out a more grounded system of value for justifying the principles of political justice.

1

The Turning Point

IN 1795, F.W.J. SCHELLING, already a precocious philosophical talent, was completing the final year of his theological studies at Tübingen in the Duchy of Württemberg. Following Hölderlin and Hegel, Schelling had joined the seminary five years earlier, soon becoming intimate with his older contemporaries. All three were in theory destined for the Lutheran ministry, associating with one another under the rallying cry of the 'Kingdom of God' even after they had abandoned strictly orthodox religion.[1] Whatever the precise nature of their ambitions during this period, the Tübingen *Stift* was traditionally seen as a prestigious route to practical influence, either through the church or in public affairs: the clergy played a prominent role in the political and cultural life of the Duchy.[2] However, by the 1790s, opportunities for professional advancement were narrowing, and students at the seminary were turning against

1. Hölderlin to Hegel, 10 July 1794, *Briefe von und an Hegel [Hegels Briefe]*, ed. Johannes Hoffmeister, 4 vols (Hamburg: Felix Meiner Verlag, 1952), 1, p. 9.

2. Martin Hasselhorn, *Der Altwürttembergische Pfarrstand im 18. Jahrhundert* (Stuttgart: W. Kohlhammer, 1958), pp. 40–46.

their elders.[3] They were sceptical about the teachings of their senior instructors and critical of prevailing attitudes among the Württemberg establishment.

In this context, Hegel, Schelling and Hölderlin, along with many of their fellows, became enthusiastic spectators of the Revolution in France. Hegel's first biographer, Karl Rosenkranz, relayed the apocryphal tale of Schelling erecting a liberty tree with Hegel one Sunday morning in the aftermath of the summoning of the Estates General.[4] By the middle of the decade, Schelling was suspected of playing a leading role in student radicalism.[5] What such reputations meant in terms of practical politics is more difficult to determine. As Rudolf Haym—himself a renegade from Hegelianism and commentator on the ideas of the period—pointed out, initial excitement about the Revolution was widespread in Germany: from Klopstock to Gentz and Fichte, opening responses tended to be exuberant. Hegel's reaction, according to Haym, was no exception.[6] Yet, for all the exhilaration, opinion among supporters was rather generalised and indeterminate. The passage of time would bring more shape to the array of amorphous attitudes. By the stage at which Hegel came to express a coherent view of the proceedings, he was in fact critical of the trajectory of events. In due course he would reveal his doubts about the enterprise altogether. The standard account

3. Martin Leube, 'Die geistige Lage im Stift in den Tagen der französischen Revolution', *Blätter für Württembergische Kirchengeschichte*, 39 (1935), pp. 149–71.

4. Karl Rosenkranz, *Georg Wilhelm Friedrich Hegels Leben* (Berlin: Duncker und Humblot, 1844), p. 29.

5. Franz Gabriel Nauen, *Revolution, Idealism and Human Freedom: Schelling, Hölderlin and Hegel and the Crisis of Early German Idealism* (The Hague: Martinus Nijhoff, 1971).

6. Rudolf Haym, *Hegel und seine Zeit: Vorlesungen über Entstehung und Entwicklung, Wesen und Werth der hegelschen Philosophie* (Berlin: Rudolph Gärtner, 1857), p. 323.

of Hegel as a cheerleader for the Revolution is not only simplifying, but fundamentally misguided.

After graduation, Hegel settled in Switzerland as a private tutor in the house of a patrician Bernese family while Hölderlin moved north-east to Waltershausen near the Thuringian Forest. In 1794, Hegel reconnected with his old comrades. That Christmas he contacted Schelling. Now about to turn twenty, Schelling was finishing a dissertation on the biblical commentary of Marcion of Sinope, under the supervision of the Tübingen professor Gottlob Storr. Hölderlin, at this point, had befriended Schiller and was based in Jena, concentrating on the writings of Kant and the Greeks, and about to discover Fichte in earnest.[7] Schelling responded to Hegel on 5 January 1795 in exultant tones. Philosophy, he declared, was not yet at an end.[8] Its substance and vocation had been transformed by Kant, yet the business still awaited completion. Events in France, along with developments in philosophy, contributed to an air of expectation. Thoroughgoing renewal seemed to be at hand.

Kant's third critique, the *Critique of the Power of Judgment*, was a central text for Schelling at this time, just as it was for Hölderlin. So too was his *Religion within the Boundaries of Mere Reason*, as well of course as the major works of the 1780s—the moral and epistemological writings alike. Schelling was trying to penetrate the significance of Kant's thinking under the influence of Fichte, whom he had met during the latter's passing visit to Württemberg in May 1794.[9] Fichte, he was convinced, was

7. Hölderlin to Hegel, 10 July 1794, *Hegels Briefe*, 1, p. 10.
8. Schelling to Hegel, 6 January 1795, ibid., p. 14.
9. Fichte to his wife, 20 May 1794, in Immanuel Hermann Fichte, ed., *Johann Gottlieb Fichtes Leben und literarischer Briefwechsel*, 2 vols (Sulzbach: J. E. Seidel, 1830–31), 1, pp. 277ff.

bringing philosophy to new heights, where more conventional followers of the Kantian message were apt to lose their bearings. He was also combining this idealist inheritance with a reworking of Spinoza which aimed to unite theoretical and practical reason.[10] At the same time, by reconciling pre-critical metaphysical aspirations with the insights of post-Kantian Idealism, Schelling believed that dogmatism could be overcome whilst vindicating the ideal of freedom. This involved a redescription of the principle of divinity in terms of the unconditioned striving of subjectivity.[11] This, then, was a period of philosophical tumult, matched by a sense of boundless future promise. Kant, Schelling announced, had dismantled 'everything'.[12] Christian superstition consequently lay in tatters. The process of reconstruction could now begin on the basis of rigorously formulated premises.

Like Schelling, Hegel associated Tübingen with a retrograde theology that sought to mitigate the challenge posed by Kant's insights. For both students, Storr was a dominant academic presence, along with other professorial figures such as Christian Schnurrer and Johann Flatt.[13] Storr appeared to exemplify what the more regressive stance involved. In his earliest years at the seminary, Rousseau rather than Kant absorbed Hegel's attention.[14] But, looking back from the middle of the decade, Hegel

10. Schelling to Hegel, 6 January 1795, *Hegels Briefe*, 1, p. 15.

11. Schelling to Hegel, 4 February 1795, ibid., p. 22.

12. Ibid., p. 14.

13. A draft *curriculum vitae*, now lost, setting out the role and influence of Hegel's teachers, is cited in the 'Preface' to *Hegels theologische Jugendschriften*, ed. Herman Nohl (Tübingen: J.C.B. Mohr, 1907), pp. viii–ix.

14. On the early influence of Rousseau, see Dieter Henrich, 'Leutwein über Hegel: Ein Dokument zu Hegel Biographie', *Hegel-Studien*, 3 (1965), pp. 39–77. According to H. S. Harris, correcting Henrich in *Hegel's Development: Toward the*

concluded with Schelling that the Tübingen professoriate lacked the spirit of critical philosophy. This was now being advanced at Jena through the writings of the neo-Kantian philosopher Karl Reinhold.[15] Schelling elucidated more concretely what the traditional approach entailed. In his view, Storr had hoped to use the sceptical results of Kantian criticism to re-establish the old assumptions of natural and revealed theology by resort to pseudo-critical procedures.[16] Towards this end, Kant's moral proof for the existence of God was wheeled out to support conventional doctrines about the deity as a personalised entity (a 'persönliche, individuelle Wesen') residing in the beyond.[17] For Schelling and Hegel alike, this was tantamount to re-establishing dogmatic metaphysics by stealth. They both believed this tendency risked a cascade of negative consequences. Even after the enlightened Friedrich Eugen succeeded his brother to become Duke of Württemberg in May 1795, Schelling believed that orthodox theology among the clergy held the threat of the rebirth of superstition. The authorities risked squandering the benefits of 'freedom of thought' (*Denkfreiheit*) and, with that, a return to moral despotism.[18]

Sunlight, 1770–1801 (Oxford: Clarendon Press, 1972), p. 108, Hegel likely first studied Kant and Fichte in 1792–93. See also G.W.F. Hegel, 'Exzerpt 43: Aus Rousseau à M. D'Alembert', in *Frühe Exzerpte (1785–1800)*, ed. Friedhelm Nicolin and Gisela Schüler (*Gesammelte Werke* 3) (Hamburg: Felix Meiner Verlag, 1991), pp. 237–38, though the excerpt may be as late as 1795.

15. Hegel to Schelling, 24 December 1794, *Hegels Briefe*, 1, p. 12. On Reinhold, see Karl Ameriks, *Kant and the Fate of Autonomy: Problems in the Appropriation of the Critical Philosophy* (Cambridge: Cambridge University Press, 2000), ch. 2.

16. On Storr and his Tübingen colleagues, see Otto Pfleiderer, *The Development of Rational Theology in Germany since Kant and Its Progress in Britain since 1825* (London: Swann Sonnenschein & Co., 1890), pp. 85ff.

17. Schelling to Hegel, 6 January 1795, *Hegels Briefe*, 1, p. 14.

18. Schelling to Hegel, 21 July 1795, ibid., p. 27.

The age therefore appeared to be turning on a pivot—
looking forward to possible deliverance but assailed by forces
of darkness leading to moral corruption. For the three Tübingen graduates, consciousness of this axial moment raised profound issues concerning social and cultural change. It threw up
questions about the causes of intellectual innovation, as well as
the relationship between the progress of knowledge and ethical
improvement. In the previous generation, as Hegel was acutely
aware, both Rousseau and Lessing had addressed these topics
in peculiarly challenging ways. In addition, Herder had explored how historical transitions highlighted the relativity of
past values. Recent developments in France only complicated
these matters, particularly regarding relations between tradition
and enlightenment—or, more specifically, between popular
sentiment and philosophical criticism. Both Hölderlin and
Hegel were self-consciously devoting themselves to popular
education (*Volkserziehung*), yet it was proving an arduous
task.[19] Hegel had no doubts about the transformative power of
ideas (*Kraft der Ideen*): philosophers could prove the intrinsic
worth of humanity, and the populace might learn to feel its
force. On that basis, members of the public could directly claim
their rights.[20] Yet a misalliance between the people and their
educators remained possible, as Schelling came to discover:
'My principal failure', he confessed to Hegel, 'was that I did not
know the *people*, that I expected too much from their good will,
perhaps even too much from their divine dispensation.'[21] Hegel
was himself sensitive to this difficulty: modern individuals remained susceptible to squandering their independence. They

19. Hölderlin to Hegel, 26 January 1795, ibid., p. 18.
20. Hegel to Schelling, 16 April 1795, ibid., p. 24.
21. Schelling to Hegel, 21 July 1995, ibid., p. 28.

were liable to undermine, in Kant's famous phrase, their self-governing 'maturity' (*Mündigkeit*).[22] This left avant-garde philosophers such as Schelling in effect transcending their age: as Hegel saw it, his comrade was too enlightened for the times.[23] Yet Hegel remained committed to the improvement of mankind, and consequently to ideas with general traction.[24] For doctrines to be effective they had to connect with existing preferences; for them to become widespread they had to engage opinions at large. Already in the final months before his move from Tübingen to Bern, Hegel had been studying epochal shifts in belief systems, and consequently the meaning of historical change. His sense that he stood at a watershed moment fostered his interest in innovation. He was above all concerned with categorical shifts in the moral history of man. This mostly meant significant changes in the history of religious consciousness. Under the aegis of religious reform, Hegel was concerned with moral progress over the course of human development. Accepting the idea in Kant that rational religion was dedicated to the goal of moral perfection, he believed that this ultimate purpose had to be compatible with 'subjective' motivations.[25] Moral

---

22. Hegel to Schelling, 30 August 1795, ibid., p. 29. Responsibility for owning up to one's majority in terms of rational freedom is enjoined by Kant in 'An Answer to the Question: What is Enlightenment?' (1784), in *Practical Philosophy*, ed. and trans. Mary J. Gregor (Cambridge: Cambridge University Press, 1996), AA 8: 35.

23. Hegel to Schelling, 30 August 1795, *Hegels Briefe*, 1, p. 31.

24. Hegel to Schelling, end of January 1795, ibid., p. 14.

25. This is the theme of Hegel's fragmentary essay from the late summer of 1793 beginning 'Religion is eine der wichtigste Angelegenheiten' (Text 16), in G.W.F. Hegel, *Frühe Schriften 1*, ed. Friedhelm Nicolin and Gisela Schüler (*Gesammelte Werke 1*) (Hamburg: Felix Meiner Verlag, 1989), and translated as 'The Tübingen Essay', in Hegel, *Three Essays, 1793–1795: The Tübingen Essay, the Berne Fragments and Life of Jesus*, ed. and trans. Peter Fuss and John Dobbins (Notre Dame, IN: Notre Dame University Press, 1984, repr. 2004), p. 33.

reasons, in other words, were animated by sentimental and customary attachments. In effect, this implied that spiritual progress could not be separated from living historical forces. Back in 1748 Montesquieu had refined how best to understand interdependence among the various components of social life.[26] The impact of Montesquieu's views in Germany has been generally recognised; his early influence on Hegel is equally apparent from a fragmentary essay that the latter drafted at the end of his Tübingen period.[27] 'The spirit of the nation [Geist des Volks]', Hegel wrote, 'is reflected in its history, its religion, and the degree of its political freedom.'[28] He now set about disaggregating the assorted elements in Montesquieu's causal nexus—laws, commerce, religion, mores—and analysing their relationship to the aspiration to morality as conceptualised by Rousseau and Kant.

As Georg Lukács would later argue, this was an exercise in religious *and* political thought.[29] There was no narrowly 'theological' phase in Hegel's early career.[30] In fact, he scarcely wrote at all, in these years, about theology as such. As Hegel put it to Schelling in the mid-1790s, religion and politics had always

26. Charles-Louis de Secondat, baron de Montesquieu, *The Spirit of the Laws* (1748), ed. and trans. Anne Cohler, Basia Carolyn Miller and Harold Samuel Stone (Cambridge: Cambridge University Press, 1989), p. 9.

27. Rudolf Vierhaus, 'Montesquieu in Deutschland: Zur Geschichte seiner Wirkung als politischer Schriftsteller im 18. Jahrhundert' (1965), in *Deutschland im 18. Jahrhundert: Politische Verfassung, soziales Gefüge, geistige Bewegung* (Göttingen: Vandenhoeck & Ruprecht, 1987).

28. Hegel, 'Tübingen Essay', p. 56.

29. Georg Lukács, *The Young Hegel: Studies in the Relations between Dialectics and Economics* (1948), trans. Rodney Livingstone (London: Merlin Press, 1975), ch. 1.

30. *Pace* Wilhelm Dilthey, *Die Jugendgeschichte Hegels* (Berlin: Verlag der Königlichen Akademie der Wissenschaften, 1905), which influenced Nohl's editorial conception of *Hegels theologische Jugendschriften*.

been co-relative enterprises.[31] He was particularly focused on the coming of Christianity as a revolutionary transition. It held out the prospect of a moral awakening at a time when public virtue was declining under the Roman Empire. Hegel proposed examining how the Christian faith took off, but also how its objectives were systematically frustrated. He studied revolutionary promise as well as unexpected reversals. As a result, his subject was not only cultural transformation, but also the pathologies inherent in historical change. It became clear that carrying out an anatomy of revolutions involved investigating how outcomes contradicted their original purposes.

II

There were six decisive episodes in particular that captured Hegel's imagination throughout the 1790s: Periclean Greece, the rise of Rome, the story of Christ, the Reformation, the thought of Rousseau and Kant, and the French Revolution.[32] Throughout his career these remained essential touchstones. What preoccupied him particularly were the transitions between these episodes.[33] For that reason, he explored each moment with resolute attention: the passage from Judaism to Christianity; the decline of the Greek city-states and the rise to ascendancy of Roman power; the emergence of the Reformation out of the

31. Hegel to Schelling, 16 April 1795, *Hegels Briefe*, 1, p. 24.

32. For Hegel, less 'reflective' cultures, such as those of Egypt and Persia, in being less critical, were less prone to revolution. See Terry Pinkard, *Does History Make Sense? Hegel on the Historical Shapes of Justice* (Cambridge, MA: Harvard University Press, 2017), ch. 3.

33. G.W.F. Hegel, *Lectures on the Philosophy of World History, Introduction: Reason in History*, trans. H. B. Nisbet (Cambridge: Cambridge University Press, 1975), pp. 62–63.

medieval Church; and the progress from Enlightenment to Revolution in France. For Hegel, each of these amounted to some kind of revolution, or drastic transformation in a determinate way of life. What drove this sequence of upheavals? Hegel began by complicating reductive accounts that opposed 'intellectual' and 'material' causes of change. In addressing the interconnections between religion, morality and politics, he focused on elucidating familiar cases of religious thought and practice. Most world religions, he observed, combined doctrinal with moral and ceremonial aspects. As potential vehicles for moral progress, religions typically brought together ethical values based on rational norms with habits grounded in human sensibility. This amalgam yielded customs which permeated the institutions of public life. The appeal of customs was often enhanced through ceremonial forms of representation. Hegel pointed to the example of Athenian dramatic festivals: 'the dramas they staged in the public theatre had a religious origin which they never disavowed, even as they became more cultivated.'[34] Thus social practices, Hegel argued, could be analysed into their rational, affective and aesthetic dimensions. He thought that many religions failed to combine each aspect in healthy proportions. Christianity, for instance, appeared to lack a sustaining sense of beauty: 'the spirit of our religion has banished all the beautiful colorations of sense as well as everything that has charm.'[35] The Greeks, once again, provided the telling counterpoint. In their world, morality, popular sentiment and aesthetic values reinforced one another. As Hegel saw it, this coalescence facilitated a political existence based on freedom. Moreover, such an artful mix of factors fulfilled a persistent

---

34. Hegel, 'Tübingen Essay', p. 56.
35. Ibid., p. 53.

'need' of reason: the reconciliation of virtue with happiness. From Hegel's vantage point, failure to coordinate these two indispensable values would pose a threat to the integrity of any civilisation.

As things appeared to Hegel around the mid-1790s, the prospects for Christianity were altogether less propitious than had been the fortunes of Athenian culture. In building his case, part of his argument was explicitly indebted to Kant. A properly rational religion (*Vernunftreligion*), Hegel agreed, was dedicated to the project of moral betterment. But, in his early writings, Hegel sought to reconcile this commitment to duty with Rousseau's conception of 'conscience' or purity of heart. In this Hegel was inspired by the Savoyard Vicar in Rousseau's *Emile*, for whom moral sensibility was rooted in feelings ('simplicity of heart') untouched by the rationalising inclinations of *amour-propre*.[36] Conscience, Rousseau argued, is the 'voice of the soul', which never deceives. However reason, when captured by the passions, does.[37] The attempt to merge Rousseau with Kant is pursued intermittently in the Tübingen essay: 'religion is a concern of the heart stemming from a need of practical reason'.[38] This underpinned Hegel's core conviction that a viable faith had to be a people's or 'folk' (*Volk*) religion: it must engage existing human affections.[39] In a challenge to Kant, he made plain his view that purity of intention, or 'holiness' of disposition, was not sufficient to propel human beings into action. Behaviour

36. Jean-Jacques Rousseau, *Emile, or On Education* (1762), ed. and trans. Christopher Kelly and Allan Bloom (Hanover, NH: University Press of New England, 2010), p. 425,
37. Ibid., p. 449.
38. Hegel, 'Tübingen Essay', p. 36. 'People's religion' seems a better translation of *Volksreligion* than 'folk religion'.
39. Ibid., pp. 33, 42.

was only incentivised by moral norms insofar as these formed part of already cherished values that spoke to our deepest sentiments. Without these conditions, a church was merely a set of 'objective' or disembodied precepts.[40]

In expounding his argument, Hegel considered the impact of enlightenment (*Aufklärung*) on cultural change. For enlightenment to be effective it had to 'determine' the will. That is, it had to change the direction of human choice. This might be effected by means of either our practical or our theoretical faculty. The latter, however, was a potential source of corruption when based on the narrow aptitudes of 'understanding' (*Verstand*). In clarifying this point, Hegel contrasted the conduct of Coriolanus and Tertullian: the former, he thought, was moved by humility, the latter by pride. Tertullian had condemned the final wish of Socrates, as relayed in Plato's *Phaedo*, that a sacrifice be offered on his behalf to the god Asclepius.[41] This, to Tertullian, was mere heathen superstition, but to Hegel it exhibited Socrates's piety on the threshold of death. Tertullian had allegedly failed to recognise an instance of conscientious rectitude on account of his subscription to theoretical dogmas that warped his judgement of virtue. This made Tertullian an 'arrogant sectarian' who traduced the promptings of conscience to service his self-regarding intellect.[42] Understanding might of course be constructively enlightened by freeing the mind of counterproductive prejudices. But it was also susceptible to vanity, especially among the learned. The influence of Rousseau's *Emile*, as well as his *Discourse on the Arts and Sciences*, is

40. Ibid., pp. 33–34.

41. See Q. *Septimi Florentis Tertulliani Apologeticum*, ed. Paolo Frassinetti (Turin: Paravia & Co., 1965), pp. 105–6; Plato, *Phaedo*, 118a.

42. Hegel, 'Tübingen Essay', pp. 38–39.

again evident here. Sophists of enlightenment merely strove to raise themselves above mass opinion, thereby losing all sense of purity of heart.[43] Wisdom (*Weisheit*) was required to yoke intellect to virtue. Such a feat was often the work of 'outstanding individuals'.[44] Yet, even then, inspired talents would have to work with the grain of history. This requirement carried with it a further burden of risk: the path on which events were already travelling might be foredoomed.

Most importantly, Christianity was consigned to its fatal course. Hegel was already preoccupied with Kant's theory of the 'highest good', the terminus where virtue and happiness would ideally meet.[45] As Hegel explained in a fragment from his Bern period, the highest good meant 'morality accompanied by the appropriate degree of happiness'.[46] The Kantian account of a prospective overlap between the moral good (the kingdom of ends) and the sum of human satisfaction (happiness) was built on a critique of Christian attempts to close the gap by resort to superstitious beliefs and fetishistic practices. Hegel worried that Kant's vision had been erected on a 'mere' ideal of reason, with the result that hopes for its realisation were disconnected from human sensibility. However, at the same time, he accepted Kant's indictment of compromised Christian orthodoxy as 'an idolatrous faith, which imagines it can curry God's favor by some means or other than a will that is in itself good'.[47] This degraded creed, based on self-abasement, was the source of modern moral despotism. Under it, responsibility was

---

43. Ibid., p. 44.

44. Ibid., pp. 42–43.

45. The best treatment of the role of the highest good in Kant is still Allen W. Wood, *Kant's Moral Religion* (Ithaca, NY: Cornell University Press, 1970), ch. 3.

46. Hegel, 'Unter objektiver Religion', in *Frühe Schriften 1*, p. 155.

47. Hegel, 'Tübingen Essay', p. 45.

sacrificed to pleas for divine recompense. It therefore derived from a misbegotten conception of providence. On Hegel's reading, the Greeks resigned themselves to the machinations of blind fate, whereas Christians were continually agitating for immediate favours from an all-powerful and omnipresent deity. Inevitable disappointment led to anger and alienation. The Greeks similarly assumed that the gods favoured virtuous conduct, but at the same time they resigned themselves to the fact of misfortune—to the necessity of luck (ἀναγκαίη Τύχη).[48] Oedipus, for example, accepted his unhappy fate (μοῖρα).[49] However Christians, for the most part, were left petitioning for relief, forever condemned to despondency and self-incurred impotence. During his years in Bern, Hegel enlarged on these ideas in a further series of fragmentary drafts. His central concern remained the contradictions internal to orthodox Christianity. His strategy was still to compare the fate of Christian belief with the plight of Judaism along with the careers of the Romans and the Greeks.

III

This comparative approach was in part carried out by juxtaposing exemplary characters. Socrates and Jesus, as outstanding personalities who shaped incipient ways of life, were the principal protagonists examined. Rome produced no equivalent instructors, Hegel believed. Its culture was dominated by a single organising virtue in the face of which dissent could not

---

48. Ibid., pp. 50–52.

49. Hegel, 'Jetzt braucht die Menge', in *Frühe Schriften 1*, p. 163. Hegel's interest in the problem of fate (*Fatum, Moira*) started early. See G.W.F. Hegel, 'Exzerpt 44: Aus Homer, Ilias', in *Frühe Exzerpte*, pp. 239–40.

be tolerated: 'deviation from Roman nature was a crime against the state'.[50] Greece—or, more specifically, Athens—was altogether different. In the fifth century BCE, a critical ethos thrived, exemplified by the ironic personality of Socrates. The institutions of democratic city-states produced open, rational inquiry. As Adam Smith had similarly noted, frankness and urbanity were shared norms; all classes, excluding slaves, freely exchanged opposing views.[51] Jesus likewise challenged prevailing Jewish values. Like Socrates, he was a charismatic countercultural force. However, both figures, Hegel emphasised, had to operate in widely divergent contexts. Their approaches were also conspicuously distinct. Socrates cultivated colleagues rather than disciples, and his interlocutors retained their independent identities along with their all-too-human attributes.[52] Jesus, on the other hand, collected disciples and apostles. From the beginning he encouraged exclusivity and discipline among those charged with disseminating his message.[53] Over time, the message came into conflict with the world in which it was obliged to function. In Hegel's mind, the problems were both structural and intellectual in nature. Contradictions steadily proliferated. To begin with, Christ's teachings were designed for an intimate fraternity, where selflessness and mutual

50. Hegel, 'Berne Fragments', in *Three Essays, 1793–95*, p. 61

51. Ibid., p. 59. Cf. Adam Smith, *Lectures on Rhetoric and Belles Lettres*, ed. J. C. Bryce (Indianapolis: Liberty Classics, 1985), p. 158.

52. Hegel, 'Berne Fragments', pp. 62–63. Cf. G.W.F. Hegel, 'The Positivity of the Christian Religion' (1795–96), in *Early Theological Writings*, trans. T. M. Knox (Philadelphia: University of Pennsylvania Press, 1975), p. 82. The essay as presented here in English is an editorial reconstruction, based on the work of Herman Nohl, from fragments dating from 1795 to 1796, principally Texts 32, 33 and 34 in Hegel, *Frühe Schriften 1*.

53. Hegel, 'Berne Fragments', pp. 61–63.

accommodation could succeed. Yet these conditions were poorly adapted to the goal of proselytism. Property, rather than communism, was cherished in wider society; and self-defence, instead of pacifism, was the standard posture of states.[54] Thus normative precepts and existing arrangements inevitably collided. Jesus could make history, but not just as he pleased.

On Hegel's analysis, this impasse shaped the history of Christianity. It influenced the character of its proponents and detractors alike. Critics recorded the sequence of Christian abominations: the crusades, the conquest of America, the slave trade. While apologists might accept that these were reprehensible failures, they still responded that the only cure was a purified Christian code.[55] Hegel cited Montesquieu's injunction against righteousness, which he took to be applicable to both sides: reproaches against churches might equally be applied to governments, yet in the end moral improvement had to be enacted with the support of existing establishments.[56] Otherworldly purity was never a real option. Nonetheless, Hegel still maintained that Christian ideology was riven by intrinsic tensions. On the one hand, Christianity was a universal system of renewal; but, on the other, it was merely an historic faith, such that adherence was contingent on accidents of birth.[57] Hegel was also perturbed by the Christian promise of salvation. While this was based on the idea of being well-pleasing to God, it was also based on faith in the divinity of Christ. By implication, the doctrine of grace was no less troubling to Hegel: on the one

54. Ibid., pp. 70–71, 75.

55. Ibid., p. 70.

56. Ibid., discussing Montesquieu's *Spirit of the Laws*, p. 460 (Cohler, Miller and Stone edn).

57. Hegel, 'Berne Fragments', p. 96.

hand deliverance depended on the character of moral behaviour, but on the other hand it was a gift based on the quality of conviction. On top of this, the idea of human depravity was fundamental. Christianity could make man virtuous only if he was already good, but inherent wickedness made the hope of renovation futile.[58]

Hegel observed that Christianity demanded forms of piety that in practice were only sustainable among intimates—inside the family, or among a dedicated brotherhood. Translating these expectations into a more diffuse society had disturbing consequences. Above all it bred a deep-seated suspicion of deviation from outwardly professed intentions. Historically, this distrust gave rise to a violation of rights—to inquisitions, confessions, penances and excommunications. The overwhelming impulse to scrutinise motives persisted through the Reformation, Hegel recognised: Luther still sought to control men's minds, with the result that hypocrisy became endemic within Protestant cultures.[59] Where Christianity was introduced into foreign countries, the populace was pitted against clerical leaders. This, for Hegel, yielded another irony: despite the initial cast of its faith, the Christian mission instituted a class-based society, starkly pitting lay society against a priestly order. The burden of discrepancies mounted. Wherever authority was used to eradicate simple traditions, reason thereafter inevitably rose to challenge the ascendancy of entrenched beliefs and their enforcement.[60]

Throughout the history of civilisations, Hegel reflected, incongruities had generated seismic adjustments in the shape of

58. Ibid., pp. 94–95.
59. Ibid., pp. 72–73.
60. Ibid., p. 99.

world revolutions. Established forms of culture eroded and broke down. Writing about epochal transitions in the 1790s, Hegel was aware that his own age was undergoing a fundamental shift. This only deepened his fascination with the dynamics of change and their underlying causes. Herbert Marcuse wrote of German Idealism in general that the ideas of 1789 largely determined its 'conceptual core'.[61] Despite speculation of the kind, historians since Friedrich Meinecke have associated changes at that time with the origins of Germany's 'deviation' from mainstream European norms.[62] Meinecke built on arguments devised by Ernst Troeltsch which were then ratified by Meinecke's student Hajo Holborn.[63] All this contributed to the spurious notion of a special intellectual path that led German society astray. By way of contrast, for Hegel there existed a European convergence, which made it all the more essential to grasp the meaning of the French Revolution. However, the complexity of Hegel's conception has scarcely been appreciated. He applauded events in the period which advanced self-government and accountability. Yet he did not approve the sequence of events following on from 1789. Nonetheless, the very idea of revolution pervaded his sensibility. Under its influence he wrote that 'tradition [. . .] entwined as it is in universal custom, can only be broken up by the most extreme state of

---

61. Herbert Marcuse, *Reason and Revolution: Hegel and the Rise of Social Theory* (1941) (Boston, MA: Beacon Press, 1960), p. 3.

62. Friedrich Meinecke, *Die deutsche Katastrophe: Betrachtungen und Errinerungen* (Wiesbaden: Eberhard Brockhaus Verlag, 1946).

63. Ernst Troeltsch, 'Naturrecht und Humanität in der Weltpolitik', *Weltwirtschaftliches Archiv*, 18 (1922), pp. 485–501; Hajo Holborn, 'German Idealism in the Light of Social History', in *Germany and Europe: Historical Essays* (New York: Doubleday, 1970).

decay coupled with the advance of reason, and even then only amidst violent convulsions.[64] Hegel was thinking partly of his home territory: the fate of France might yet await the situation in Württemberg. Reason could tip decline into a fall. For Hegel, this made it crucial to understand the descent of French affairs into spiralling zealotry and violence.

There were those who would lament the departure of bygone worlds, dissolved under mounting pressure from rational scrutiny. Notoriously, in 1799, Novalis deplored the demise of medieval Europe and its replacement by a regime of commercial acquisitiveness.[65] Earlier, he had singled out Burke's *Reflections on the Revolution in France* as a 'revolutionary' tract against the Revolution and the mercenary attitudes established in its wake.[66] He had in mind Burke's regret for the passing of the 'age of chivalry'.[67] Yet Hegel had no patience with belated anguish of the kind. He suggested that we are drawn to such lingering residues out of fear that value in general would perish with the loss of particular goods. This accounted for nostalgic 'portrayals of the age of chivalry'. On that basis, Hegel concluded that it was 'the tendency of the present age to confuse the disappearance of those once moving associations with the demise of ethical life as such that provokes its lamentations'.[68] Typically, Hegel believed, as one form of life succeeded

64. Hegel, 'Berne Fragments', p. 66.

65. Novalis, 'Christianity or Europe: A Fragment' (1799), in *The Early Political Writings of the German Romantics* (Cambridge: Cambridge University Press, 1996), p. 63.

66. Novalis, 'Pollen' (1798), in ibid., p. 29.

67. Edmund Burke, *Reflections on the Revolution in France* (1790), ed. J.C.D. Clark (Stanford, CA: Stanford University Press, 2001), p. 238.

68. Hegel, 'Berne Fragments,' p. 67.

another, primordial simplicity was first sacrificed to the tenets of clerical learning, but later, as was happening at the close of the eighteenth century in France, the dominion of priestcraft would be undermined by rational criticism. The job of philosophy was less to rue these dislocating reversals than to monitor the direction of travel. Philosophy's task in that sense was partly historical in nature.

For Schelling, Hölderlin and Hegel, it was above all Kant who had illustrated the potential impact of reason on human affairs. As he was completing his dissertation on biblical hermeneutics in 1795, Schelling revealed to Hegel his determination not to be buried in antiquarian dust, but rather to be swept along by the tide of his 'own time'.[69] It was Kant who had opened the gate to an incipient rebirth. The *Critique of Pure Reason* itself, Schelling later asserted, had spawned a 'revolution'. The completion of this task sometimes seemed more distant than initial hopes suggested: 'the revolution, which should be effected through philosophy, is still far off'.[70] But the source of all promise remained undisputed: 'with Kant the dawn rose'.[71] In this spirit, Hegel reminded Schelling that 'Reason and Liberty' was still their slogan, and an 'invisible church' (*unsichtbare Kirche*) the goal of their communion.[72] This was a deliberate invocation of Kant's *Religion within the Boundaries of Mere Reason*. As Kant framed the matter, religion strove to realise an ethical association with the aid of ecclesiastical establishments. The question for Hegel was whether the 'visible' institution was compromising the 'invisible' objective. What was not

69. Schelling to Hegel, 6 January 1795, *Hegels Briefe*, 1, p. 14.
70. Schelling to Hegel, 21 July 1995, ibid., p. 28
71. Schelling to Hegel, 4 February 1795, ibid., p. 20.
72. Hegel to Schelling, end of January 1795, ibid., p. 18.

in doubt was the inspiration behind Hegel's forecast: 'From the Kantian system and its highest completion, I expect a revolution in Germany.'[73] The means of this transformation lay in principles already available. These awaited application to all inherited schemes of thought. Ultimately, Hegel would apply them to Kant himself.

73. Hegel to Schelling, 16 April 1795, ibid., p. 23.

2

Kant, Religion and Revolution

THE IDEA OF A TRANSFORMATIVE insight leading to a sudden break is fundamental to Kant's understanding of his achievement in the *Critique of Pure Reason*. As is well known, this conception of his project was crystallised in the 'Preface' to the second edition of the work, published in 1787. A dramatic shift in perspective, Kant argued, could completely remodel a science. Famously, he recalled the case of Copernicus, who, to make sense of 'the celestial motions', switched perspective from the stars to the position of the spectator, yielding the thought that while the latter was in motion the former were at rest.[1] The Copernican challenge began as a hypothesis, subsequently tested by a series of experiments.[2] As with Copernicus, Kant

---

1. Immanuel Kant, *Critique of Pure Reason* (1781), ed. and trans. Paul Guyer and Allen W. Wood (Cambridge: Cambridge University Press, 1998), B xvi.

2. N. R. Hanson, 'Copernicus's Role in Kant's Revolution', *Journal of the History of Ideas*, 20: 2 (April 1959), pp. 274–81, argued that the idea of a Copernican hypothesis appeared nowhere in Kant's works. But see Immanuel Kant, 'The Blomberg Logic' (1770s), in *Lectures on Logic*, ed. and trans. J. Michael Young (Cambridge: Cambridge University Press, 1992), AA 24: 222–24. Cf. Immanuel Kant, *The Conflict of the Faculties* (1798), in *Religion and Rational Theology*, ed. and trans. Allen W. Wood and George di Giovanni (Cambridge: Cambridge University Press, 1996), AA 7: 83.

went on to argue, so also with his own philosophy: an 'alteration in our way of thinking' promised to place a whole system
of knowledge on a new footing.[3] Circular groping in metaphysics could, accordingly, graduate to 'the secure course of a
science'.[4] The new Kantian conception proposed that our experience of the world is formed into knowledge through the
faculty of cognition. In this way, a pioneering philosophical
intuition had given rise to what Kant himself dubbed 'an entire
revolution'.[5] Kant pointed to 'the restless striving' of reason as
the source of this species of innovation.[6] He picked out three
examples of successful intellectual reorientation undertaken
before his own attempt to renovate metaphysics. These were
logic, mathematics and natural science respectively. In each
case, a form of knowledge discovered a new way of 'constructing' its object, as illustrated by Euclid in the case of geometry.[7]
In this instance, 'a new light broke' upon a gifted pioneer. Although the flowering of natural science had been slower, with
the breakthrough coming in the sixteenth and seventeenth
centuries, here too 'a light dawned'.[8] In fact, in each of these
examples, 'a sudden revolution in the way of thinking' had delivered up a new world. This pointed to the active role of our
mental faculties in determining the shape of things: 'reason

On the Copernican 'turn' (Wende), see Hans Blumenberg, *Die kopernikanische
Wende* (Frankfurt am Main: Suhrkamp, 1965).

3. Kant, *Critique of Pure Reason*, B xviii.

4. Ibid., B viii.

5. Ibid., B xxii.

6. Ibid., B xiii.

7. Kant to Christian Gottfried Schütz, 25 June 1787, in Immanuel Kant, *Correspondence* [*Kant Correspondence*], ed. Arnulf Zweig (Cambridge: Cambridge University
Press, 1999), AA 10: 489, makes clear that he had Euclid specifically in mind.

8. Kant, *Critique of Pure Reason*, B xii–B xiii.

has insight only into what it produces according to its own design'.[9] It is never merely a passive pupil, but always also a dynamic teacher.

Kant's focus, then, was on intellectual change—on new departures in the history of reason. But, for all that, the consequences of a drastic shift in perspective affected life more generally. As Kant saw it, the revolution in geometry, for example, was even more significant than the 'discovery of the way around the famous Cape'.[10] It was clear that the rounding of the African continent in 1488, opening access to the markets of the East to the Portuguese, had changed Europe and the world, both politically and commercially, forever. However, it was equally plain that without the application of the principles of geometry, this feat of navigation would itself not have been possible. What struck Kant in the cases of logic, mathematics and empirical science, and perhaps now too in metaphysics, was less the process of incremental development than the spectacle of 'a revolution brought about all at once'.[11] Given this emphasis on sudden conceptual innovation, it is notable that the final chapter of the first *Critique*, 'The History of Pure Reason', is a mere two and a half pages long. This is partly accounted for by the fact that the chapter was only a placeholder, a provisional summary to be 'filled in the future'.[12] But it is also a consequence of Kant's tendency to view philosophy in terms of positive results alone, without much interest in the process whereby insights were acquired. As he surveyed the history of philosophical endeavour at the close of the *Critique of Pure Reason*,

9. Ibid., B xiii.
10. Ibid., B xi.
11. Ibid., B xvi.
12. Ibid., A852/B880.

he confessed that he could see 'edifices' across this landscape, yet each of them lay in 'ruins'.[13] From this viewpoint, past exercises in philosophy added up to a simple history of error. Accordingly, narratives such as Johann Jakob Brucker's *Historia critica philosophiae*, much like Diogenes Laërtius's *Lives of the Philosophers*, recorded only a litany of false starts.[14] Before a given decisive breakthrough, there was only 'stumbling about' (*herumtappen*).[15] There was no reason to dwell on the sequence of blunders unless one stage was related to the next. It was Hegel who would in due course strive to provide these linkages.

Kant tended to disregard the value of historical knowledge per se. In the first *Critique* itself, he followed Christian Wolff's *Discursus praeliminaris de philosophia in genere* of 1728 in distinguishing between received learning and principled discrimination. The former was associated with merely historical understanding, the latter with rational discourse. Historical knowledge, as Kant presented it, is passively received, or just taught, either on the basis of direct experience or by means of recorded narratives.[16] This form of education was at bottom 'imitation': 'one only learns to walk by first being led'.[17] Cultures that were pre-philosophical were largely imitative, in Kant's view. Among the Chaldeans, the Babylonians and even the Egyptians, the role of thinking was confined to priestly and administrative circles: 'All the philosophers of the most ancient peoples were to be found among the priests'. Before it could separate itself from clerical and governing elites, Kant went on,

---

13. Ibid.
14. Both Brucker and Laërtius are cited in the first *Critique*. See ibid., B xi; A316.
15. For 'stumbling about' before the advent of science, see ibid., B vii.
16. Ibid., A836/B864–A837/B865.
17. Kant, 'Blomberg Logic', AA 24: 17.

philosophy could not 'really be produced'.[18] Nonetheless, some degree of reflection emerged in even the most static societies. This activity tended to begin with thought about the deity and its characteristics. The rational cognition of such subjects judged its material on the basis of principles. It did not simply absorb, it also criticised. Kant thought that the historical progress of criticism revealed the 'labors' of reason over time.[19] The first seed of constructive enlightenment sprouted when the gods were regarded as favourably disposed to good conduct. Thus, moral theory and speculative inquiry, or ethics and metaphysics, together spawned philosophy.[20]

Kant followed Rousseau in believing that a misalliance between the two corrupted human thought and behaviour. Recalling the *Discourse on the Arts and Sciences*, Kant registered that 'Rousseau is of the opinion that the sciences have brought more harm than good'.[21] When the vanity of empty speculation compromises the impulse to fellow-feeling, a monstrous disproportion between our aptitudes arises, and virtue loses out to bogus sophistication.[22] The cure for this malady, Kant believed, lay in the procedures of his own critical philosophy: 'The critical path alone is still open,' he wrote.[23] This course involved reconceptualising the relationship between theoretical and practical reason altogether. It entailed subjecting the former to self-limiting critique and employing the latter as the basis for belief in such ideas as made up the subject matter of speculative metaphysics. Before this Kantian turn, all previous

18. Ibid., AA 31–32.
19. Kant, *Critique of Pure Reason*, A852/B880.
20. Ibid., A853/B881.
21. Kant, 'Blomberg Logic', AA 24: 65.
22. The point is developed in Rousseau, *Emile*, p. 455.
23. Kant, *Critique of Pure Reason*, A855/B883.

inquiry seemed to be mere floundering. There was no need, Kant thought, to chart the string of misadventures. And yet, despite his apparent indifference to the cumulative process of the history of ideas, Kant did acknowledge some developments as changes for the better. This implied that momentum might actually matter. To begin with, Kant's own project, in seeking to transcend Rousseau's indictment of crooked reason by showing how ethics could help secure rationality against self-corruption, at the same time upended our concept of moral value.[24] For Hegel, Hölderlin and Schelling, this was an example of moral progress. It derived, Kant himself claimed, from the critique of reason itself, which, by comparison with ancient philosophy, 'assigned the human being a thoroughly active existence in the world'. This meant that the individual was itself 'the original maker of all its representations and concepts, and ought to be the sole author of all its actions'.[25]

Kant's was not the only revolution in morals. In the 'Jäsche Logic', he declared that the 'most important epoch of Greek philosophy starts finally with Socrates'.[26] This was a familiar view, similarly held by Hegel, who explicitly named Socrates as a 'revolutionary' figure.[27] For both Kant and Hegel, this was because Socrates provided citizens with practical orientation. He redirected attention from the nature of things to human behaviour. At the same time, he proved his case both in argument and by

24. Rousseau's actual position is complex and beyond the scope of the discussion here. In any case, Kant associates his arguments with what he termed 'misology', or hostility to reason. See p. 326 below.

25. Kant, *Conflict of the Faculties*, AA 7: 70.

26. Kant, 'The Jäsche Logic' (1800), in *Lectures on Logic*, AA 9: 29.

27. G.W.F. Hegel, *Vorlesungen über die Philosophie der Geschichte* (1837), vol. 12 in *Werke*, ed. Eva Moldenhauer and Karl Markus Michel, 21 vols (Frankfurt: Suhrkamp, 1986), p. 329.

his own conduct.[28] This suggested that Socrates provided ethics with a new content, though Kant refrained from identifying what this comprised. Relevant to this context, in the 'Vienna Logic' Kant distinguished between the analytic and synthetic import of philosophy, the first of which could sharpen while the second could feed thinking. In theory, Socrates nourished his listeners with the practical substance of morality. Yet when Kant presented him as acting as a 'midwife' to his auditors, he took him to have helped them better reflect on what they already knew.[29] The material significance of his message went unmentioned. Therefore, on the one hand, we are led to expect that the Socratic revolution established a new regime of value yet, on the other, we are only shown how he developed new procedures. Nonetheless, despite all this, Kant did believe in a process of moral refinement. In the *Critique of the Power of Judgment*, he devoted considerable energy to explicating the 'culture of the human being' (*Kultur* des Menschen), amounting to the development of mental capacity in two dimensions: first, the improvement of rational skills in terms of instrumental calculation; and second, the cultivation of moral self-restraint (*Zucht, Disziplin*).[30]

Moral progress for Kant was not simply a matter of heightened self-control, but also a function of enlightenment. While this involved developing a conception of the moral life, it also implied a view of its enabling circumstances. As he argued in his famous essay on the meaning of 'Enlightenment', for autonomy to prosper conditions of freedom had to prevail.[31]

28. Kant, 'Blomberg Logic', AA 24: 36.

29. Kant, 'The Vienna Logic' (1780s), in *Lectures on Logic*, AA 24: 843.

30. Immanuel Kant, *Critique of the Power of Judgment* (1790), ed. and trans. Paul Guyer (Cambridge: Cambridge University Press, 2000), AA 5: 430–32.

31. Immanuel Kant, 'An Answer to the Question: What is Enlightenment', passim.

While, in Kant's treatment, the substance of enlightenment in Socrates remained obscure, it became more transparent in the case of Rousseau. In the remarks to his *Observations on the Beautiful and Sublime*, Kant revealed how 'Rousseau has set me right'—by teaching him how to honour human beings. This was apparently based on a new conception of the rights of humanity.[32] Yet it was Christianity, for Kant, which constituted the aboriginal revolution in consciousness. Essentially, he took Rousseau to have clarified the Christian message by associating the moral faculty with purity of heart grounded in a conception of freedom.[33] In the *Critique of Pure Reason*, Kant wrote of moral concepts being 'determined' and 'purified'. This came about under the influence of what he termed the 'extremely pure moral law of our religion'.[34] Christ introduced a breakthrough on which Rousseau helped to build. Kant's work was a further extension of this process of elucidation. It was not until 1792, when he started to publish a series of essays in J. E. Biester's *Berlinische Monatsschrift*, all of which would appear together as *Religion within the Boundaries of Mere Reason*, that Kant turned more closely to thinking about the history of moral reasoning, and thus the stages involved in the perfection of virtue. Six months after the first essay had appeared, an admiring interlocutor, Ludwig Borowski, presumed to compare Kant with the figure of Jesus Christ. While Kant protested that any suggestion of equivalence was hyperbolic, he conceded that there was a basic alignment of principles between 'Christian'

32. Immanuel Kant, 'Remarks' (1764–65), in *Observations on the Feeling of the Beautiful and Sublime and Other Essays*, ed. and trans. Patrick Frierson and Paul Guyer (Cambridge: Cambridge University Press, 2011), AA 20: 94.

33. See Rousseau, *Emile*, pp. 444, 448–49, on which Kant drew.

34. Kant, *Critique of Pure Reason*, A817/B845.

and 'philosophical' morality. Christ was a conspicuously 'hallowed' figure, Kant underlined, while he himself was merely 'a pathetic bungler trying to interpret the former as well as he can'.[35] There was considerable room for innovation in finessing an interpretation, yet the broad thrust of the Kantian programme was evident enough in this formulation.

II

As already indicated, Kant considered Christianity to have triggered 'a revolution in the human race'.[36] Like other moments of epochal transition in the Kantian repertoire, this involved a sudden mutation in an existing mindset. The seed of properly moral judgement was implicit in all religions, yet it was the Christian faith that above all helped this rational capacity to evolve: 'there lies in it (invisibly)—as in a shoot that develops and will in the future bear seeds in turn—the whole that will one day enlighten [*erleuchten*] the world and rule over it'.[37] There was, Kant was arguing, a rational kernel within the mystical shell. For the shoot (*Keim*) to blossom, the right conditions had to emerge. Kant believed that Christianity, as a universal programme with a pure message, would prove the most efficient delivery mechanism for disseminating religion as a project of moral betterment. To begin

---

35. Kant to Borowski, 24 October 1792, *Kant Correspondence*, AA 11: 380. For Borowski's letter to Kant of 12 October 1792, see AA 11: 373. For the sketch to which Kant was responding, see L. E. Borowski et al., *Immanuel Kant: Sein Leben in Darstellungen von Zeitgenossen* (Darmstadt: Wissenschaftliche Buchgesellschaft, 1978), pp. 41ff.

36. Immanuel Kant, *Religion within the Boundaries of Mere Reason and Other Writings*, ed. and trans. Allen Wood and George di Giovanni (Cambridge: 1998), AA 6: 63.

37. Ibid., 6: 122.

with, it brought about an alteration at once in theology and ethics. Under it, expectations of behaviour were modified alongside a reconceptualisation of the relationship between God and man. This was signalled by the teachings of Christ as a human divinity (or 'God-man').[38] His doctrines proposed a fundamental adjustment to Jewish ideas—both to the Jewish interpretation of the nature of the deity and of relations between the creator and human agents. Judaism, for Kant, was a religion of outward service. This it shared with all religions that reconciled virtue with happiness by the intercession of divine favour. In the Jewish case, supplicants sought redemption through practices of petition: forms of worship were taken to lead to a remission of sins. From Kant's viewpoint, the Jewish theocracy kept alive the idea of moral value, although in practice this was degraded under the influence of worldly incentives and the notion that virtue could be compelled by inducements.[39]

It was this worldview that was shattered by the advent of Christ. Whatever the truth of the life of Jesus, as an ideal he was the prototype of morality made flesh.[40] Whereas Judaism, much like other cult-based systems of belief, rejected the idea of the self-improvement of reason, labouring instead under the idea of human impotence, Christ established a 'religion of *good life-conduct*'.[41] This involved a wholesale repudiation of forms of supernatural solicitation in favour of an emphasis on moral attitudes or dispositions (*Gesinnungen*). A *Gesinnungsethik* of the kind had to be rooted in human freedom: 'it is a fundamental principle that, to become a better human being, everyone

38. Ibid., 6: 119.
39. Ibid., 6: 79–80.
40. Ibid., 6: 63.
41. Ibid.

must do as much as it is in his power to do.'[42] This was a religion of self-imposed continence in which moral choice was determined by freely conforming the will to duty. In the history of all known forms of public faith, Christianity alone began with this intuition.[43] Kant believed that his own thought, much like Rousseau's, was a detailed elucidation of this revolutionary insight. It represented an altogether new 'moral dominion.'[44] But while the Christian religion amounted to a metamorphosis in this way, it drew upon primeval human capacities or 'predispositions' (Anlagen).[45] So, while the Christian revolution was in one sense a straightforward breach consisting of a radically new approach to morality, the nature and the process of renovation was complicated.

The need for renovation derived from the condition of human beings. For Kant, our nature was afflicted by a radical and ineliminable 'propensity' (Hang) for evil.[46] This was neither a natural nor a hereditary predicament, but a product of self-willed corruption. Kant's Pelagianism is evident in his emphasis on imputability: humanity did not originally 'lie in sin', but rather elected to submit to its own proclivity for evil.[47] Kant advanced an elaborate conjectural moral psychology to justify this claim. He proposed that our natural predispositions

42. Ibid., 6: 51. The term Gesinnungsethik (ethics of disposition) is Weber's, not Kant's, but it is close to the latter's meaning. See Max Weber, Wissenschaft als Beruf (1917–1919); Politik als Beruf (1919), ed. Wolfgang J. Mommsen and Wolfgang Schluchter (Tübingen: J.C.B. Mohr, 1994), p. 79.

43. Kant, Religion, AA 6: 52.

44. Ibid., 6: 83.

45. Ibid., 6: 26.

46. Ibid., 6: 28–29.

47. On Pelagianism in Kant, see Allen W. Wood, Kant and Religion (Cambridge: Cambridge University Press, 2020), pp. 62, 161, 178–79.

were fundamentally benign: the appetite for self-preservation ('animality'), the desire for happiness ('humanity') and the capacity for moral reciprocation ('personality') were all harmless as primitively constituted.[48] However, in social life the development of rational self-love bred self-conceit. As a result, the instinct for self-preservation was liable to abuse, instrumental reason was prone to self-aggrandisement and our moral faculty was readily subverted. It was not 'personality', as such, that was debased: respect for the good could never itself be extirpated from the mind. Rather, reason was seduced into self-corruption. This happened when the 'dear self' (*das liebe Selbst*) intruded itself into moral judgement.[49] Self-love enabled the 'incorporation' of self-serving maxims into the practical will.[50] In effect, a choice contrary to the moral law is prompted by the culpable subordination of the rationally more potent incentive to mere sensory inclination. This pathological yet universal frame of mind sprang from an underlying 'temptation to be tempted' for which human choice was itself responsible. It found expression in different levels of corruption, ranging from frailty through impurity to depravity.[51] The propensity to corruption might yield heinous acts—or 'vices of hatred'—such as malice, vengeance, envy and domination.[52] Yet immorality for the most

---

48. Kant, *Religion*, AA 6: 26–28.

49. Immanuel Kant, *Groundwork of the Metaphysics of Morals* (1785), ed. and trans. Mary Gregor and Jens Timmerman (Cambridge: Cambridge University Press, 2012), AA 4: 407.

50. Kant, *Religion*, AA 6: 23–24. On the concept of evil and the 'incorporation' thesis in Kant, see Henry E. Allison, *Kant's Theory of Freedom* (Cambridge: Cambridge University Press, 1990), pp. 5–6, 146–61.

51. Kant, *Religion*, AA 6: 29–30.

52. Immanuel Kant, *The Metaphysics of Morals*, ed. Lara Denis, trans. Mary Gregor (Cambridge: Cambridge University Press, 2017), AA 6: 458–61; Kant, *Religion*, AA 6: 93–94.

part was a product of devious rationalisation (*Vernünfteln*).[53] It proceeded, that is, from self-deception: from the covert importation of self-interest into putatively moral choices. While Kant was deeply convinced of the depravity of the will, he was equally committed to the hope of regeneration.[54] No matter how all-encompassing the impulse to self-love might be, the germinal concept of meritorious action remained indelible within consciousness: it 'resounds', as Kant put it, 'unabated in our souls'.[55] The question was how to render this faint possibility actual in practice. The Christian revolution was a step in the right direction: it conveyed the possibility of purity of heart through persuasive doctrinal formulations, reinforced by the conduct and sufferings of Jesus. But Christianity itself was soon debauched. Having inaugurated a far-reaching rebirth—a radical 'change of heart' (*Herzensänderung*)—the descent into decadence promptly materialised. Christ's intervention occurred when Judaism was 'ripe for revolution'.[56] Groaning under the weight of ecclesiastical ordinances, and exposed to the influence of new waves of Greek thought, the people were ready for a rejuvenating message.[57] Christ signalled a dramatic about-turn, a completely new mode of thinking (*Denkungsart*).[58] This mental shift was a precondition for ongoing practical change. The spiritual about-face would stand in need of constant application ('incessant laboring'), a relentless programme of cultivation.[59] Kant described this as a process of

53. Kant, *Groundwork*, AA 4: 37; Kant, *Religion*, AA 6: 42.
54. Kant, *Religion*, AA 6: 37, 44.
55. Ibid., 6: 45.
56. Ibid., 6: 80.
57. Ibid., 6: 128.
58. Ibid., 6: 47.
59. Ibid., 6: 48.

incremental 'reform' succeeding the initial 'revolution'.[60] Yet tangible reversals immediately loomed.

The earliest stage of Christian evolution was missing from the historical record. Kant noted that the Roman historians immediately following the death of Christ never addressed themselves to the character of the early church. By the time that a learned public existed to register and describe its affairs, the faith had already degenerated, shaping the course of future progress.[61] This reversal amounted to a reconfiguration of the primary Christian credo. Whereas salvation, Kant thought, ought to be based on 'works'—on the quality of intentions and their corresponding deeds—the frailty of the human mind typically subverted the appropriate *ordo salutis*. This inversion persisted within Lutheran orthodoxy. Under its rules, forgiveness was made reliant on the profession of faith.[62] According to Kant, there had occurred within Catholicism and Lutheranism alike a corruption of purely moral religion dedicated to the enhancement of autonomous duty. Here, then, was the actual fate of the 'visible' church of Christian belief charged with creating an 'ethical community'.[63] Yet, despite this setback, Kant held that a rational core still resided within the ecclesiastical casing. This 'invisible' shoot aimed at realising an association under the laws of virtue.[64] For human creatures, such an ambition required assistance from the 'idea' of providence as well as institutional means of embodiment. Any pure moral faith always stood in need of historical expression. This was because, pending the

---

60. Ibid., 6: 47: 'a revolution [. . .] in the mode of thought but a gradual reformation in the mode of sense'.
61. Ibid., 6: 130.
62. Ibid., 6: 116–17.
63. Ibid., 6: 95–96.
64. Ibid., 6: 101.

arrival of moral perfection, behaviour needed to be incentivised: religion could not afford to bank on the stimulus of duty
alone. Ideas of reason had to be animated through sensible
representations which could at once galvanise and transmit a
model of upright conduct. Ordinarily, Kant recognised, motivation was derived from external prescriptions deriving their authority from a scheme of revelation. It remained to be shown
what constituted the most effective vehicle for realising the
invisible goal of ethical community. In Kant's mind, since this
objective involved collecting the 'totality' of human beings
within a 'republic of virtue', only a church of universal scope
could hope to bring about the fulfilment of that purpose.

With due deference to Moses Mendelssohn's *Jerusalem*, yet
fundamentally dissenting from its conclusions, Kant took Judaism to be an unpromising vehicle for the promotion of a universal moral faith.[65] Still, there were correspondences between
Christian and Judaic tenets, too. Like the Jewish religion, Christianity enjoyed the advantage of basing instruction on scripture. By
comparison with indoctrination through tradition, propagation by
means of scripture ensured the survival of an historical faith,
ultimately generating scholarship and a clerisy to facilitate its
adaptation and preservation: 'history proves that never could
a faith based on scripture be eradicated by even the most devastating political revolutions'.[66] Kant later applied the same
principle to 1789 in France: because the event had been publicly
recorded, it could never be forgotten.[67] Judeo-Christian doctrine was likewise ineradicable. However, unlike Judaism,

65. For the character of Kant's response to Mendelssohn, see, again, Wood, *Kant's
Moral Religion*, pp. 200–209.

66. Kant, *Religion*, AA 6: 107.

67. Kant, *Conflict of the Faculties*, AA 7: 88.

Christianity was intended as a comprehensive faith, transcending the local conditions of its formation. This made it a fitting 'integument' for the aim of universal conversion.[68] At the same time, it advocated purity of intention to replace what Kant regarded as a mercenary cult. Yet despite the hope that could reasonably be invested in the Christian mission, what is most striking in Kant's narration is the devastation of its primary purpose over the course of its development. In other words, the revolution was succeeded by the most catastrophic regression. At this point Kant resorted to Lucretius: 'tantum religio potuit suadere malorum!' (such evils could religion induce);[69] except that for Kant, the culprit was not heathenism, but Christianity itself. His depiction of Christian carnage was unsparing: in the wake of Jesus's revolutionary evangelism, steady deterioration ensued. Monkishness, superstition, orthodoxy, priestcraft and sectarianism rolled in with the centuries. Tyranny in the Eastern church and papacy in the West confirmed the process of decline. Later the Reformation introduced disfigurements of its own, including an escalation in fanaticism and strife. Altogether, the visible church permitted 'that turmoil which has wrecked the human race, and still tears it apart'.[70] Nothing is more remarkable in the philosophy of Kant than his adherence to the hope of future progress in moral refinement together with an abhorrence of the products of civilisation. Although history remained a site of ultimate promise, its record was unremittingly bleak.

There were three main indices of promise for Kant. First, as we have seen at length, came the Christian revolution itself. But

68. Kant, *Religion*, AA 6: 121.
69. Ibid., 6: 131, citing Lucretius, *De rerum natura*, 1.101.
70. Kant, *Religion*, AA 6: 131.

then there were improvements in philosophy as well, even if the gains were inconclusive and haphazard. Stoicism, for instance, had seemed a bonus to Kant: whereas it tended, unhelpfully, to deprecate sensibility, it also usefully championed the 'dignity of human nature'.[71] The Spinozist emphasis on the role of philosophy in augmenting the moral vocation of religion was also beneficial, even if, in general, Kant discounted Spinoza's ideas.[72] The insights of Rousseau and, more generally, the ideal of toleration, had likewise made overwhelmingly positive contributions. But finally, for Kant, beside the career of philosophy, it was the French Revolution which amounted to the most auspicious event in the history of civilisation since the coming of Christ. Comparison between the Christian and French revolutions was not uncommon. 'It is one of the decisive epochs of world history,' Georg Forster commented on events in France: 'since the birth of Christianity there has been nothing like it.'[73] But for Kant, unlike the radical initiatives which he catalogued in the cases of logic, mathematics and natural science, a moral revolution presented its own peculiar difficulties. With mathematics there occurred a transformative intuition, and a new intellectual universe eventuated. Similarly, physical science was launched by means of mutinous hypotheses which were then confirmed and explained by calculated 'experiments' (*Versuche*). But, in Kantian thought, a coup in the world of ethics was significantly different. New insights were not followed by

71. Ibid., 6: 57n.

72. For Kant's more critical approach, see, perhaps most interestingly, Immanuel Kant, 'What Does It Mean to Orientate Oneself in Thinking' (1786), in *Religion and Rational Theology*, ed. and trans. Allen W. Wood and George di Giovanni (Cambridge: Cambridge University Press, 1996), AA 8: 143n.

73. Georg Forster, *Werke*, ed. Gerhard Steiner, 4 vols (Frankfurt: Insel, 1967–70), 4, p. 794.

constructive experiments so much as by failed 'attempts' (*Versuche*) at implementation. It remains to be shown where this leaves the example of the French Revolution itself. Kant believed that the event may well have misfired, although he also assumed that the failure of a scheme did not invalidate its legitimacy if residual hope was still lodged in its original purpose.

The Christian revolution had dramatised the difference between action and intention, between an external effort at manipulating behaviour and an internal adjustment in attitude. The history of the church had shown that mechanical alterations left the dispositional mindset unconverted. For all its promise, Christ's message of emancipation was undermined by countervailing forces. The simple overthrow of one regime could not by itself bring about the objective invested in another. Kant's indictment of the process of Christian decadence was clearly intended to echo his verdict on the French Revolution. Anticipating the completion of rational religion, he forecast the end of arbitrary inequality. Concretely, he expected that the 'degrading distinction between *laity* and *clergy*' would cease, ushering in an era of equal self-legislation.[74] While purity of heart was the rational goal of church government, clerical authority was only an aid to enlightenment, and should ultimately yield to self-determination. This revealed Kant's optimism about ecclesiastical structures receding, not his vision of social and political organisation. Yet it is notable how he emphasised that no such renovation could be accomplished by means of an 'external revolution' alone. Any pre-emptive institutional overhaul, he wrote pessimistically, depended on 'fortuitous circumstances' liable to tip events into 'turbulence and violence'.[75] Not only

74. Kant, *Religion*, AA 6: 122.
75. Ibid.

was an attempt to force morality a contradiction in terms, but it was also bound to fall victim to the exigencies of power.

III

Around the time Kant was reflecting on the conditions of violence, Prussia was at war with France. The Prussian ruler, Frederick William II, had been pledged since 17 August 1791 to restore the authority of the French king. The following year, he was drawn into support for Austria against France. The Brunswick Manifesto of 25 July 1792 intensified hostility between the Revolutionary regime and the European allies ranged against it. With an invasion of French territory imminent, several Paris sections prepared to move against Louis XVI, with insurgents storming the Tuileries on 10 August. The inchoate project to establish a constitutional monarchy in France now lay in ruins. In the early period of the Revolution, Kant had referred in the third *Critique* to 'a recently undertaken transformation of a great people into a state'.[76] Recasting a people as a 'state' meant replacing arbitrary administration with the rule of law. The enterprise was informed by a normative 'idea', but it could not guarantee its own effective implementation. Since its early articulation as an ideal, the project had met with grave impediments. A succession of 'fortuitous circumstances', as we have seen Kant put it, had indeed interceded. This led to protracted political upheaval, as well as a military contest at home and abroad. The exact point at which Kant might have thought this process of *dérapage* to have set in cannot be precisely determined, but at least the scale of the abysmal descent became increasingly evident between the French king's flight to

76. Kant, *Critique of Judgment*, AA 5: 375n.

Varennes in the spring of 1791 and the overthrow of the crown the following summer.[77] As the monarchy imploded in Paris, in Königsberg Kant was concerned about the outlook for his essays on religion in the face of the censorious attitude of the Berlin court. At the end of August 1792, as the French Constitution of 1791 unravelled, Kant submitted his work for evaluation to the Faculty of Theology at his own university. It was in this body of writing that he aired his doubts about the prospects for 'external revolution'.[78] A revolution that was merely 'external' placed power at odds with principle. The moment of compromise constituted the point of deviation. For Kant, the situation was by then irrecoverable: 'what is thus for once put in place at the establishment of a new constitution is regrettably retained for centuries to come'.[79] The aberration inevitably casts a long shadow, since the career of power is subject to the vicissitudes of struggle.

This raised the question of how political miscalculation might best be corrected. The costliest course, as far as Kant was concerned, was to stage a revolution against the revolution, as was happening in France in the summer of 1792. A political ideal, like a rational religion, could not be wished into existence by an audacious coup. Transitions were tortuous, drawn-out and oblique, and so dependent on incremental adjustments. A

77. The term *dérapage* (skidding off course) was first used in this context by François Furet and Denis Richet in *La Révolution* (Paris: Hachette, 1965–66), to depict the deviant course of the Revolution. Furet later came to argue that the trajectory was not anomalous, since the enterprise had been aberrant in its very conception. Cf. François Furet, *La Révolution: De Turgot à Jules Ferry, 1770–1880* (Paris: Hachette, 1988).

78. Kant to the Theological Faculty, late August 1792, *Kant Correspondence*, AA 11: 358–59.

79. Kant, *Religion*, AA 6: 122.

decisive improvement, Kant argued, could only be 'carried to effect, inasmuch as it is to be a human work, through gradual reform'.[80] All attempts to shorten the course, by resort to violent regime change, would surely prove abortive. Just as a moral religion was contradicted by an ethos of ecclesiastical service, so a republican constitution would be destroyed by its despotic implementation. Any effort to establish freedom by a process requiring its intermediate eradication was bound to miscarry. For the most part in his life and writings, Kant avoided direct political engagement. His interest in politics was largely focused on the goals of moral philosophy, extending over time into constitutional theory. At the same time, he was acutely aware of the Prussian state's determination to control debate, having experienced first-hand its resolution in stifling open discussion. Not least among the attempts to interfere with Kant was a *Kabinettsordre* issued by the Prussian king and signed by Johann Christoph Wöllner, the minister of justice, charging him with abusing the terms of his academic employment.[81] It is therefore unsurprising that Kant was circumspect about public affairs. When Carl Spener, a Berlin-based book merchant, wrote to him in the spring of 1793 encouraging him to update his 'Idea for a Universal History' with a view to including an assessment of the current situation, Kant bluntly declined. To begin with, he candidly admitted that he valued his own skin. At the same time, he considered himself a 'pygmy' confronted by overwhelming might. Besides, there was no audience for moderation under the current

---

80. Ibid.
81. Friederich Wilhelm II to Kant, 1 October 1794, *Kant Correspondence*, AA 11: 525. On Frederick William II and Wöllner, see James J. Sheehan, *German History, 1770–1866* (Oxford: Oxford University Press, 1989), p. 292.

dispensation.[82] Given this outlook, it is perhaps unsurprising that Kant secreted his views on the Revolution in an essay on the tensions between true religion and church government.

Nonetheless, on a philosophical plane at least, Kant did offer some assessment of proceedings in France in his essays on political theory published in the 1790s. Back in 1784, he had suggested that a revolution might well succeed in dismantling an oppressive apparatus of rule. Yet, he went on, political action of the kind could never rehabilitate society. Genuine political reconditioning, he believed, presupposed a moral transformation. An institutional overhaul implied only a change in administration which, however much it might profess the cause of justice, could not accomplish its goal without a reformation in attitudes: 'new prejudices will serve just as well as the old ones to harness the great unthinking masses'.[83] Successful revolution thus presupposed enlightenment. This last, in turn, could more easily advance under a regulated monarchy than a popular state (Freistaat).[84] In making this judgement, Kant was applying the lessons of Montesquieu to the case of Prussia: 'the power of the people has been confused with the liberty of the people', Montesquieu had remarked.[85] Similarly, for Kant, freedom was not a matter of placing initiative directly in the hands of an unincorporated populace. Government, instead, had to be enlightened. In the first Critique, Kant had pressed for a creative redeployment of Platonic insights.[86] His essay on 'Enlightenment' developed this approach. The receptiveness of kings to

82. Kant to Carl Spener, 22 March 1793, Kant Correspondence, AA 11: 417.
83. Kant, 'What is Enlightenment?', p. 18.
84. Ibid., p. 22.
85. Montesquieu, Spirit of the Laws, p. 155.
86. Kant, Critique of Pure Reason, A 315/B 372. Cf. Kant, Conflict of the Faculties, AA 7: 91.

direction from philosophers would make it possible to correct the wayward influence of 'guardians' (*Vormünder*).[87] Nonetheless, for enlightenment to flourish, discipline was required. Freedom to philosophise usually came under threat where mass opinion governed the state. A more streamlined authority structure was a boon to intellectual freedom, which in turn facilitated moral self-legislation. The occurrence of Revolution in France obliged Kant to spell out how he viewed relations between theory and practice, and thus, by extension, how the institutions of government ought to be organised. In the first place, what mattered to Kant was the achievement of a regulated system of government. Toward this end, he conceded that an 'absolute monarch' could rule 'in a republican manner.'[88] Yet it was better to offer security to that arrangement, which meant giving the people's representatives control over legislative provisions, above all the right to reject the resort to war.[89]

IV

In its earliest phase, the French Revolution sought to combine a powerful monarch with a parliamentary system of legislation, yet without resolving how relations between the organs of state might be harmonised. Kant notoriously condemned the resort to resistance whilst justifying the 'idea' of a republican regime.[90]

---

87. Kant, 'What is Enlightenment?', pp. 17–18.

88. Immanuel Kant, 'Drafts for *Conflict of the Faculties*', in *Lectures and Drafts on Political Philosophy*, ed. and trans. Frederick Rauscher (Cambridge: Cambridge University Press, 2016), AA 19: 610.

89. Ibid., 19: 606.

90. On this, see Gareth Stedman Jones, 'Kant, the French Revolution and the Definition of the Republic', in Biancamaria Fontana, ed., *The Invention of the Modern Republic* (Cambridge: Cambridge University Press, 1994); Arthur Ripstein, *Force and*

To reconcile these two distinct pledges, he defended the events of June 1789 along 'Tory' lines. The change of regime had resulted, he contended, from an unwitting if still voluntary abjuration of royal authority in favour of the Estates General.[91] This was to present the Revolution as a process of constitutional transition rather than a violent overthrow of the state, a description which Kant reserved instead for 10 August 1792.[92] It is well known that Kant deplored insurrection of any kind. In preference to dissolving the condition of right, the people ought to endure even 'unbearable abuse', while the execution of the head of state should be regarded as beyond the pale.[93] Eight years before the Revolution, Kant had already promoted the ideal of a republic in which *the freedom of each to exist together with that of others'* would be maximised.[94] The implications of this commitment were not fully worked out by Kant until the completion of the 'Doctrine of Right' which formed the first part of his 1797 *Metaphysics of Morals*. But, more immediately, he came under pressure to elaborate what this paradigmatic notion of

---

Freedom: Kant's Legal and Political Philosophy (Cambridge, MA: Harvard University Press, 2009), ch. 11; Reidar Maliks, *Kant's Politics in Context* (Oxford: Oxford University Press, 2014), ch. 4.

91. Kant, *Metaphysics of Morals*, AA 6: 341. Cf. Kant, 'Reflections on the Philosophy of Right', in *Lectures and Drafts*, AA 19: 595–96. The Tory defence of the Glorious Revolution is discussed in J. P. Kenyon, *Revolution Principles: The Politics of Party, 1689–1720* (Cambridge: Cambridge University Press, 1977). Kant's awareness of the relevant positions is evident from his discussion of 1688 in his 'On the Common Saying: That May Be Correct in Theory, but Is of No Use in Practice' (1793), in *Practical Philosophy*, AA 8: 303, where he satirises those who 'preferred *to attribute* a voluntary abdication of government to the monarch they frightened away'.

92. For the contrast between 1789 and 1792 in Kant's mind, see Reidar Maliks, *Kant and the French Revolution* (Cambridge: Cambridge University Press, 2021), particularly the interpretation of the *séance royale* of 23 June 1789.

93. Kant, *Metaphysics of Morals*, AA 6: 320–21.

94. Kant, *Critique of Pure Reason*, A316/B373.

republicanism might mean in practical terms. Notwithstanding scholarly speculation on the subject, Kant never endorsed any of the constitutional models retailed in France.[95] In fact, it seems safest to assume that he did not approve of any of the proposals hatched in the years following 1789. He supported the principle that the French should 'republicanize' themselves, and believed that the National Assembly had initiated that process, but did not endorse specific partisan arrangements.[96] Nonetheless, he was taken by many followers to have captured the 'spirit' of the Revolution in his writings. He had also experienced the defection of students from critical philosophy to various forms of empiricism in the aftermath of 1789, and so felt obliged to clarify his views on French events.

Most shades of opinion in the German lands regarded the early days of the Revolution with optimism. It sparked enthusiastic anticipation in Schlözer, Müller, Klopstock, Wieland, Schubart, Richter, Herder and Voss. Only a minority—for instance, Goethe, Schiller, Möser, Rehberg and Brandes—exercised reserve.[97] Friedrich Gentz, who had studied under Kant at Königsberg in the 1780s, fell under the spell of Burke in the very early 1790s. By that stage, Reinhold had already associated Kant with the spirit of 1789. Four years before the Revolution, he described Kant's ideas as 'harbingers of one of the most far-reaching and beneficent revolutions that has ever occurred at one and the same time

---

95. Kant appears as an enthusiast for the Revolution in Manfred Kuehn, *Kant: A Biography* (Cambridge: Cambridge University Press, 2001), pp. 340–43. There is discussion of his relationship to Sièyes in Jacques Droz, *L'Allemagne et la revolution française* (Paris: Presses Universitaires de France, 1949), p. 158.

96. Kant, 'Drafts for *Conflict of the Faculties*', AA 19: 604: 'a people [. . .] who have now republicanized themselves'.

97. G. P. Gooch, *Germany and the French Revolution* (London: Longmans, 1927).

in the scholarly and moral world'.[98] In the revised 1790 edition of the same work, Reinhold identified Kant still more explicitly with the tendencies of the age, which had witnessed a 'shaking of all previously known systems', at the centre of which stood the ferment in metaphysics spearheaded by the Critique of Pure Reason.[99] The same pattern was evident in a series of allegedly interconnected events, spanning the decline of monasticism, the ascent of freedom of the press, the termination of serfdom and 'the North American, French and Dutch revolutions'.[100] However, Kant delayed providing a considered response to French developments until 1793. Then, in his essay on 'Theory and Practice', he petitioned against the revolutionary scramble to guard the public happiness, whilst also arguing in favour of a legitimate commonwealth devoted to the security of 'inalienable rights'.[101] According to Kant, such a condition of public right could not be discovered by the application of prudence based on an assessment of the people's welfare. An approach of that kind underpinned the creation of the British constitution following the Glorious Revolution, just as it shaped the course of the French Revolution, in both instances leading to serious defects. Instead, for Kant, political justice could only be validated by an appeal to rational principles which provided criteria against which existing arrangements could be judged.

Biester, who was responsible for the publication of Kant's essay in Berlin, was explicit in his assessment of the tangible

98. Karl Leonhard Reinhold, Letters on the Kantian Philosophy, ed. Karl Ameriks, trans. James Hebbeler (Cambridge: Cambridge University Press, 2005), p. 5.

99. Ibid., pp. 131–36. For discussion, see Michael Morris, 'The French Revolution and the New School of Europe: Towards a Political Interpretation of German Idealism', European Journal of Philosophy, 19: 4 (December 2011), pp. 532–60.

100. Reinhold, Letters, p. 133.

101. Kant, 'Theory and Practice', AA 8: 290, 304.

significance of the framing depicted in 'Theory and Practice'. Above all else, he was grateful to Kant for dispelling the rumour that he had approved what Biester dubbed 'the ever increasingly repulsive French Revolution'. French politics, Biester went on, had shattered 'the universal principles of constitutional law and the concept of a civil constitution, as I now learn from your essay'.[102] Yet it was not until 1795 that Kant fully formulated what a constitution based on an 'original' contract entailed. In his essay on 'Perpetual Peace', again written for Biester's *Berlinische Monatsschrift*, Kant distinguished the forms of sovereignty—which located authority in the power of either the one, the many or the few—from the nature of government, which could be exercised either despotically or with a proper regard for external freedom.[103] Jacobinism, for Kant, was plainly a form of popular despotism.[104] True republicanism, by comparison, distinguished executive from legislative power. The independence of the legislature could be measured by the security of civil liberty. Since international warfare militated against the achievement of absolute justice, domestic right depended on the achievement of perpetual peace. Thus, for Kant, the prototype of a patriotic regime that looked toward eliminating the detrimental effects of war was signalled but not realised by the French Revolution. It was left to the philosophy of history to show how the ideal of a morally grounded politics could be credited, if not actualised.

Although Kant declined to update his 'Idea for a Universal History' as requested by Spener in 1793, he more or less

102. Biester to Kant, 5 October 1793, *Kant Correspondence*, AA 11: 456.

103. Immanuel Kant, 'Toward Perpetual Peace' (1795), in *Practical Philosophy*, AA 8: 352.

104. See his comments on Danton in Kant, 'Theory and Practice', AA 8: 302. Cf. Kant, *Conflict of the Faculties*, AA 7: 86n, where 'innovation, Jacobinism and mob action' are censured.

succumbed to the proposal in an essay written in 1795 and published three years later in the *Conflict of the Faculties*. The essay addressed, as the title formulated it, 'An Old Question Raised Again: Is the Human Race Constantly Progressing?' The query was directly posed in connection with the French Revolution, an event contrived by a 'talented people' (*geistreichen Volks*) whose purpose was universally admired across the states of Europe.[105] Kant took that purpose (or 'idea') to be self-evident, and reducible to two principles: first, that a constitution should by right enjoy popular approval; and second, that it should aim to realise justice by rejecting offensive warfare. These features, for Kant, defined what he termed a 'republican constitution'—'republican at least in essence', meaning a form of politics that was cherished in principle, even where the ideal was not to hand, as in the case of contemporary Prussia, where equally the model should not be forced [106] It was not the mere existence of this idea that raised Kant's expectations, but the enthusiastic yet disinterested reception it received among spectators.[107] What this widely shared response demonstrated, in Kant's mind, was the advance of a mode of thinking among mankind which disposed them to a morally purified kind of politics. In point of fact, the promising ideal might backslide—it may, Kant conceded, 'succeed or miscarry', potentially, in the latter case,

---

105. Ibid., 7: 85. 'Ingenious' might be a better rendition of *geistreich* than 'talented'.

106. Ibid., 7: 85, 86n.

107. 'Enthusiastic' here is based on the German *Enthusiasmus*, utterly distinct from the word *Schwämerei* (a form of derangement), usually likewise rendered as 'enthusiasm' in English. For the role of *Enthusiasmus* in Kantian moral theory, see Immanuel Kant, *Anthropology from a Pragmatic Point of View*, ed. and trans. Robert B. Louden (Cambridge: Cambridge University Press, 2006), pp. 152, 169, 216. *Enthusiasmus* is an affect aroused by a moral idea, akin to the modern 'idealism'.

leaving a trail of atrocities.[108] However, even though the experiment might fail, the existence of a sensibility well disposed to justice needed only the right circumstances to accomplish its goal in the end. Given an endless succession of potential trials, only one chance need prevail to vindicate the whole series, and at least one triumphant opportunity would one day come around.

In Kant's eyes, the French Revolution laid the foundation for a quasi-Copernican revolution capable of transforming the interpretation of the moral universe. He contended that human affairs only looked disappointing because of the angle from which they were usually observed. Unlike explanations for the cycle of the planets, there was no hypothesis applicable to social life that could guarantee predictions short of the achievement of providential wisdom.[109] However, Kant developed a point of view that gave rational grounds for hope, based around the change of heart inaugurated by the French Revolution. Now it could be seen that the Christian Revolution was a preparation for current events in France. This latest development did not represent the final days, Kant realised. But it did show how a radical switch would eventuate at some point, since a disposition tending in the right direction only needed a single break. Across the expanse of secular time, one successful shot would be sufficient. This is what Kant's philosophical chiliasm amounted to in practice. The length of time that would intervene before mundane deliverance obtained was admittedly incalculable, but belief in final salvation was nonetheless rationally grounded, according to the principles of Kantian moral theory.

108. Kant, *Conflict of the Faculties*, AA 7: 85.
109. Ibid., 7: 83.

3

The Christian Revolution
and its Fate

GERMAN PHILOSOPHICAL CULTURE through the nineteenth
century was engrossed by the spectacle of a 'transvaluation'
(*Umwertung*) of values. The idea became central to Nietzsche's
indictment of priestcraft as a denial of life.[1] It continued to
shape the philosophy of Heidegger, culminating in his notion
of historical 'forgetting' (*Vergessenheit*) by which the era of post-
Platonic metaphysics was imposed upon an earlier relationship
to the world.[2] In both Nietzsche and Heidegger, the process
of revaluation represented a moment of epochal depreciation.
Philosophy became a struggle against the legacy of history,
an insurgency against a misbegotten world. The past was not
an inheritance to be shaped, so much as an experience to be

1. Friedrich Nietzsche, *Zur Genealogie der Moral* (1887), in *Werke: Kritische Gesamtausgabe*, ed. Giorgio Colli and Mazzino Montinari, 30 vols (Berlin: De Gruyter,
1967–), VI, vol. 2 (1968), p. 281.

2. Martin Heidegger, 'Seinsvergessenheit', *Heidegger Studies*, 20 (2004),
pp. 9–14.

overcome (*überwindet werden*).[3] The concept of revolution that had been developed by Kant and Hegel still haunted this project. Images of rupture and destruction remained integral to the analysis. However, these tokens of disjunction were scarcely episodes in a meticulously itemised historical process. Equally, they pointed to a programme of wholesale abandonment, rather than a plan of recovery. With this slide into abstraction came a loss of traction. From a Hegelian perspective, the post-Idealist tradition represented by Nietzsche and Heidegger was an exercise in seeking to 'overleap' (*überspringen*) the world.[4] By comparison, Hegel had been preoccupied with future possibilities immanent in his own age. Value had to be salvaged from the world directly encountered, not from a time already lost. From this perspective, philosophy had to take the form of historical reconstruction. As we have seen, despite Kant's roots in the rationalist tradition, the historical vocation of philosophy was a Kantian bequest.[5] Nowhere was its legacy more apparent than in Hegel's evolving conception of revolution.

Throughout his years in Bern and Frankfurt, Hegel continued to explore the heritage of Christianity through the prism of Kantian ethics. Integral to this project was a sustained attempt to make sense of world-historical transitions. This was undertaken with an acute awareness of his own era as a time of upheaval, a distinct moment of passage. It was the job of philosophy to penetrate the significance of these developments.

---

3. Hans-Georg Gadamer, 'Heidegger and the History of Philosophy', *The Monist*, 64: 4 (October 1981), pp. 434–44.

4. This is to draw upon an insight from the 'Preface' to G.W.F. Hegel, *Elements of the Philosophy of Right*, ed. Allen W. Wood, trans. H. B. Nisbet (Cambridge: Cambridge University Press, 1991), pp. 21–22.

5. On this, see Karl Ameriks, *Kant and the Historical Turn: Philosophy as Critical Interpretation* (Oxford: Clarendon Press, 2006).

That historical mission was cultivated by Hegel throughout his Frankfurt and Jena periods, ultimately constituting the basic argument of his mature thought. In his 1801 work on *The Difference Between Fichte's and Schelling's System of Philosophy*, Hegel presented his task as a form of historical diagnosis: the 'need' for philosophy was relative to the wider culture in which it operated.[6] For this reason Fichte's thought, understood as an elaboration of the authentic spirit of Kant, amounted to an 'epoch-making system': it raised problems which his contemporaries could not circumvent. Yet even Fichte remained inadequate to the demands of the age, which manifested themselves in a deeper urge to overcome the dichotomies that dominated post-Kantian thought. For Hegel, that impulse could be seen in the yearning manifested by Schleiermacher's writings as much as in the art and poetry of the age. Philosophy, accordingly, was charged with articulating conditions integral to current circumstances. It explicated the meaning of 'time's inner core'.[7] A year later, in *Faith and Knowledge*, Hegel traced the symptoms of this philosophical 'grief' to what he termed the 'principle of the North'.[8] By this he meant the culture of the European Enlightenment under the shadow of the Protestant Reformation. Philosophy was a form of historical analysis, although the explanation it offered was not reducible in the last instance to either ideal or material causes, since neither concept was sufficient to account for the dynamics of change. As Hegel saw it, the axis of change turned on the relationship between thought

6. G.W.F. Hegel, *The Difference between Fichte's and Schelling's System of Philosophy* (1801), ed. and trans. H. S. Harris and Walter Cerf (New York: State University of New York Press, 1977), pp. 89ff.

7. Ibid., pp. 82–83.

8. G.W.F. Hegel, *Faith and Knowledge* (1802), ed. and trans. H. S. Harris and Walter Cerf (New York: State University of New York Press, 1977), p. 57.

and its context. However, that process was not formed by an opposition between ideas and their empirical conditions. Understanding revolution required a form of explanation in which 'given' conditions were always already a product of human initiative.

To make sense of the nature of revolution in his own day, Hegel set about grasping the character of epochal shifts more generally. In the draft materials that make up the essay on 'The Positivity of the Christian Religion', Hegel included reflection on the extraordinary feat by which paganism was supplanted by the Christian religion. This was, he wrote, 'one of those remarkable revolutions [*wunderbaren Revolutionen*] whose causes the thoughtful historian must labor to discover'.[9] The strangeness of the event prompted the general inquiry: how can an emerging system of belief successfully supplant another whose tentacles have spread throughout the lifeworld of a powerful and self-confident culture? Hegel was asking what made the transition from the ancient to the modern world possible. There were two sides to the question. First, the decline and fall of Roman greatness had to be explained. The very topos of 'decline and fall' stretched back from Gibbon and Montesquieu to the ancient historians themselves, offering a rich seam of historical investigation.[10] Second, the emergence and transformation of an alternative form of life, inaugurated by the teachings of Christ, had to be analysed. This involved elucidating the transmutation of Christianity from a moral religion into a system of

9. Hegel, 'Positivity', p. 152. The material here derives from 'Jedes Volk', Text 34 in *Frühe Schriften 1*.

10. On this, see J.G.A. Pocock, *Barbarism and Religion: The First Decline and Fall* (Cambridge: Cambridge University Press, 2003).

'positive' dogmas. Such an exploration was inevitably a study in the typology of revolution more generally.

Already by the middle of the 1790s, Hegel's various accounts of radical supersession discarded the Kantian notion of a 'Copernican' turn. The displacement of a comprehensive worldview by an alternative was not a matter of straightforward intellectual succession. Fresh insights were not sufficient to uproot an all-inclusive viewpoint. Hegel believed, on the one hand, that change was never one-dimensional; on the other, he thought, it could not be induced by the operation of 'cold syllogisms'.[11] Explanation had to take account of multiple dynamics reaching into the recesses of the imagination of peoples. Altogether, this venture was a self-conscious attempt to deepen the Kantian philosophy of history. It involved a process of excavation in which the past was dredged more carefully for causal determinants. Kant's vision turned on a synoptic narrative of progression which moved from an original 'possibility'— the innate capacity for moral personality—to the Christian understanding of this germinal potentiality which prized purity of intention over external conformity. Yet the Christian breakthrough went awry, leaving modern societies with only the hope of recovery. At this point, Kant applied himself to showing how this hope was rational. In Hegel's eyes, the Kantian scheme was itself in effect a revolution, a break with orthodox Christian accounts of moral justification, although it stood in need of its own revaluation. Over time, this prompted Hegel to undertake a fundamental reappraisal of the Kantian theory of morality. This was a slow and incremental process which also gave rise to broad reflection on the course along which the history of

11. Hegel, 'Positivity', p. 153.

ethical life unfolded, extending from Judaism and Christianity to the Reformation and the French Revolution.

II

While Hegel moved later in the 1790s towards a more critical engagement with Kantian ethics, in the middle of the decade he remained committed to extending Kant's conception of Christianity as essentially a form of philosophical morality. In this spirit, he contended that 'the aim and essence of all true religion, our religion included, is human morality'.[12] Jesus was presented as defining the purpose of the Christian vision in terms of a project of liberation: 'He undertook to raise religion and virtue to morality and to restore to morality the freedom which is its essence'.[13] Hegel saw this elevation as effecting its own transvaluation. It entailed a dramatic break with the predominant culture of Judaism, although the departure at the same time involved a return, a reclamation of first principles already delineated in the Hebrew Pentateuch, notably in Deuteronomy and Leviticus.[14] The history of the Jewish faith had sullied the import of these inaugural principles, leading to a society based on mechanical obedience such as prevailed throughout Judea in the era of Roman dominance around the first century CE. In response, Jesus sought to found an approach to virtue based on the quality of its 'disposition' (*Gesinnung*).[15] In overcoming slavish acquiescence in Jewish

12. Ibid., p. 68.

13. Ibid., p. 69.

14. Ibid., p. 69n: Hegel compares Matthew 22:37, 7:12 and 5:48 with Deuteronomy 6:5 and Leviticus 19:18.

15. Hegel, 'Positivity', p. 70.

statutes, the hypocrisy of merely appearing to be good would be supplanted by an ethics of conscientious integrity. Hegel represented the desired transformation in explicitly Kantian terms, as an assignment based on sacrifice and renunciation focused on a struggle against inclinations (*Neigungen*).[16] However, as Kant too had asserted, the Christian enterprise backfired. On Hegel's analysis, the causes of the miscarriage could be uncovered by studying the intersection between Christ's embassy and the setting in which it strove to prosper.

In Hegel's retelling, the career of Jesus exemplified the complex role of philosophy in history. It illustrated the difficulty of analysing the impact of thought on society generally. The form of thought in the case of Christ was a species of moral instruction whose content was best illustrated by the ethical precepts articulated during the Sermon on the Mount and in the new commandment of the Last Supper.[17] In Hegel's summary, the fate of these tenets depended on three factors: the moral capacity of human beings; the circumstances in which the edicts were circulated; and the manner in which they were disseminated. The operation of these variables during the spread of Christianity ensured that the inner vocation of the faith would meet with adversity. Ultimately, as Hegel put it, Christ's plan became a 'shipwreck'.[18] Both 'external circumstances' and the 'spirit of the times' brought disappointment to the business of self-willed moral renewal.[19] Underlying this defeat was the absence of 'inherent goodness' in human nature.[20] Humanity had a

---

16. Ibid.
17. Matthew 5–7; John 13:33–35.
18. Hegel, 'Positivity', p. 70.
19. Ibid., p. 73.
20. Ibid.

capacity for normative self-government, but the functioning of this aptitude was limited in practice. Under the conditions of religious life in ancient Bethlehem and Jerusalem, there were powerful obstacles to the realisation of autonomy. Judaism, in Hegel's depiction, was descending into a monastic cult characterised by slavish obedience to rigid formulae.[21] There had been mounting opposition to this degradation, epitomised by the asceticism of mystic sects such as the Essenes and the stance of John the Baptist.[22] Jesus himself was unaffected by the 'contagious sickness of the age'.[23] But, Hegel noted, he still had to function within it. Preaching in this atmosphere would never prosper as purely rational discourse: it had to appeal to existing norms. For this reason, as Hegel reported it, Christ was forced to invoke the will of God, to demand faith in his own person, and so in effect to reduce his audience to tutelage.[24] His mode of persuasion made use of the full panoply of devices: the idea of a Messiah, the image of resurrection, and the wizardry of miracles. Purity of principle lapsed into 'positive' forms of authority.[25]

Whilst struggling to thrive where there was a limited fund of virtue along with counterproductive canons of belief, the spread of the gospel was also dependent on the character of the apostles. These were simple craftsmen enthralled by the charisma of Jesus, yet still immersed in the axioms of their old faith. Their reason, in this situation, could at best be 'receptive', certainly not 'legislative'.[26] A limited band of brothers inevitably became

21. Ibid., pp. 68–69.
22. Ibid.
23. Ibid., p. 70.
24. Ibid., pp. 75–77.
25. Ibid., pp. 71–73.
26. Ibid., p. 85.

consumed by a cult of personality. Their own homilies, delivered on transitory visits to far-flung districts, were also bolstered by the appeal to authority. On Hegel's analysis, the full text of the apostle Mark's proselytising injunction—'Go ye into the world and preach the gospel'—bore the marks of positivity and superstition.[27] The emphasis on belief, baptism and magical powers was remote from the truly Christian message of mercy and philanthropy. Accordingly, although an ethos of self-sacrifice did permeate the early church, the self-restraint characteristic of such a 'a small band of sectaries' was dependent on the limited extent of the association.[28] The alliance among Christ's followers was of a nature to dilute both family and civil ties. This restricted the opportunities to broaden into a larger society. When expansion did come, Hegel observed, the cohesiveness of the sect found itself at odds with the culture of the state. As the sectarian clique developed into an ecclesiastical structure, the moral rigour of the Christian faithful steadily abated Donations to the church replaced major personal sacrifice, and the powerful, rather than the poor, became the beneficiaries of contributions.[29] Hypocrisy, at the same time, became pervasive. As with Jewish manners in the era of decline, Christianity descended into 'lip-service'.[30] In due course, the scrutiny of motives became a central clerical endeavour. The revolution had devoured its children.

So the wheel, Hegel concluded, had come full circle. The Christians had become Jews again, though with additional layers of surveillance, thanks to supervision by over-vigilant

27. Mark 16:15–18, discussed in Hegel, 'Positivity', p. 83.
28. Hegel, 'Positivity', pp. 86–87.
29. Ibid., p. 88.
30. Ibid., p. 79.

churches.[31] As the society of 'friends' became co-extensive with a territorial polity, the church itself became a 'spiritual state' (*geistliche Staat*) under which reason was sacrificed to the will of the community.[32] Judgement had been forfeited to ecclesiastical representatives, who were themselves a kind of '*status in statu*' (state within a state).[33] The national religion sought to educate customary attitudes, leaving external coercion to the civil authorities. Yet both bodies usurped the autonomy of the will in the name of a communal enterprise. Over time, the spiritual state even came to prevail over the civil, in Protestant and Catholic countries alike. This resulted in a situation in which, across Europe, 'no dissenter can obtain civil rights'.[34] In this revolution which had rebounded on itself, the original values championed were tarnished, if not extinguished. The main ideals sponsored in Hegel's account of Christianity were identical with the slogans of the French Revolution: Jesus had been an advocate for liberty, equality and fraternity. Yet, as the Christian transformation proceeded, each of these aspirations was undone. The freedom of moral self-legislation gave way to the jurisdiction of confessors and prelates.[35] The equality of the faithful—under which 'the slave was the brother of his owner', and moral worth was esteemed above social standing and distinguishing talents—was replaced by a regime of private property in which parity only existed in the eyes of heaven.[36] Fraternity, likewise, proved unsustainable as the circle of Christian friendship grew to cosmopolitan proportions. In theory, 'every

31. Ibid., p. 140.
32. Ibid., pp. 98–101.
33. Ibid., p. 107.
34. Ibid., p. 108–9.
35. Ibid., pp. 69, 98, 101, 104.
36. Ibid., pp. 87–89.

Christian should have found in every other, the Egyptian in the Briton, wherever he might chance to meet him, a friend and a brother'.[37] In practice, however, the bonds of association steadily loosened. Cohesion was in reality superficial, more an obligation imposed than a connection felt.

In this way, Hegel makes clear that it was the destiny of Christianity to subvert its original purpose. As already noted, it also unseated a rival order of faith and politics. The causes of this revolution were to be found in the 'secret' dynamics by which Christian belief could capitalise on the demise of the ancient commonwealths.[38] The Greek and Roman religions were suited to the mores of self-governing city-states. Under these conditions, the idea of the *patria* gave meaning to individual endeavour. However, the Romans conquered the Mediterranean world of autonomous republics, relinquishing in the process their own independence. This development was facilitated by the extension of aristocratic influence abetted by the disappearance of patriotic values. Property, luxury, comfort and egoism eradicated the ethic of public and military service.[39] A remote and hierarchical system of rule deprived citizens of all sense of collective membership. In the face of atomisation, the old gods lost their currency. Death, Hegel observed, became 'terrifying'.[40] The civilisation which made the lamentations of Lucian, Longinus and Iamblichus resound also fostered a yearning for the Messiah.[41] In the language of the *Phenomenology*, the 'unhappy consciousness' had appeared, and worshippers pined

37. Ibid., p. 103.
38. Ibid., p. 152.
39. Ibid., p. 164.
40. Ibid., p. 158.
41. Ibid., p. 159.

for the 'unattainable *Beyond*' by the empty grave of Christ.[42] Not only had the character of society been warped but— influenced by the predominant mindset of the time—humanity as such was considered depraved by nature.

III

In the final years of the 1790s, Hegel continued to try to discern the 'fate' (*Schicksaal*) of Christianity. This, however, was not a purely historical enterprise. It was part of his attempt to comprehend the forces that had shaped the modern world, with a view to ascertaining what it held in store. Towards the end of his stay in Bern, Hegel had highlighted the special achievement of the era in which he was living. It was, he believed, the calling of his age to reclaim the treasures that had habitually been squandered on heaven. Yet, so far, this recovery of the gods for human powers had only been staked as a theoretical right. What period, Hegel demanded, would be in a position to put that claim to use: 'what age will have the strength to validate this right in practice and make itself its possessor?'[43] Hegel believed that answering this question involved figuring out relations between religion, morals and politics. This included grasping the historical shift from life under the ancient city-states to civil existence under the Roman Empire. Later, notably in his study of the constitution of the Holy Roman Empire on which he was working at the turn of the century, Hegel would explore the passage from the Middle Ages down to the eighteenth century.

42. G.W.F. Hegel, *The Phenomenology of Spirit* (1807), ed. and trans. Michael Inwood (Oxford: Oxford University Press, 2018), §217.

43. Hegel, 'Positivity', p. 159.

As we have seen, throughout these researches, he was also concerned to fathom the transition from Judaism to Christianity, as well as the connection between Christian principles and the thought of Kant. Crucially, after his move to Frankfurt, his assessment of Kant's role altered. This modified his analysis of the succession of past stages in moral and religious thought, as well as his estimate of the potentialities latent in his own time. Launching a critique of Kantian moral theory meant reconceptualising the relationship between morality and social life. The very term 'morality' now acquired a negative connotation, distinguishable from the richer idea of an ethical relationship designated by the word 'love'.[44] A fragmentary comment from the Frankfurt period is revealing: 'a man that is only moral is a miser who accumulates and preserves without enjoying anything.'[45] Hegel fleshed out his indictment by contrasting Kant's doctrine with the original teachings of Christ. He also expanded his account of the legacy of Judaism to Christianity, identifying what he termed the 'spirit' of each, and seeking to unravel their peculiar destinies. It was the lot of these forms of consciousness to struggle against the world. It was a battle that sometimes led to conflict and violence. The anatomy of this dynamic formed an essential background to Hegel's narration of the path followed by the French Revolution.

Christianity, like Judaism, was a revolt against nature, although both systems turned against reality in different ways.[46] It was

44. See G.W.F. Hegel, 'Welchem Zwekke' and 'So wie sie mehrere Gattungen', Texts 49 and 50 in *Frühe Schriften 2*, ed. Walter Jaeschke (*Gesammelte Werke 2*) (Hamburg: Felix Meiner Verlag, 2014).

45. G.W.F. Hegel, 'Zu der Zeit da Jesus', Text 52 in *Frühe Schriften 2*, p. 120.

46. On this, see Steven B. Smith, 'Hegel and the Jewish Question: In Between Tradition and Modernity', *The History of Political Thought*, 12: 1 (Spring 1991), pp. 87–106.

Abraham, Hegel asserted, who was the true progenitor of the Jewish people.[47] He represented an altogether new consciousness, a particular response to the hostility of nature symbolised by the story of the flood. His strategy was contrasted with the approach of Nimrod as represented in Josephus's *Antiquities of the Jews*, insofar as Abraham sought to tame the elements through belief in a higher being.[48] The price of Abraham's trust was absolute subjection to God's law. Unlike their equivalents in Greek mythology, both descendants of Noah raged against necessity. But Nimrod relied on the 'law of the stronger' to regulate human needs, whereas Abraham deferred to the mastery of a higher power.[49] As part of this submission, Abraham, a shepherd, cut his remaining intimate ties in asserting his independence from natural bonds. With subjection thus came disseverance, a denial of ordinary human affect: 'Abraham wanted *not* to love, wanted to be free by not loving.'[50] This was essentially the 'spirit' of Judaism, its governing principle of association, which in practice amounted to a policy of dissociation. In wandering with his flocks, Abraham maintained his distance from nature. At the same time, in fencing himself off from others, he detached himself from all community outside his immediate progeny: 'He was a stranger on earth, a stranger to the soil and to men alike.'[51] As such, his spirit helped

47. G.W.F. Hegel, 'The Spirit of Christianity and Its Faith' (1797–99), in *Early Theological Writings*, p. 182. This essay is an editorial reconstruction, originally by Herman Nohl, of fragments, mostly mini-essays, from the Frankfurt period. Two versions of this fragment are presented as 'Mit Abraham', Text 61 in *Frühe Schriften* 2.

48. Josephus, *Antiquities of the Jews*, 1.4, cited by Hegel, 'Spirit of Christianity', pp. 184.

49. Hegel, 'Spirit of Christianity', pp. 183–85.

50. Ibid., p. 185. This and the following citations down to p. 205 of 'The Spirit of Christianity' are from 'Abraham in Chaldäa geboren', Text 48 in Hegel, *Frühe Schriften* 2.

51. Hegel, 'Spirit of Christianity', p. 186.

to determine his fate, and so also the portion of his people, which became in effect a rebellion against the natural disposition of humanity. He stood alone against partnership (*philia, amicitia*) under a jealous God.[52]

Hegel considered the Abrahamic legacy to be still operative down through Jacob, even though the latter succumbed to a life of settled agriculture. For instance, the heritage was evidenced by the extirpation of the Shechemites, carried out by Jacob's sons for the rape of Dinah.[53] The legislation delivered by Moses, Hegel alleged, was a further extension of the 'soul' of Abraham: it pitted the Jewish nation against the remainder of the human race—fostering an '*odium generis humani*'—as manifested by the campaign of annihilation against the Canaanites.[54] This mixed culture of interpersonal hostility combined with servitude to divine authority persisted when the nomadic Jews settled down to agriculture. But this shared life with their neighbours did not result in easy affiliation: the 'genius of hatred' persisted. Continuing in the midst of the acquisition of property, it led to a life of passivity and consumption—the 'sheer empty need of maintaining their physical existence'.[55] Jewish equality, unlike the equality of the Athenians and Spartans as stipulated by Solon and Lycurgus, amounted to uniformly bland subjection: 'there was strictly no citizen body at all'.[56]

52. For the development of Hegel's views, see Peter Hodgson, 'The Metamorphosis of Judaism in Hegel's Philosophy of Religion', *The Owl of Minerva*, 19: 1 (Fall 1987), pp. 41–52.

53. Genesis 34:15–31; Hegel, 'Spirit of Christianity,' pp. 188–89.

54. Numbers 21:2–3; Deuteronomy 7:1–2; Joshua 6:17, 21; Hegel, 'Spirit of Christianity', pp. 191, 194, 201.

55. Hegel, 'Spirit of Christianity', p. 194.

56. Ibid., pp. 197–98.

The Jews, then, were 'made of misfortune and made for misfortune', though their spirit was in its genesis self-wrought.[57] They were afflicted by a peculiar tragedy, whose nearest dramatic representation was Macbeth: his defection from the path of humanity evoked neither pity nor fear since his communion with darker spirits was less a flaw than an aberration.[58] Jesus, in seeking to transcend this tragic plight, became instead its victim. Yet, departing from his earlier views, Hegel no longer equated the Christian triumph over obsequiousness with Kantian self-command. Instead, 'morality' based on reason was itself associated with self-inflicted subordination to an alien standard. This was yet another kind of self-annihilation, a denial of desire in the name of purely 'objective' norms—an 'ought' separated from the world of value as it 'is'.[59] The Kantian agent thus carried 'his lord in himself'.[60] One might have expected, Hegel reflected, that Jesus would adopt the Kantian solution of opposing the mere legality of behaviour with a self-imposed universal norm. Yet this, he now concluded, was exactly what Christ rejected. Kant's understanding of duty took love itself to be pathological, insofar as his concept of obligation opposed sensible inclinations to universal norms.[61] Overcoming this cleavage, which involved the 'fulfilment' or 'plērōma' (πλήρωμα)

---

57. Ibid., p. 195.

58. Ibid., pp. 204–5. For 'flaw' or 'error' (in Aristotle, ἁμαρτία) Hegel has 'the inevitable slip of a beautiful character'.

59. Ibid., pp. 206–9. This and the following citations down to p. 224 of 'The Spirit of Christianity' are from 'Jesus trat nicht lange', Text 55 in *Frühe Schriften 2*.

60. Hegel, 'Spirit of Christianity', p. 211. Hegel is criticising Kant's conception of love as base feeling (*Empfindung*), and thus as pathological, as set out in the *Metaphysics of Morals*, AA 6: 401.

61. Hegel, 'Spirit of Christianity', p. 211.

of duty in the practical sphere, now became the principal objective of Hegel's ethics and the basis for his repudiation of Kant.[62] He developed this disavowal through a number of stages, first in his essay on 'Natural Law' in 1802–03, and later in the *Phenomenology*, the *Encyclopedia* and the *Philosophy of Right*. As Hegel saw matters around 1798, there remained a residual element of positivity in Kant, a sacrifice of freedom carried out in the name of freedom. Hegel associated a similar deficit with the political ideas of Rousseau, which he thought ramified through the wayward course of the French Revolution. In each of these cases, autonomy was at odds with the attachments of common life—with publicly avowed values and established social preferences. A similar, if still different, fate had awaited Jesus. Although Christ sought to restore 'completeness' (*Ganzheit*) to humanity by overcoming its degradation, he did not do so on the basis of the legal commands enjoined by reason. Instead, Hegel claimed, he sought to 'fulfil' (*erfüllen*) and 'annul' (*aufheben*) morality as an imperative command.[63] Even so, for this new light to facilitate an unaccustomed form of life, symbolised by Christ as the Kingdom of God, prevailing Jewish habits would have to be receptive to an unfamiliar message, which of course they were not. To promote his cause, Jesus was obliged to attack the dominant mode of existence, which fomented in him an 'ever increasing bitterness against his age and his people', notably against the Pharisees.[64] This made him,

---

62. For 'plērōma', see ibid., pp. 214–15: it was a term prominent among gnostics, and associated with Paul the apostle.

63. Ibid., p. 212, though 'completeness' is mistranslated as 'humanity'.

64. Ibid., p. 283. This and the following citations down to p. 301 of 'The Spirit of Christianity' are from 'Mit dem Muthe', Text 60 in *Frühe Schriften* 2.

Hegel later remarked, a determined rebel.[65] Instead of building a social movement, Christ formed an exclusive sect disconnected from the larger society and passively divorced from the state—a 'narrow-souled consciousness' (*engherzigen Bewußtseyn*) under alien domination.[66] This characteristic was reproduced in many of Jesus's followers. With that, spiritual pride became a latent inclination within Christianity.

Hegel dubbed this tendency 'enthusiasm' (*Schwärmerei*), associating it both with Christ and the more militant among his adherents.[67] This attitude bred an attachment to a species of liberty that was hollow. Jesus could find freedom, as Hegel put it, 'only in the void [*Leere*]'.[68] He fled relationships in the actual world on the grounds that all available ties were fatally compromised. This resolution became an integral if ominous part of his embassy: 'Do not assume that I have come to bring peace to the earth; I have not come to bring peace, but a sword.'[69] In carrying the kingdom of virtue in his heart alone, he relinquished actual life in favour of another possible life. This severance (*Trennung*) from happiness took the shape of a war on impulse, which passed through innumerable brutal conflicts over the course of history—a series of flights 'into the void' unleashing 'atrocities

65. G.W.F. Hegel, *Lectures on the Philosophy of Religion: The Lectures of 1827*, ed. Peter C. Hodgson, trans. R. F. Brown, P. C. Hodgson and J. M. Stewart (Oxford: Clarendon Press, 2006), pp. 460, 463n.

66. Hegel, 'Spirit of Christianity', p. 284.

67. Ibid., pp. 281, 288, though Knox unhelpfully translates *Schwärmer* as 'dreamer'. For discussion of the idiom in the European Enlightenment, see J.GA. Pocock, 'Enthusiasm: The Antiself of Enlightenment', *Huntington Library Quarterly*, 60: 1/2 (1997), pp. 7–28. See also Richard Bourke, 'Jon Elster's "Enthusiasm and Anger in History"', *Inquiry*, 64: 3 (2021), pp. 308–20.

68. Hegel, 'Spirit of Christianity', p. 285.

69. Matthew 10:35, cited by Hegel, 'Spirit of Christianity', p. 286.

and devastations'.[70] The implied echo of disturbances in Hegel's time is unmistakable, though it would be wrong to conclude that he saw the French Revolution as a rebirth of religious enthusiasm. There was no 'eternal recurrence of the same' in Hegel's scheme of thought. But he did believe that the Revolution was animated by a form of fanaticism which similarly failed to join righteousness to a spirit of accommodation. Hegel had reinterpreted the Kantian Revolution and placed it in the context of the history of religion and morals, encompassing the legacies of Abraham, Christ and Socrates. It remained for him to explain the impact of the Reformation on the character of modern freedom as it struggled to take shape with such devastating consequences after 1789.

IV

Hegel barely addressed the character of the Reformation in his early writings. He preferred to explore the original meaning of Christianity. However, implicit in this exploration was a verdict upon Christ's legacy. Comparison between the values of the primitive church and the doctrines of the reformers would have been uppermost in the minds of Hegel's contemporaries. For them, the Reformation was a cardinal moment in the German past. Interpreting its meaning was one of the goals of sacred history. In his mature works, Hegel delivered a more explicit assessment of its implications. Particularly in his lectures on the philosophy of history and on the history of philosophy, he directly tackled the corruptions of the medieval church and evaluated the impact of attempts at its reform.

70. Hegel, 'Spirit of Christianity', p. 288n.

Hegel's engagement with the subject was presented in the context of his avowed orthodoxy. Towards the end of his life, he described himself to Friedrich Tholuck, a Pietist enthusiast, as 'completely confirmed in Lutheranism'.[71] Writing earlier in the same year to the Prussian education minister, Karl von Altenstein, he proclaimed himself unambiguously to be 'a Lutheran Christian'.[72] Yet it is also plain that a commitment to the national faith was a condition of Hegel's tenure as a professor at the University of Berlin. He pictured himself as unravelling the truths of Lutheranism by means of philosophy. However, this philosophical rendition involved a new interpretation.[73] From the point of view of accepted doctrine, Hegel's ideas represented a departure from tradition. He was aligned with the official position in his criticisms of Catholicism, which he claimed undermined conscience through the exercise of clerical authority. This had the effect, he argued, of dividing the world into two polar kingdoms: one secular and the other in the great beyond.[74] Protestantism, by comparison, represented a return to mundane existence. It stood for an incipient reconciliation with actuality, although not with things as they currently stood.

Hegel contended that Lutheranism abolished the categorical distinction between laity and priesthood. This was part and parcel of an acceptance of earthly life as the focus of human

71. Hegel to Tholuck, 3 July 1826, *Hegels Briefe*, 4 (2), p. 61.

72. Hegel to von Altenstein, 3 April 1826, *Hegel: The Letters*, trans. Clark Butler and Christiane Seiler (Bloomington, IN: Indiana University Press, 1984), p. 531.

73. Here I agree with Michael Rosen, *The Shadow of God: Kant, Hegel, and the Passage from Heaven to History* (Cambridge, MA: Harvard University Press, 2022), p. 13.

74. G.W.F. Hegel, *Vorlesungen über die Philosophie der Weltgeschichte 4: Nachschriften zum Kolleg des Wintersemesters, 1830/31*, ed. Walter Jaeschke (*Gesammelte Werke* 27.4) (Hamburg: Felix Meiner Verlag, 2020), p. 1495.

concern. Chastity yielded to the sanctity of marriage; the cult of poverty gave way to the pleasure of work; and unquestioning obedience was replaced by the value of conscience located in the recesses of the heart. These advances registered the 'principal revolution' introduced by the zeal for reform. According to Hegel, the leading figure in this process was neither Wycliffe nor Hus, but Luther, who by this account relocated divinity in human actuality.[75] At the same time, the value of humanity was now based on 'interiority' (*Innigkeit*). This referred to the inner dimensions of the person. With this new-found emphasis on subjectivity, feeling and personal faith gained new standing in religion. So too, however, did the sense that the world was out of joint. Sensibility was now dominated by repentance, contrition and guilt. That was the price of freedom in its Lutheran guise. It remained for philosophy to resolve these inchoate emotions and decipher the meaning of their symbolic representation. The 'stage' reached by Luther, who was still guided by revelation, fell short of properly philosophical comprehension and was therefore not yet 'mature'.[76] Nonetheless, reformed religion was a necessary prelude to reconciling conscience with a world being shaped to meet its expectations. In the aftermath of the Reformation, the sovereignty of the will occupied the centre of human conduct.[77] Social existence would have to be brought to meet its standards.

These developments in religious life led to a transformation in attitudes in all sections of German society. Yet equivalent

75. G.W.F. Hegel, *Vorlesungen über die Geschichte der Philosophie 3*, vol. 20 in *Werke*, ed. Eva Moldenhauer and Karl Markus Michel, 21 vols (Frankfurt: Suhrkamp, 1986), pp. 49–50.

76. Hegel, *Philosophy of Right*, 'Preface', p. 22.

77. Hegel, *Philosophie der Weltgeschichte: 1830/31*, pp. 1537–40.

moral progress was denied to Catholic France. Much like Protestantism, Jesuit thought became preoccupied with the complexities of volition, though this was largely a means of exempting individuals from responsibility.[78] The old servitude in the face of prelacy continued. As the following chapters in this book will show, Hegel thought it was the lack of an antecedent revolution in principles that led to the fury of the French Revolution. The groundwork for political renewal had not been laid in moral rebirth. In Germany, rehabilitation had already been initiated through religion. As Hegel argued in his final lecture on world history in 1823, 'without a change in religion, no truly political change can happen.'[79] He went on to observe that constitutional arrangements in Protestant Europe—in Denmark, England, the Netherlands and Prussia—were widely divergent. Yet in each case the image of government as serving the common good was highly evolved. This reconciled their populations to public institutions. On the other hand, in Catholic countries—in Spain, Ireland, France and Italy—criticism had descended into violence against the state. In each case, a moral energy confronted an obdurate positive force. The causes of these upheavals lay deep in Europe's past, encompassing relations between religion, morals and politics. The French Revolution only made sense in world-historical perspective.

78. Ibid., p. 1541.
79. G.W.F. Hegel, *Vorlesungen über die Philosophie der Weltgeschichte 1: Nachschriften zum Kolleg des Wintersemesters, 1822/23*, ed. Bernadette Collenberg-Plotnikov (*Gesammelte Werke* 27.1) (Hamburg: Felix Meiner Verlag, 2015), pp. 460–61, 461n.

PART II

Hegel and the French Revolution

Introduction

AFTER HIS 'COPERNICAN' REVOLUTION in epistemology, Kant unleashed a revolution in the relationship between virtue and happiness. He rejected all links between conduct and rewards as formulated across the spectrum of traditional religions. The value of an action lay in the purity of its motivation rather than in the consequences connected to behaviour. History, Kant contended, promised to realise this new orientation. Yet he also claimed that the path towards its fulfilment had been strewn with mishaps. In the absence of an account of the reasons for these miscarriages, Kant could only explain the failure in terms of a shortfall in morality. He proposed that evil persisted because selfishness corrupted ethical standards. Hegel sought to offer a more complete analysis of the causes behind successive missteps in the progress of ethical life. This drew his attention to the significance of historical transitions. Consequently, as we have seen, the passage from Judaism and Christianity to the Reformation and the French Revolution came to occupy the centre of both his historical and his philosophical concerns.

The relevant transitions often appeared as a brutal rupture. The journey from a given 'shape of spirit' to a new form of consciousness revealed itself in the guise of a definite break. Hegel represented this kind of fracture as a 'qualitative leap', since a completely new normative order replaced an older settlement. Nonetheless, behind the instant of nativity, Hegel recognised an extended process. The French Revolution, as with other episodes of historical transformation, had been a product of long-term growth. In one sense, it was a new dawn, but in another it was part of a protracted development. The reason for the appearance of a sudden rift was the violence of its proceedings. However, this disorder did not actually bring about real change. It registered a massive reorientation in thought, although it failed to secure a sustainable arrangement. A more compelling reconstruction of political values presupposed an alignment between insurgent moral energy and the received norms of social life. The chapters that make up the second part of this book are concerned with Hegel's search for reconciliation between subversive righteousness and stable institutions. This involved a reappraisal of the course of European history as it passed from the medieval to the modern world. The key moment was the shift from feudal monarchy to the constitutional state.

Just as Hegel had criticised the Christian flight into the void, he also indicted the purity of Rousseauean and Kantian principles as these were directed against the institutions of ethical life (*Sittlichkeit*).[1] He claimed that the French Revolution involved a rebellion of this kind against the external edifices of society

---

1. G.W.F. Hegel, *Elements of the Philosophy of Right* (1821), ed. Allen W. Wood, trans. H. B. Nisbet (Cambridge: Cambridge University Press, 1991), §29R.

and state. The insurrection hijacked the levers of government which had controlled France since Richelieu's reforms from the 1620s.[2] The concentration of power in the hands of a strong executive was not the only result of these seventeenth-century developments. So too was the disintegration of the Holy Roman Empire, against which, according to Hegel, Richelieu had conspired by means of the Treaty of Westphalia. Hegel noted that the German lands had long resisted subordination to an organised structure of command. After 1648, he went on, the forces of disaggregation steadily intensified. This process occurred in Germany against the background of a reconfiguration of values across Europe. Hegel described this in terms of the decline of birth as the defining feature of social rank. Even as a role for corporations survived in Germany, the connection between nobility and political office weakened. This remodelling was observable alike in England, Austria, Prussia and France long before 1789. The new dispensation called for a reorganisation of political forces in the struggle between universalism and hereditary privileges.[3] Social relations, constitutional theory and the system of representation would have to be overhauled. From the late 1790s on, in major publications such as the *Phenomenology of Spirit* and the *Philosophy of Right*, among others, Hegel sharpened his conception of what was required to achieve this goal.

---

2. G.W.F. Hegel, *Vorlesungen über die Philosophie der Weltgeschichte 4: Nachschriften zum Kolleg des Wintersemesters, 1830/31*, ed. Walter Jaeschke (*Gesammelte Werke 27.4*) (Hamburg: Felix Meiner Verlag, 2020), p. 1561.

3. G.W.F. Hegel, *Lectures on Natural Right and Political Science: The First Philosophy of Right*, ed. and trans. J. Michael Stewart and Peter C. Hodgson (Oxford: Oxford University Press, 2012), §125A.

4

The Holy Roman Empire
and the French Revolution

EARLY IN HIS JENA PERIOD, around 1803, Hegel addressed the topic of transitional epochs. Such periods of change, he believed, usually gave rise to decisive individuals who helped remodel the cultural world around them. Such figures, he thought, could rouse 'the still slumbering shape of a new ethical world to waking'. Consummate revolutionaries of the kind came armed with a philosophy bearing a new world within it. Alexander the Great was Hegel's favoured example: he 'passed out of the school of Aristotle to become conqueror of the world'.[1] A new mode of life depended on transformative thought and action as well as the means of translating between the two. Yet this, for Hegel, was no simple process. In fact, the difficulties involved in understanding radical change posed the greatest challenge to both philosophy and history. The issue could hardly be productively addressed without deploying the resources of both forms of inquiry. Ideas and affairs had to be analysed together. They

1. Karl Rosenkranz, *Georg Wilhelm Friedrich Hegels Leben* (Berlin: Duncker und Humblot, 1844), pp. 189–90.

operated, moreover, within a larger social context shaped by the labour of whole populations. There were reasons to explore the thought of extraordinary thinkers, just as it made sense to examine the activities of remarkable leaders. However, neither simply made the world in which they functioned. Machiavelli showed how preeminent mythological and historical leaders— such as Moses, Cyrus, Romulus and Theseus—had displayed their capabilities (*virtù*) in shaping the material they encountered 'into the form that seemed best to them'.[2] Hegel was clearly drawn to this facet of Machiavelli's teaching.[3] He also agreed that initiatives undertaken by gifted rulers were constrained by the pressing contexts in which they worked. It was the intricacy of these contexts that stood in need of examination, as well as the opportunities for innovation within them.

Also during his early Jena years, Hegel pondered the idea of outstanding genius. A truly inventive individual, he contended, had to cooperate with their cultural milieu. For this reason, a work of art was necessarily a 'universal' possession. It was not the product of a lone pioneer, but 'a discovery of the people as a whole'.[4] The same principles applied in the case of political revolution (*Staatsrevolution*). Hegel developed his argument by recounting an imaginary scenario in which a community was buried beneath the surface of the earth, above which was

2. Niccolò Machiavelli, *The Prince*, ed. Quentin Skinner and Russell Price, trans. Price (Cambridge: Cambridge University Press, 1988), p. 20.

3. See Hegel's excerpt transcribed in 1801–2 from book 26 of Machiavelli's *Prince*, covering the same ground, in G.W.F. Hegel, *Schriften und Entwürfe (1799–1808)*, ed. Manfred Baum (*Gesammelte Werke 5*) (Hamburg: Felix Meiner Verlag, 1998), pp. 205–6. The extract formed a plank of the argument in G.W.F. Hegel, 'The German Constitution', in *Hegel: Political Writings*, ed. Laurence Dickey and H. B. Nisbet, trans. Nisbet (Cambridge: Cambridge University Press, 1999), pp. 79–80.

4. Rosenkranz, *Hegels Leben*, pp. 180–81.

positioned an imposing lake. Each individual in the group applied themselves to their own purpose. The members of the
crowd hacked at the masonry above, hoping to improve their
underworld existence by putting the available stone to constructive use. As they proceeded, their surrounding conditions
changed. Inexplicably, they grew restless, drilling ever deeper
into the vault above. Gradually, they became thirsty, yet they
pressed on, until finally the facade became transparent over
their heads and, unexpectedly, the water surged in. It *'drinks
them'*, Hegel wrote, while 'they *drink it*'.[5] It is clear that in this
fable of revolutionary change, the transformative endeavour
was the work of all, even if an individual spearheaded the final
breakthrough. In Hegel's model, there is no dispensing with
exceptional contributions. Audacious innovators commonly
bring matters to a crunch. Yet, in this vision, enterprise owes its
achievement to the conditions on which it capitalises.

These same concerns made an appearance in the 'Preface' to
Hegel's *Phenomenology of Spirit*, the main text of which he was
completing in the autumn of 1806. In that year, on 14 October,
Prussian forces faced the emperor Napoleon at the battle of
Jena. The contest was a defining episode in the progress of the
French Revolution. The army of the Prussian monarch, Frederick William III, crumbled before the might of the French military. Prior to the decisive confrontation, the city of Jena itself
was heavily bombarded, obliging Hegel to seek refuge on the
far side of the town.[6] The Prussian army, now under the general command of Duke Ferdinand of Brunswick, had last
endeavoured to outmanoeuvre the French battalions in 1792,

5. Ibid., p. 181.
6. Terry Pinkard, *Hegel: A Biography* (Cambridge: Cambridge University Press,
2000), p. 228.

culminating in ignominious defeat at Valmy on 20 September, and followed by the prompt withdrawal of the Prussians from French territory.[7] Now, fourteen years on, Brunswick, at the age of seventy-one, faced his enemy once more. Along with chief advisers in the monarch's administration, including both Karl von Hardenberg and Baron vom Stein, he was desperate to bolster Prussia's position in northern Germany, especially as Napoleon seemed intent on extending himself into the far reaches of the European continent.[8] Hegel at this point wrote to his friend, Friedrich Niethammer, confessing that everyone in the surrounding area, including himself, was eager for a French victory. The evening before the decisive assault, he caught sight of the emperor himself—'this world-soul' (*Weltseele*)—leaving the town on reconnaissance.

Hegel found the French emperor 'impossible not to admire': 'It is indeed a wonderful sensation to see such an individual, who, concentrated here at a single point, sitting on a horse, reaches out over the world and masters it.'[9] By the following evening, Napoleon had conclusively routed his opponents. Brunswick himself was fatally wounded in action at nearby Auerstedt. Days later, on 18 October, Hegel dispatched the final sheets of the *Phenomenology* to his publisher, followed by the 'Preface' in early February. In the intervening period, as

7. T.W.C. Blanning, *The French Revolutionary Wars, 1787–1802* (London: Arnold, 1996), ch. 3.

8. Paul Schroeder, *The Transformation of European Politics, 1763–1848* (Oxford: Clarendon Press, 1994), pp. 302ff; Brendan Simms, *The Impact of Napoleon: Prussian High Politics, Foreign Policy and the Crisis of the Executive, 1797–1806* (Cambridge: Cambridge University Press, 1997), pp. 285–91.

9. Hegel to Niethammer, 13 October 1806, *Briefe von und an Hegel* [*Hegels Briefe*], ed. Johannes Hoffmeister, 4 vols (Hamburg: Felix Meiner Verlag, 1952), 1, p. 120.

Napoleon advanced through central Europe, a string of Prussian fortresses fell to the French. After entering Berlin on 27 October 1806, followed by a pilgrimage to Potsdam, Napoleon gave notice of his plan to deprive the Prussians of their possessions west of the Elbe, an arrangement confirmed the following summer under the Treaty of Tilsit. In addition, a crushing indemnity was imposed. The remnants of the Prussian state were only permitted to survive in order to serve as a buffer against Russia.[10] It was a time, as Hegel put it in his 'Preface', 'of birth and of transition to a new period'.[11] In less than two decades, the French system of government had been repeatedly overhauled. Established principles of social organisation had been revised. The balance of power in Europe had been radically undermined. Between 1797 and 1803, annexations and incorporations transformed the map of the continent. The majority of imperial cities lost their autonomy under the Empire. The Confederation of the Rhine was established, following the battle of Austerlitz, on 12 July 1806. A month later, the Holy Roman Empire was finally dissolved. Ecclesiastical territories were swept aside, while numerous jurisdictions across Germany were mediatised. Württemberg, Baden and Bavaria increased their territories. Substantial tracts of the erstwhile Reich fell under the immediate control of Napoleon. Yet, as Hegel repeatedly emphasised, throughout the same period since 1789, philosophy was being reborn. He intended his observations on a tottering world to carry epic resonance. The French Revolution

---

10. Christopher Clark, *Iron Kingdom: The Rise and Downfall of Prussia, 1600–1947* (London: Allen Lane, 2006), pp. 307–11; Hajo Holborn, *A History of Modern Germany, 1648–1840* (New York: Alfred A. Knopf, 1964), p. 385.

11. G.W.F. Hegel, *The Phenomenology of Spirit* (1807), ed. and trans. Michael Inwood (Oxford: Oxford University Press, 2018), §11.

and its aftermath enjoyed world-historical significance, and Hegel regarded his own work as integral to the drama. Thomas Nipperdey described the advent of modern Germany in the following terms: 'In the beginning was Napoleon.'[12] For Hegel, however, matters were more complex. Despite his fascination with trailblazing characters, he emphasised the role of 'spirit' (*Geist*) in effecting seismic change. The nature of this agent has posed a problem for interpretation. In major portions of the literature, 'spirit' has been cast as a disembodied abstraction.[13] It has gradually been accepted that this depiction involves distortion.[14] Nonetheless, Hegel's frequent poetic constructions often serve to mangle his meaning. Commonly enough, spirit is personified as an individual actor.[15] The 'Preface' to the *Phenomenology* provides numerous examples. For instance, Hegel tells us in §11, in the context of his portrayal of the 'birth and transition' characteristic of the age, that *Geist* 'has broken with the previous world of its life and ideas.'[16] It might seem as though spirit were a kind of substratum, a ghostly equivalent of Spinoza's *natura naturans*. At the same time, since spirit acts, it

---

12. Thomas Nipperdey, *Deutsche Geschichte, 1800–1866: Bürgerwelt und starker Staat* (Munich: C. H. Beck, 1983), p. 11. Rival views that still take the period around the French Revolution to mark a definitive break can be found in Hans-Ulrich Wehler, *Das deutsche Kaiserreich, 1871–1918* (Göttingen: Vandenhoeck and Ruprecht, 1994), pp. 20ff; Heinrich August Winkler, *Der lange Weg nach Westen*, 2 vols (Munich: C. H. Beck, 2000), 1, p. 5.

13. A prominent version in the anglophone literature is Charles Taylor, *Hegel* (Cambridge: Cambridge University Press, 1975).

14. Robert Pippin, *Hegel's Idealism: The Satisfactions of Self-Consciousness* (Cambridge: Cambridge University Press, 1989), pp. 3–15.

15. This has prompted misconceptions, as with G. A. Cohen, *Karl Marx's Theory of History: A Defence* (Oxford: Clarendon Press, 1978), pp. 1ff, where Hegel's abstract personification is recast as a literal individual: 'world spirit is a person'.

16. Hegel, *Phenomenology*, §11.

would appear to possess a will, and so while some are tempted to regard it as an occult metaphysical substance, it has the evident characteristics of an active mind, a replica of self-consciousness as theorised by Kant and Fichte. One thing, in any case, is certain: post-Kantian theories of subjectivity played an essential role in Hegel's construction of the concept. The world of 'substance', as he put it, 'is essentially subject'.[17]

The truth, then, is that—much like Kant's reason—Hegel's *Geist* is reflexively self-critical. For ease of comprehension, we might envisage spirit in the way that we sometimes think of 'culture', even though *Bildung* in Hegel's usage refers to a subsidiary aspect of *Geist*.[18] Spirit is not an inert reservoir of customs, or a complex of indifferently inherited traditions; it is an interconnected system of principles and commitments.[19] The culture of the early nineteenth century, Hegel wanted to say, had broken from a previous form of life. The rupture was in some respects cataclysmic. Yet underlying the eruption was a steady process. There was the semblance of an abrupt disjunction, like a human birth, but behind the sudden breach was a continuous development, and ahead lay a lengthy stretch of maturation. Hegel was concerned with both the nature of the chasm and the steady action by which the culture evolved. This

17. Ibid., §25. For discussion, see Robert Pippin, *Hegel on Self-Consciousness: Desire and Death in the 'Phenomenology of Spirit'* (Princeton, NJ: Princeton University Press, 2011); Sally Sedgwick, *Hegel's Critique of Kant* (Oxford: Oxford University Press, 2012), ch. 5; Terry Pinkard, 'Subjectivity and Substance', *Hegel Bulletin*, 36: 1 (May 2015), pp. 1–14.

18. Raymond Geuss, '*Kultur, Bildung, Geist*', in *Morality, Culture, and History: Essays on German Philosophy* (Cambridge: Cambridge University Press, 1999), argues that *Kultur* cedes to *Geist* in the German philosophical context under Hegel's influence. For *Bildung* as a facet of *Geist*, see Hegel, *Phenomenology*, §442.

19. Robert Brandom, *A Spirit of Trust: A Reading of Hegel's 'Phenomenology'* (Cambridge, MA: Harvard University Press, 2019), pp. 9ff.

required minute attention to the details of incremental adaptation. Above all, it demanded an analysis of the shifting forms of legitimation which accompanied this gradual advance. In addition, Hegel was interested in the very principle which lent momentum to the unfolding process, the source of movement as *Geist* progressed. Without the existence of critical self-reflection within society, a given culture would either be static, or passively mutating. In the absence of self-consciousness, a culture could not be fashioned: it would simply happen. 'Only spirit', as Jean Hyppolite put it, 'has a history.'[20]

II

For Hegel, then, the shape of a new world can become apparent 'like lightning, all of a sudden.'[21] Yet the roots and consequences of this transformation require excavation, an effort at digging into a 'wide-ranging revolution in various forms of culture [*Bildungsformen*]'.[22] This involves attending to the minutiae of the relevant factors—to the very 'entrails' (*Eingeweide*) of the elements under review, as Hegel put it in describing scientific procedure in the age of Bacon.[23] Such inspection had to reach across all sectors of human behaviour. This necessarily included conceptual innovation, since otherwise adjustments would have to be viewed as purely reactive—in which case it would be natural rather than cultural evolution, and thus strictly speaking not an historical development at all. With Hegel's focus on new

20. Jean Hyppolite, *Genesis and Structure of Hegel's 'Phenomenology of Spirit'* (Evanston IL: Northwestern University Press, 1974), p. 33.
21. Hegel, *Phenomenology*, §11.
22. Ibid., §12.
23. Ibid., §241.

ideological directions, social change included self-motivated shifts in the character of self-consciousness. There was no suggestion that this process was not explicitly concrete, nor that ideology was an emanation rather than a mundane force. Hegel's point, instead, was that ideological structures could never come into existence if there was no incipient role for self-aware human agents. By their mutually modifying interaction, these actors brought social norms into existence. Historical explanation thus had to account for normative change by analysing the process of *sich bildende Geist* (self-cultivating spirit).[24] This included examination of stark historical fractures as well as of the steady labour out of which cleavages sprang. Since Hegel saw his era as a moment of disruption, his approach included investigation of contemporary conditions. Napoleon was a factor relevant to the circumstances, but he was neither an ultimate cause nor an absolute beginning. The reasons for change lay deep in the antecedent culture, whose tentacles were manifest in every dimension of life.

The triumph of Napoleon over Prussia in 1806–7 came after a period of neutrality under Frederick William III during the War of the Second Coalition. That contest was fought out between France and her remaining European enemies, including Austria, Britain and Russia, from 1798 to 1802. By the end of the military confrontation, French control over its Westphalian territories was confirmed, Napoleon had expanded into northern and central Italy, and the German lands were forced to accept their weakened position.[25] Having already established the Batavian Republic in 1795 and gained recognition for its control

24. Ibid., §12.
25. Michael Rowe, *From Reich to State: The Rhineland in the Revolutionary Age* (Cambridge: Cambridge University Press, 2003), ch. 3.

of the regions it occupied on the west bank of the Rhine under the Peace of Basel, French forces had more than redressed their early losses against the allies. At the same time, resentment on account of Prussia's pursuit of its own narrow interests spread across southern German territories. Austrian power was then reduced in 1797 under the Treaty of Campo Formio, with losses confirmed four years later under the Treaty of Lunéville, more or less concluding the War of the Second Coalition. Hegel later quoted Napoleon on the significance of Campo Formio in his lectures on the philosophy of right, stating in effect that the French Republic had 'no more need of recognition than the sun'.[26] By 1801, the Holy Roman Empire was divided strategically into competing spheres of interest comprising the Prussian north, the Austrian south, and the remaining western regions poised between France and Germany, principally along the Rhine.[27] Acutely conscious of these developments, Hegel was at work between 1799 and 1803 on a study of the 'German Constitution', essentially a critique of the current condition of the German Reich, and implicitly an exploration of how it might be rejuvenated. This involved comparison with the situation in France, including the impact of the Revolution in both territories. It amounted to a detailed contextualisation of the fallout from 1789, considered on a European scale. More important than the sudden burst of change—the 'qualitative leap', as Hegel phrased it in the *Phenomenology*—was the long gestation in terms of which more proximate events had to be explained.

26. Hegel, *Philosophy of Right*, §331A. Cf. G.W.F. Hegel, 'Vorlesungsnachschrift, K. G. v. Griesheim, 1824–5', in *Vorlesungen über Rechtsphilosophie, 1818–1831*, ed. Karl-Heinz Ilting, 4 vols (Stuttgart: Frommann-Holzboog, 1973–74), 4, p. 741.

27. Joachim Whaley, *Germany and the Holy Roman Empire*, vol. 2: *The Peace of Westphalia to the Dissolution of the Reich, 1848–1806* (Oxford: Oxford University Press, 2012), ch. 61.

At the end of his career, in his final lectures on the philosophy of world history, Hegel declared his astonishment at the outbreak of the Revolution. His comments recall the mood at Tübingen in the early 1790s. The very occurrence, he revealed, seemed to him a brilliant 'sunrise'.[28] Remarks of the kind go some way toward explaining Hegel's reputation as an eager supporter of the Revolution. But which Revolution, we need to ask, is he supposed to have endorsed? The decade following 1789 is not reducible to a single episode. The Revolution is better understood as a series of insurrections, including counterstrokes against the original revolt. Despite this, Joachim Ritter claimed that everything in Hegel's thought proceeded from his early Revolutionary 'enthusiasm'. Throughout his career, Ritter went on, Hegel consistently 'affirmed' the event: 'there is nothing more unambiguous than this affirmation'.[29] The evidence counts against blank statements of the kind; even so, biographers have essentially followed Ritter's lead.[30] Everything is referred to an isolated milestone, as if the age had turned about a single point while the interpretation of the watershed stood still.[31] We are often reminded of Hegel's habit of toasting the Revolution every year on 14 July as a token of ongoing devotion.[32] The meaning

28. Hegel, *Philosophie der Weltgeschichte: 1830/31*, p. 1562.

29. Joachim Ritter, *Hegel and the French Revolution: Essays on the Philosophy of Right*, trans. Richard Dien Winfield (Cambridge, MA: MIT Press, 1982), pp. 44–46.

30. Klaus Vieweg, *Hegel: Der Philosoph der Freiheit* (Munich: C. H. Beck, 2019), p. 67; Pinkard, *Hegel: A Biography*, pp. 22ff.

31. Jürgen Habermas accepted this verdict, though he added to it the curious and unsubstantiated claim that Hegel applauded revolution whilst rejecting the activities of revolutionaries. See his somewhat opaque essay, 'Hegel's Critique of the French Revolution', in *Theory and Practice*, trans. John Viertel (London: Heinemann, 1974).

32. Friedrich Förster relayed this story following a visit to Dresden in July 1820. See G.W.F Hegel, *Hegel in Berichten seiner Zeitgenossen*, ed. Günther Nicolin (Hamburg: Felix Meiner Verlag, 1970), pp. 207, 213–14.

of the gesture is less frequently examined, let alone contextualised. The 'daybreak' of 1789 certainly made an indelible impres-
sion. In fact, expressions of idealistic warmth are most conspicuous in Hegel's final semester of lectures on world history,
delivered just a year before his death. He reckoned that every
thinking person celebrated the symbolic import of the Declaration of the Rights of Man and the Citizen. A fervour, he recalled, infused the period. It was, he stressed, a Copernican
transformation: 'For as long as the sun had stood in the firma-
ment and the planets revolved around it, it had not been appreciated that human beings were centred in their heads—that
is, in thought—and actuality constructed according to its standards.' Anaxagoras had argued, as Hegel registered, that it was
'mind' (νοῦς) which regulated the phenomenal world. Yet
never before the Revolution in France had it been recognised
that ideas governed the moral universe.[33] However, for all the
breathless emotion of these remarks, Hegel's attitude was in fact
profoundly sceptical.

Although critical, Hegel's reaction was also nuanced and
multifaceted. What he admired was the ambition to discipline
politics through philosophy, to regulate power by resort to
principles. At the same time, he had no doubt that the attempt
had failed in practice, that the very endeavour had ensured its
own ruinous defeat. Equally, he was certain that any assumption that the fiasco might have been avoided was naïve, even
self-absorbed. The origins of the Revolution lay deep in history. It was therefore necessary to distinguish between local

33. Hegel, *Philosophie der Weltgeschichte: 1830/31*, p. 1561. The same observation
about Anaxagoras appears in the section on the Peloponnesian War in G.W.F. Hegel,
Vorlesungen über die Philosophie der Geschichte (1837), vol. 12 in *Werke*, ed. Eva Moldenhauer and Karl Markus Michel, 21 vols (Frankfurt: Suhrkamp, 1986), p. 328.

symptoms and long-term causes, and to view events with reference to far-reaching consequences. While the broad outlines of the future should be accepted, each step in the process did not have to be approved. Hegel was scathing about the methods employed to advance the 'rights of man'. Specific harbingers of things to come could legitimately be deplored even if they pointed to the shape of a better world. Hegel had detailed access to developments on the ground, lending authority to his dismay at the course of events. Copies of *Le Moniteur Universel* were widely read in Germany for its coverage of Revolutionary news and debates. Hegel inquired of Schelling in 1794 whether the citizens of Württemberg still had access to the French papers as residents in Bern did.[34] He also regularly consulted Johann Wilhelm Archenholz's *Minerva*, a periodical first established in 1792. He was therefore familiar with the writings of Konrad Engelbert Oelsner, a Silesian contributor to *Minerva* who fled to Switzerland in May 1794 having been forced out of Paris after a series of imprisonments at the hands of the authorities.

Oelsner, much like Joachim Heinrich Campe, published his own eyewitness accounts of the situation in Paris, and increasingly turned from sympathy for the regime to bitter opposition to the Jacobin terror.[35] During these years, he had established connections with German publicists in France—including Georg Forster, Karl Friedrich Reinhard, Georg Kerner and

---

34. Hegel to Schelling, 24 December 1794, *Hegels Briefe*, 1, p. 12.

35. See Konrad Engelbert Oelsner, 'Briefe aus Paris, über die neuesten Begebenheiten in Frankreich', in *Minerva: Ein Journal historischen und politischen Inhalts*, vol. 3 (1792), pp. 326–88, 551–75; vol. 4 (1792), pp. 1–64, 103–14, 175–89; vol. 5 (1793), pp. 127–84, 284–368, 493–564; and Joachim Heinrich Campe, *Briefe aus Paris zur Zeit der Revolution* (Braunschweig: Schulbuchhandlung, 1790).

Gustav von Schlabrendorff—along with the Abbé Sieyès.[36] Given Oelsner's access to political circles and the army, as well as his familiarity with the struggles of the capital and the provinces, he was arguably the most important German observer of events.[37] Hegel reported meeting him in December 1794 before delivering his own verdict on the actions of Jean-Baptiste Carrier, a committed Jacobin and member of the Revolutionary Tribunal charged with carrying out mass executions just north of the Vendée region. Carrier was convicted and sentenced to death on 16 December 1794. His trial laid bare— much as Oelsner had done—what Hegel termed the 'complete ignominy' (*ganze Schändlichkeit*) of the Robespierre faction in the National Convention.[38] Later, receiving the endorsement of the Committee of Public Safety, Carrier had inflicted brutal violence on thousands of defenceless opponents, real and imagined. His victims died in their droves—by firing squad, forced drowning or under the guillotine. Adolphe Thiers later painted him as a petty functionary who behaved during the drownings at Nantes as a monster of vindictiveness.[39] These

---

36. Oelsner published a preface to a collection of Sieyès's political writings. See Emmanuel-Joseph Sieyès, *Politische Schriften, 1788–1790: Vollständig gesammelt von dem deutschen Übersezer nebst zwei Vorreden über Sieyes Lebensgeschichte, seine politische Rolle, seinen Charakter, seine Schriften*, ed. Konrad Engelbert Oelsner, 2 vols (Leipzig: Wolff, 1796).

37. Klaus Deinet, *Konrad Engelbert Oelsner und die Französische Revolution: Geschichtserfahrung und Geschichtsdeutung eines deutschen Girondisten* (Munich: Oldenbourg, 1981).

38. Hegel to Schelling, 24 December 1794, *Hegels Briefe*, 1, p. 12. On the impact on Hegel of the drownings carried out by Jean-Baptiste Carrier, see James Schmidt, 'Cabbage Heads and Gulps of Water: Hegel on the Terror', *Political Theory*, 26: 1 (February 1998), pp. 4–32.

39. Adolphe Thiers, *The History of the French Revolution*, trans. Frederic Shoberl, 5 vols (New York: D. Appleton, 1854), 3, p. 69.

drownings, cynically dubbed 'immersions' and 'national baptisms', soon became infamous for their calculated cruelty. In the darkest period of the Revolution, Hegel was repelled by the needless carnage. But he would come to see the terrorism as an integral product of the original idealism, not a peculiar or unaccountable perversion.

III

Over the following years, certainly by 1798, the depth of Hegel's suspicions became even more discernible. It was not just the wholesale destructiveness of proceedings that disturbed him. He was more generally perplexed by the approach to politics exhibited across the range of Revolutionary initiatives, not least the adoption of principles and measures which were bound to prove counterproductive under conditions as they existed. In the fragmentary remains of a pamphlet dealing with the proposition 'That the Magistrates should be Elected by the People', Hegel made plain the various forms of representation he rejected. The pamphlet was drafted as a response to the unfolding situation in Württemberg where, in 1797, its autocratic duke, Friedrich Eugen, had been forced to reconvene the Estates of the diet (*Landtag*) after a period of dissolution that had lasted from 1770.[40] Long-standing controversy between the claims of the diet and the executive was suddenly reanimated as the constitutional principles defining the Duchy came under scrutiny.[41] With an end to the French occupation of the territory in

40. James Allen Vann, *The Making of a State: Württemberg, 1593–1793* (Ithaca, NY: Cornell University Press, 1984).

41. Laurence Dickey, *Hegel: Religion, Economics, and the Politics of Spirit, 1770–1807* (Cambridge: Cambridge University Press, 1987), ch. 3.

sight, the parlous state of the finances triggered a crisis when the standing committee (*Ausschuß*) of the diet proved unwilling to agree a constructive way forward with the duke. Faced with the imminent summoning of the Württemberg Estates, the opportunity for reform was widely trumpeted, including the possibility of a comprehensive revision of the very basis on which representatives were selected. Hegel was keen to avoid the electoral experiments which had in his view destabilised France since the early 1790s. With this experience in mind, he declared that it made no sense to introduce popular elections into a hereditary monarchy where the population was unenlightened and accustomed to blind obedience. This lesson applied equally to south-west Germany: 'as long as the people were ignorant of their rights, as long as public spirit [*Gemeingeist*] was absent, as long as the power of officials was not restricted, popular elections would only serve to bring about the complete overthrow of our constitution.'[42] At the turn of the century he acknowledged the need for some form of representation whilst again indicting French innovation in the area as being aberrant and destructive.

These views were plainly not those of a revolutionary *ingénu*. Yet Hegel's doubts did not focus only on the dangers of popular enfranchisement. He was equally scathing about the impulse toward centralisation, evident during the Revolution as well as the centuries before it. It was this wider perspective that he cultivated in his draft materials on the 'German

42. G.W.F. Hegel, *Daß die Magistrate von den Bürgern gewählt werden müssen* (1798), in *Frühe Schriften 2*, p. 108. Extract originally reported by Rudolf Haym, *Hegel und seine Zeit: Vorlesungen über Entstehung und Entwicklung, Wesen und Werth der hegelschen Philosophie* (Berlin: Rudolph Gärtner, 1857), p. 66.

Constitution'. The subject of this work was the likely future of the German Reich, currently under pressure from Napoleon. Through the 1790s, as the French Revolution impacted directly on the geopolitics of central Europe, debate about the condition of the Holy Roman Empire became widespread.[43] As Hegel set about composing his own contribution to the discussion, the Second Congress of Rastatt was deliberating on the future configuration of the German states-system.[44] By now, the likelihood of some measure of secularisation affecting ecclesiastical territories had been accepted, and delegates at Rastatt were considering annexations and compensation plans, although wrangling seemed only to lead to deadlock. For many, the Treaty of Campo Formio had already sounded the death knell of the polity, yet for Hegel it was just the last in a sequence of capitulations stretching back to the Treaty of Westphalia, cumulatively signalling the demise of the state. Germany, he boldly proclaimed, 'is no longer a state'.[45] While the statement implied a judgement about what constituted statehood, Hegel built his case on comparative analysis, juxtaposing the trajectory of the German Empire since its inception with the experience of France after the Wars of Religion.

Much of Hegel's treatment involved a tirade against moralism, an indictment of philanthropic attitudinising in politics

43. Whaley, *Germany*, ch. 64; Karl Otmar von Aretin, *Das Alte Reich, 1648–1806*, 4 vols (Stuttgart: Klett Cotta, 1993–2000), 3, pp. 454–56; Wolfgang Burgdorf, *Reichskonstitution und Nation: Verfassungsreformprojekte für das Heilige Römische Reich Deutscher Nation im politischen Schrifttum von 1648 bis 1806* (Mainz: Verlag Philipp von Zabern, 1998).

44. Hegel mentions the Congress, and the Treaty of Lunéville, in 'German Constitution', pp. 7, 32.

45. Hegel, 'German Constitution', p. 6.

which disdained the realities of power and unavoidable clashes of interest. Frederick the Great was singled out for blame as the would-be philosopher-king given to elevating principles over the means of fulfilling them. Sometimes, Hegel coolly remarked, drastic means were required: 'gangrenous limbs cannot be cured by lavender-water'.[46] Against sanctimonious sermonising, Hegel adopted a posture of vigorous realism, espousing coordinated German government as a matter of necessity, and invoking Machiavelli as a presiding genius who himself had sought to recover the fortunes of Italy by 'uniting it into a single state'.[47] Why was it, Hegel asked rhetorically, that from Hippolytus à Lapide to Voltaire, Germany had become a byword for anarchy and disintegration?[48] His answer lay in the historical development of the Reich, culminating in the *Reichsdeputationshauptschluss* of 1803,[49] a resolution of the German Imperial Diet which in effect restructured the Empire along lines dictated by France, leading to the incorporation of around 112 territories into larger jurisdictions, with over three million subjects finding themselves under new

46. Ibid., p. 80.

47. Ibid., pp. 60, 69–70, 79ff. Cf. G.W.F. Hegel, *Jenaer Systementwürfe 3: Naturphilosophie und Philosophie des Geistes*, ed. Rolf-Peter Horstmann (Hamburg: Felix Meiner Verlag, 1987), p. 236.

48. Hegel, 'German Constitution', pp. 6, 74. Hippolytus à Lapide was a pseudonym for the historian and legal publicist Bogislaw Philipp von Chemnitz. Cf. G.W.F. Hegel, *Review of the Proceedings of the Estates Assembly of the Kingdom of Württemberg, 1815–1816*, in *Heidelberg Writings*, ed. and trans. Brady Bowman and Allen Speight (Cambridge: Cambridge University Press, 2009), pp. 33–34. See Mack Walker, *German Home Towns: Community, State, and General Estate, 1648–1871* (Ithaca, NY: Cornell University Press, 1971), pp. 17ff.

49. The last fragmentary portions of the text are dated to February 1803 in G.W.F. Hegel, *Schriften und Entwürfe, 1799–1808*, ed. Manfred Baum (*Gesammelte Werke 5*) (Hamburg: Felix Meiner Verlag, 1998), pp. 552–53.

rulers.[50] Württemberg itself was raised to become an Electorate, at the same time acquiring new territories. The public accommodation of the German constitution to conditions imposed by a foreign hegemon appeared to Hegel to indicate a loss of national sovereignty. The achievement of self-government, he believed, required that a 'mass of people' be 'united for the common defence of the totality of its property'.[51] The lack of a coherent German polity animated by a sovereign will distinguished the loose combination of states under the Empire from the situation in Britain and Spain, as well as, most importantly, from France.[52] Above all, the organisation of the military and finances under the German Reich pointed to the collapse of a functioning authority.[53] In France, the Revolution had consolidated government; in Germany, organised power had declined. Hegel sought the causes in the 'spirit' of the laws.

IV

The echo of Montesquieu was deliberate. While Hegel had invested considerable effort in distinguishing his own idea of *Geist* from the metaphysical context in which Montesquieu had developed his notion of *esprit*, both concepts sought to pick out systematic historical relations driven by 'inner' or fundamental causes. The contemporary state of affairs, Hegel argued, was an external 'appearance' that should be explained in

50. John G. Gagliardo, *Reich and Nation: The Holy Roman Empire as Idea and Reality, 1763–1806* (Bloomington, IN: Indiana University Press, 1980), pp. 239–43.

51. Hegel, 'German Constitution', p. 15.

52. Ibid., p. 77.

53. Ibid., pp. 26ff.

the light of a governing causal nexus reaching back into a more distant past. The state of the German Reich revealed a crumbling edifice in which the features of an emerging structure could be discerned. Yet, at the same time, the shattered state of the building was a product of gradual change, an incremental process of construction and deconstruction. Historical study uncovered the 'necessity' driving that process, the unstoppable force embedded within a 'system of events'.[54] This involved identifying the underlying culture, the governing normative framework, which determined the fate of German political life.

Hegel traced this to the 'German' idea of freedom. The concept had its origins in accounts of the German (or Teutonic) tribes as variously relayed by Boulainvilliers, Montesquieu and Tacitus.[55] Tacitus was most likely Hegel's immediate source: in his *Germania*, he had drawn a picture of tribal society in which authority was controlled from the bottom up and participation in affairs was widespread. On 'major matters' (*de maioribus*), as Tacitus put it, everybody (*omnes*) deliberated.[56] Herein lay the original source of the subsequent German 'drive for freedom'. It was this impulse which accounted for the entrenched national character which combined obduracy with the spirit of independence.[57] These features were formed in Europe's pre-feudal past, and persisted in the territories of the German Reich

54. Ibid., pp. 7–8.

55. See Michael Sonenscher, *Before the Deluge: Public Debt, Inequality, and the Intellectual Origins of the French Revolution* (Princeton, NJ: Princeton University Press, 2007), pp. 137ff. Boulainvilliers's role figured prominently in Emmanuel-Joseph Sieyès, *What Is the Third Estate?* (1789), trans. Michael Sonenscher, in *Sieyès: Political Writings; including the Debate between Sieyès and Tom Paine in 1791*, ed. Sonenscher (Indianapolis: Hackett, 2003), p. 99.

56. Tacitus, *Germania*, ch. 11.

57. Hegel, 'German Constitution', p. 57.

so as to inhibit the emergence of 'a common political authority'. Self-willed individuality resisted 'universality', or subjection to an impersonal structure of supreme command. The current German mass of states began life as a 'people' reluctant to acquiesce in the impersonal discipline of civil community. The legacy of this pre-political spirit was that associations under the Empire thrived in disaggregated forms—as principalities, corporations, cities, ranks, dynasties and guilds—whilst resisting limitation through submission to the state.[58] This made for diversity, and a culture of ad hoc privileges, along with a dearth of concerted political action on the part of the polity as a totality: 'The German political edifice is nothing other than the sum of the rights which individual parts have extracted from the whole.'[59] Hegel would hold to this negative verdict down to his years at Heidelberg and beyond.[60]

In accordance with the standard historical narrative of recovery after the fall of the Roman Empire, Hegel presented the 'German' spirit as a European norm. The whole continent, he reaffirmed, had been the creation of 'Germanic peoples'. However, during the course of development, most states pursued a course different from that of Germany proper: 'France, Spain, England, Denmark and Sweden, Holland, and Hungary each grew into a single state.'[61] Only Italy and Poland, along with Germany, managed to buck the trend. Various forces in German history inhibited progress in the more usual direction. These included the influence of religion in the aftermath of the Reformation; the constant experience of international interference,

58. Ibid., pp. 10–12.
59. Ibid., p. 13.
60. Hegel, *First Philosophy of Right*, §§121A, 125A.
61. Hegel, 'German Constitution', p. 62.

before and after the Treaty of Westphalia; and unequal concen-
trations of wealth and power among the estates of the Reich.[62]

Yet none of these was necessarily fatal to the establishment
of national cohesion. Instead, disintegration was caused by the failure to coordinate the plethora of separate regimes under the overarching authority of a unified Empire. This led the more powerful
members of the Reich–above all Austria and Prussia—to pursue their own strategic interests, to the detriment of supreme
authority. Across Europe, before the seventeenth century,
decision-making depended on concerted action between mon-
archs and parliaments made up of representative estates. Representation, Hegel observed, was not a feature of the participa-
tory politics of the original Germania, but equally not a product
of recent constitutional struggle in France. It was a consequence
of specialisation under the feudal system of estates. Correspondingly there emerged a division of society into distinct
orders. Yet, over time, the tenacity of separation into exclusively
defined ranks declined. At the same time, in many states, the
power of the executive increased. This meant that, for Hegel,
feudalism had not been supplanted by the French Revolution.
It had, rather, been in decline over the preceding centuries. The
'new birth' of 1789 was in truth an extended process. The sudden
'sunrise' was merely an apparent rupture whose real meaning
was to be found in a longer transformation.

Hegel believed the most important change was the shifting
role of nobilities throughout Europe, gradually modified as social relations were recast. Steadily, the rigidities of status had
abated. Hegel noted in this connection that the British prime
minister William Pitt the Younger had had to make his way in
the world much like any other gentleman: he had no privileged

62. Ibid., pp. 50ff., 56ff.

access to a seat in Parliament or offices of state. Individual talent, or 'personal' qualities, had come to matter above all else. Even in Austria, 'the way to the highest military and political offices is open to everyone'.[63] Likewise in Prussia, access to civil affairs was enjoyed by a range of educated elites who lacked the trappings of nobility or distinction by birth. In this vein, Hegel observed that the cause of France's 'misfortune' did not lie in the sudden collapse of the *noblesse* following the summoning of the Estates General, but in the reconstruction of the social orders over the course of the previous age. As Tocqueville would similarly notice half a century later, in numerous prominent states across the seventeenth-century continent, hereditary aristocracies had progressively forfeited their political role.[64] Voltaire had explored the consequences of this reversal in France in the age of Louis XIV.[65] With this background assessment in mind, the central thrust of Hegel's argument becomes clear. The impact of the protracted fall of feudalism had played out differently in the various states of Europe, triggering fragmentation in Germany and a revolution in France. Importantly, neither fate had any appeal for Hegel, especially as he viewed the options between 1799 and 1803. In short, he was hardly a wide-eyed enthusiast for the repercussions of the French Revolution.

As Hegel saw it, the quintessence of the feudal relationship was the reciprocal bond of trust (*fides*) between lord and vassal, either on the level of interpersonal relations or between

---

63. Ibid., p. 66.

64. Alexis de Tocqueville, *The Old Regime and the Revolution* (1856), ed. François Furet and Françoise Mélonio, trans. Alan S. Kahan, 2 vols (Chicago: Chicago University Press, 1998), 1, p. 118.

65. Voltaire, *Le Siècle de Louis XIV*, 2 vols (Berlin, 1751), 2, pp. 138–41.

preeminent and subordinate political communities. From this perspective, the independence of powerful states within the German Reich already pointed to the end of feudal ties.[66] In the French case, this transformation was similarly evident: the provincial power of the aristocracy had diminished as they set their sights on winning favour at court. In general, the link between heredity and public standing had been broken. For Hegel, this meant that, well before the Revolution, prestige was detached from specified civil roles, leading to increased competition between the social orders along with a rise in the incidence of resentment.[67] On Hegel's analysis, much of this was a consequence of Richelieu's far-reaching reforms. Accordingly, he observed that the seeds of dissolution which led to fragmentation in Germany had equally been originally present in France. A multiplicity of regional laws operated within the one state— Breton, Burgundian, Roman, and so on—while both a powerful patrician order and a body of disaffected Huguenots compromised the integrity of the regime. It was the genius of Richelieu, we are told, that had successfully tackled each of these potent sources of division—first, by making 'political offices dependent on the state', and second, by extending toleration to religious dissenters.[68] To achieve both, authority was therefore concentrated in a powerful executive. Yet, Hegel added, Richelieu was sure to bring about the opposite result in Germany, as he used the negotiations preceding the Treaty of Westphalia to engineer the enfeeblement of a potential rival. He capitalised, Hegel believed, on the 'spirit' of German freedom. This entailed indulging the native proclivity for 'individuality' at the expense

66. Hegel, 'German Constitution', p. 56.
67. Ibid., p. 65.
68. Ibid., p. 76.

of the 'universal' interest of the state. From that point onwards, as far as Hegel was concerned, Germany became a mere shadow of a state (*Gedankenstaat*) instead of an actual force in the world.[69] By comparison, France, much like Prussia, concentrated political initiative at the centre, and so became what Hegel termed a 'machine' state, anxiously acquiring a superabundance of prerogatives at the expense of subordinate powers. The Revolution had only succeeded in intensifying this process.

This amounted, in Hegel's estimate, to 'dangerous' experimentation rather than the deliverance of justice for mankind.[70] The term 'liberty' had secured prominence as a catchphrase in the eighteenth century, not least during the aftermath of 1789. However, in Hegel's estimation, it increasingly wore the appearance of empty declamation.[71] The experience of Germany had shown that 'freedom is possible only when a people is legally united within a state'.[72] Yet, at the same time, the history of France had made plain that the ambitions of centralised administration were liable to undermine the tangible liberties of the people. The modern state, based on securing individual rights, was perfectly compatible with the devolution of authority to 'subordinate systems and bodies'—'every estate, city, village, commune, etc. can enjoy the freedom to do and implement for itself what lies within its province'.[73] Sovereignty and consent by means of representation were regarded by Hegel as indispensable attributes of modern politics. However, he also considered

69. Ibid., pp. 41–44.
70. Ibid., pp. 21, 67.
71. Ibid., p. 93.
72. Ibid., p. 80.
73. Ibid., p. 21.

the French attempt to reconcile freedom and authority to have upset the natural rhythms of political life. In sacrificing nobility altogether as lever of state, it dispensed with a means of blunting the force of administration and reconciling the general interest with the existence of distinct ranks.[74] Social orders needed to cooperate with one another rather than aim at mutual annihilation. In abstracting the ideal of freedom from prevailing circumstances, the Revolution had resorted to naked force in order to remodel the political world, without regard for the actual contours of society.

74. Ibid., pp. 65–66.

5

Absolute Freedom and Terror

HEGEL'S BEST-KNOWN analysis of the character of the French Revolution occurs in a subsection of the *Phenomenology of Spirit* under the title 'Absolute Freedom and Terror'. This subsection forms one component of the sixth chapter of the work, dedicated to the theme of 'Spirit' (*Geist*). The 'Spirit' chapter comprises one of the six principal parts of the *Phenomenology*— preceded by accounts of 'Consciousness', 'Self-Consciousness' and 'Reason', and followed by treatments of 'Religion' and 'Absolute Knowing'. During the final stages of the book's production, these six headings were superimposed upon an earlier structure which divided the work into eight chapters, with each of these being further separated into additional subdivisions, giving rise to a somewhat labyrinthine architecture, sometimes baffling readers of the text. Commentators have been especially perplexed by the transitions between the leading topics. The movement from the book's opening epistemological preoccupations, which dominate the first three chapters, to its more historically rooted practical concerns has posed perhaps the greatest difficulty. However, much of the confusion has been quite unnecessary. Since theoretical and practical reason were distinguishable yet ultimately inseparable for Hegel, it made sense for him to show how the functioning of the one inevitably led to an analysis of the other, as set out in the transition from 'Consciousness' to 'Self-Consciousness'.[1] Hegel encapsulated this insight by observing that how we know the world depends upon the way we come to act within it. 'Self-consciousness', he argued, 'is *desire* in general'.[2] As he developed the point in his 'Reason' chapter, the state of our knowledge depends on the conditions of its ratification—on a prevailing system of norms or 'shape of spirit'. Reason is 'actualized' in the 'life of a people'.[3]

Whilst the relationship between theoretical and practical reason forms the subject of the *Phenomenology* as a whole, it is also the specific focus of the part of the work devoted to *Geist*, in which the subsection on the French Revolution appears. The *Geist* portion of the book is divided into three main sections concerned with ethical life (*Sittlichkeit*), culture (*Bildung*) and morality (*Moralität*) respectively. The section on ethical life addresses Periclean Athens, constructed around an interpretation of Sophocles's *Antigone*. Given this focus on tragic drama, the section deliberately excludes consideration of the rise of philosophy, beginning around the period of the Peloponnesian War and culminating in its aftermath with the dialogues of Plato. What interested Hegel in this account was the emergence of conflict between the principal elements that made up Greek society—essentially, the family and the public life of the city-state—along with the conditions of equilibrium between them. As the *Phenomenology* presented the situation, equilibrium within Greek society depended on a functioning harmony between individual action and established custom, between

---

1. On theoretical and practical reason, see Hegel, *Philosophy of Right*, §4A.
2. Hegel, *Phenomenology*, §167.
3. Ibid., §350.

'consciousness' and 'substance', in Hegel's terms.[4] Ultimately, over the course of the fifth and fourth centuries BCE at Athens, these two facets of life were prised apart—pitting philosophy against the polis, thought against prevailing circumstances, criticism against tradition. As Hegel would later argue in his *Lectures on the Philosophy of World History*, 'subjective reflection' under the Sophists menaced public institutions by basing allegiance on internal conviction instead of implicit trust in the existing order of things.[5] The emphasis of the first section of the *Geist* chapter in the *Phenomenology* is therefore on the rise of critical self-reflection from within the ethical life of the Greeks, leading to the dissolution of this customary form of life. In Hegel's terse narrative, this is then succeeded by a ruthless and hollow regime of right under the '*universal* commonwealth' of Rome.[6] From Rome the story moves to the 'Unhappy Consciousness' of early Christianity, the emergence of feudalism, the rise of the church, and then the creation of the modern monarchical state. The world of culture in chapter 6 of the *Phenomenology* refers to relations under the system of unlimited government exemplified by Louis XIV and his successors down to 1789.

The section on *Bildung* following that on *Sittlichkeit* concerns the advent of modern society, which Hegel later dubbed the rise of 'civil society' (*bürgerliche Gesellschaft*).[7] The chapter as a whole is thus a comparative study of the ancient and modern worlds. Whereas the ancient world was conceptualised in terms of the relationship between family and polis, its modern

4. Ibid., §§439–40.
5. Hegel, *Philosophie der Geschichte*, p. 309.
6. Hegel, *Phenomenology*, §§475ff.
7. Hegel, *Philosophy of Right*, §182A.

counterpart was differentiated into society and state. This framework is now a standard one in Western historiography. The ancient structure is taken to have cohered through public trust in the absence critical self-consciousness, whereas the modern structure is seen as riven by the competing elements that constitute society.[8] In the end, those elements would collide to produce the Revolution in France. Both the ancient and modern arrangement were further complicated by including the category of religion, dramatised in the Athenian case in terms of a tension between 'human' and 'divine' law and in the post-classical case by a collision between government, society and church.[9] Hegel's anatomy of modern conflict ranges widely across assorted 'productions' of spirit, including public power, the system of estates, ecclesiastical institutions, forms of wealth and intellectual attitudes.[10] Crucial is the collision between philosophy and authority. One dimension of this contest is the clash between faith (*Glaube*) and enlightenment (*Aufklärung*) which spills over into the struggles of the French Revolution explored in the third subsection of Hegel's account of the fate of *Bildung*. His analysis of the Revolution therefore pivots around the emergence of *Aufklärung* in a society infused with the values shaped by *Bildung*.

A generation before the publication of the *Phenomenology*, Moses Mendelssohn remarked, in an essay which Hegel had transcribed during his schooldays, that the terms *Aufklärung*, *Kultur* and *Bildung* were all recent additions to the German language, or at least newly minted pieces of specialised

8. Hegel, *Phenomenology*, §492.

9. Ibid., §§466.

10. See the editorial note in G.W.F. Hegel, *La Phénoménologie de l'esprit*, trans. Jean Hyppolite, 2 vols (Paris: Aubier, 1939–41), 2, p. 55 n. 14.

vocabulary.[11] The social role of each of them had become matters of general concern, soon to play a decisive role in the writings of Kant and Goethe. Above all, the terms had come to occupy a significant place in histories of human progress, with evident debts to Rousseau and Scottish social theory.[12] Central to the debate was the role of philosophy in society, including its impact on religion, morals and government.[13] Plainly this controversy did not begin in 1780s Prussia: it had raged in Britain and France earlier in the eighteenth century, as a result of which the German category of 'enlightenment' has come to acquire a broader range of application, sometimes being used to refer to the period as a whole. Yet the German debate had its own peculiar complexion, determined in part by Frederick the Great himself. For him, as for Kant, the age, though not yet fully enlightened, was at least an 'age of enlightenment', since honesty guided policy and the freedom to publish protected criticism.[14]

11. Moses Mendelssohn, 'Ueber die Frage: Was heißt aufklären?' (1784), in *Was ist Aufklärung? Beitrage aus der Berlinischen Monatsschrift*, ed. Norbert Hinske (Darmstadt: Wissenschaftliche Buchgesellschaft, 1981), p. 444. For Hegel's transcription, see Johannes Hoffmeister, *Dokumente zu Hegels Entwicklung* (Stuttgart: Fr. Frommanns Verlag, 1936), pp. 140–43.

12. Frederick Neuhouser, *Foundations of Hegel's Social Theory: Actualizing Freedom* (Cambridge, MA: Harvard University Press, 2000); Norbert Waszek, *The Scottish Enlightenment and Hegel's Account of 'Civil Society'* (Dordrecht: Kluwer Academic Publishers, 1988).

13. James Schmidt, 'The Question of Enlightenment: Kant, Mendelssohn, and the *Mittwochsgesellschaft*', *Journal of the History of Ideas*, 50: 2 (April–June 1989), pp. 269–91.

14. Frederick the Great, *Anti-Machiavel, ou essai de critique sur le Prince de Machiavel* (Gottingen: Abram. Vandenhoeck, 1741), ch. 18; Immanuel Kant, 'An Answer to the Question: What is Enlightenment?' (1784), in *Practical Philosophy*, ed. and trans. Mary J. Gregor (Cambridge: Cambridge University Press, 1996), AA 8: 40. On freedom of publication, see Eckhart Hellmuth, 'Aufklärung und Pressefreiheit: Zur

Elsewhere, Frederick expressed more scepticism about the utility of truthfulness, or the wisdom of complete honesty with all sections of the public. This contrasted with the arguments of one of his philosophical correspondents, Jean-Baptiste le Rond d'Alembert.[15] Their disagreement raised general questions about how to enlighten the multitude, leading the king, at d'Alembert's prompting, to hold an essay competition under the auspices of the Berlin Academy of Sciences on whether there were benefits to deceiving the people at large.[16] Hegel later recalled the subject of the competition while examining 'The Struggle of Enlightenment with Superstition' in the *Phenomenology*.[17] He then invoked the episode again in his discussion of public opinion in the *Philosophy of Right*.[18] In explaining the persistence of popular superstition, Frederick had derided instruction in schools and universities.[19] For his part, Wilhelm Möhsen, a prominent member of the secret Berlin Wednesday Society, wondered why prejudice was still widespread across the territory despite the celebrated efforts of the monarch

---

Debatte der Berliner Mittwochsgesellschaft während der Jahre 1783 und 1784', *Zeitschrift für Historische Forschung*, 9: 3 (1982), pp. 315–45.

15. Lester G. Crocker, 'The Problem of Truth and Falsehood in the Age of Enlightenment', *Journal of the History of Ideas*, 14: 4 (October 1953), pp. 575–603.

16. Shiru Lim, 'Frederick the Great and Jean Le Rond d'Alembert on Philosophy, Truth, and Politics', *The Historical Journal*, 61: 2 (October 2017), pp. 357–78; Hans Adler, ed., *Nützt es dem Volke, betrogen zu werden? Die Preisfrage der Preussischen Akademie für 1780*, 2 vols (Stuttgart: Frommann-Holzboog Verlag, 2007).

17. Hegel, *Phenomenology*, §550.

18. Hegel, *Philosophy of Right*, §317R. Cf. G.W.F. Hegel, 'Die "Rechtsphilosophie" von 1820, mit Hegels Vorlesungsnotizien, 1821–1825', in *Vorlesungen über Rechtsphilosophie, 1818–1831*, 2, p. 784.

19. Frederick the Great, *De la littérature allemande* (Berlin: G. J. Decker, 1780).

himself.[20] Kant noted, in the same spirit, that dispelling the prejudices of the masses would prove both complicated and protracted. It was not a matter for precipitate revolution: 'a public', he wrote, 'can achieve enlightenment only slowly'.[21] Relatedly, in his theory of public right, published in the shadow of the French Revolution, Kant distinguished the role of 'active' from that of 'passive' citizens in securing the state against the influence of dependent members of the polity.[22]

Mendelssohn, Kant and Hegel—much like Lessing, Herder, Schiller and Fichte—took an interest in the dynamics of enlightenment in the context of a more general concern with the education of the human race. They wished, that is, to contribute to a debate about the intellectual and moral development of the species. The terms 'vocation', 'perfectibility' and 'culture' were integral to the discussion. In his *Lectures on the Philosophy of World History*, Hegel proposed that history itself should be viewed as a kind of accumulated 'discipline' (*Zucht*). It involved the gradual schooling of the human will, whereby natural or 'immediate' inclinations were increasingly subject to rationalisation.[23] Rousseau had termed this capacity

20. J.K.W. Möhsen, 'What Is to Be Done toward the Enlightenment of the Citizenry?' (1783 lecture), trans. James Schmidt, in *What Is Enlightenment?: Eighteenth-Century Answers and Twentieth-Century Questions*, ed. Schmidt (Berkeley, CA: University of California Press, 1996), p. 50.

21. Kant, 'What is Enlightenment?', p. 18.

22. Immanuel Kant, *The Metaphysics of Morals*, ed. Lara Denis, trans. Mary Gregor (Cambridge: Cambridge University Press, 2017), AA 6: 314.

23. Hegel, *Philosophie der Geschichte*, p. 134. Kant's term for this process is 'Kultur', as in his discussion of the culture of 'skill' (*Geschicklichkeit*) and the culture of 'discipline' (*Zucht*), in Immanuel Kant, *Critique of the Power of Judgment*, ed. and trans. Paul Guyer (Cambridge: Cambridge University Press, 2000), AA 5: 432.

'the faculty of *self*-perfection' (la faculté de *se* perfectionner).[24] Central to the experience of discipline for Hegel was precisely the activity of self-discipline. Raw impulses were 'perfected'— that is, refined—by self-reflection under the influence of both instrumental and moral reasoning. This process of cultivation explained the advance of spirit: *Geist* progressed by means of a process of *Bildung*.[25] Hegel's argument drew indirectly on analyses of the passage from rudeness to refinement formulated in the works of Hume, Smith, Ferguson and Millar. Yet his position was clearly informed by the German Idealist insight that civilisation was as much a product of free self-development as it was an effect of the forces of nature. This did not mean that humans made their history as a matter of pure choice. It meant, instead, that they cultivated their desires even as they were subject to the effects of their appetites: 'they interpose [...] between the urgency of the drive and its satisfaction'.[26] This aptitude was the basic building block of civilisation, distinguishing the uneventful character of animal existence from the ever-changing variety of human life.

24. Jean-Jacques Rousseau, *Discours sur l'origine et les fondements de l'inégalité parmi les hommes* (1755), in *Oeuvres complètes*, ed. Bernard Gagnebin and Marcel Raymond, 3 vols (Paris: Gallimard, 1964), 3, p. 142 (emphasis added). For Hegel's adoption of Rousseau's term 'perfectibility', see G.W.F. Hegel, *Lectures on the Philosophy of World History, Introduction: Reason in History*, trans. H. B. Nisbet (Cambridge: Cambridge University Press, 1975), pp. 125, 149. Cf. Hegel, *Philosophy of Right*, §343.

25. G.W.F. Hegel, *Lectures on the Philosophy of World History: Manuscripts of the Introduction and the Lectures of 1822–3*, ed. and trans. Robert F. Brown and Peter C. Hodgson, with William G. Geuss (Oxford: Clarendon Press, 2011), p. 155. Cf. G.W.F. Hegel, *Lectures on the History of Philosophy, 1825–6*, ed. and trans. Robert F. Brown, 3 vols (Oxford: Oxford University Press, 2006), 2, pp. 111–13.

26. Ibid., p. 149.

II

Whereas *Bildung* in Hegel generally refers to the process of refinement and cultivation that underlies the development of *Geist*, it also has a narrower meaning applicable to society in seventeenth- and eighteenth-century France. In this context it denotes the system of manners that began to prevail in the age of the Sun King. In his *Lectures on the History of Philosophy*, Hegel noted the extent to which Prussia under Frederick the Great had sought to ape the 'culture' of the French—their 'manners, operas, gardens, dresses'.[27] In the *Lectures on the Philosophy of World History*, the perfection of these vehicles of social mobility is taken to have elevated France above the rest of Europe.[28] At the same time, the underlying norms of sociability in which this world of fashion prospered assisted Louis XIV in depressing the power of the nobility. This led to conflict between the institutions of power and the ranks of society arrayed beneath them as well as covert hostility among the social orders themselves. The section of chapter 6 of the *Phenomenology* devoted to 'The World of Self-Alienated Spirit', comprising two subsections on 'Culture' and 'Faith' respectively, covers the fate of society and religion in this era of politeness. Given Hegel's habit of economy and compression, it takes some care to separate out the elements of the conflict.

The world of modern culture, much like civil society in general, is for Hegel a condition of universal alienation in which mutual dependence thwarts concrete freedom. On the one

27. G.W.F. Hegel, *Lectures on the History of Philosophy*, ed. and trans. E. S. Haldane and Frances H. Simson, 3 vols (Lincoln, NE: University of Nebraska Press, 1995), 3, p. 391. Cf. Hegel, *World History 1822–3*, p. 515.

28. Hegel, *Philosophie der Geschichte*, p. 513.

hand, this is a state-society insofar as peaceable interaction requires public adjudication. In his 1817–18 Heidelberg lectures on
the philosophy of right, Hegel described this as a 'state' based on
the satisfaction of needs, a *Notstaat*.[29] But he was also clear that
it is a system of social relations which exists outside the purview
of political authority: one in which members of society seek to
advance their interests unmolested by the government. It follows, in turn, that state and society are made up of discrete self-
conscious persons. In the modern age of conscience and personal conviction, each individual judges the value of the benefits
that state and society provide. However, this judgement finds no
durable object of affirmation; for every advantage, there is a corresponding sense of detriment. At the same time, all relations
are mediated by the pursuit of wealth. The state depends on society for its material sustenance, just as society depends on the
state. Equally, society and state rely on their individual members.
Yet in no case does dependence provide satisfactory harmony.
Viewed negatively, the state is a source of oppression in usurping
prestige and initiative; society is a mechanism of estrangement
in sapping its members' independence; and self-consciousness
is frustrated by the loss of self-ownership. Even self-interest, in
reality, is a function of the common interest.[30] As Hegel presented the situation, individuals operated through the medium
of 'opinion', so while they might aspire to secure their own particular goals, these objectives were already defined by their social
context. As a result, attempts at personal self-definition would
inevitably end in the adoption of prescribed roles: 'Although this
world has come about through individuality,' Hegel wrote, 'it is
for self-consciousness something immediately alienated and has

29. Hegel, *First Philosophy of Right*, §89.
30. Hegel, *Phenomenology*, §494.

for it the form of immobile actuality.'[31] Every person loses their particularity and dissolves in the general currency. The individual becomes a mere 'type' or an 'espèce'.[32]

Hegel's use of the French term is followed by a quotation from Diderot's novel *Rameau's Nephew*, which had highlighted the figure of the *espèce*, contrasted in the period with a person of substance. Hegel encountered the novel in Goethe's annotated translation of 1805 which retained the French word in preference to the German term *Art*. Hegel himself noted Goethe's resort to Diderot's original usage in lieu of a German rendition by means of 'Kind [*Art*] or *good of its kind*.'[33] As Hegel commented, the German *Art* lacked the required pejorative connotation. Diderot's novel had been written between 1761 and 1774, with the manuscript being passed to Schiller in the early nineteenth century. Schiller forwarded it to Goethe, whose translation Hegel read before he composed the *Geist* chapter of the *Phenomenology*.[34] Viewed from Weimar and Jena at the turn of the century, *Rameau's Nephew* offered a revelatory snapshot of social relations in pre-Revolutionary France. Integral to that picture was the idea of a 'type', a person who filled a role but lacked all standing. Understood in this way, an *espèce* was a nobody, therefore constituting, as Diderot put it, 'the most dreadful [*redoutable*] of all epithets because it indicates mediocrity and the last degree of contempt.'[35] This line appears verbatim in Hegel's text.

---

31. Ibid., §§489, 495.

32. Ibid., §489.

33. Hegel, *Phenomenology*, §489.

34. Lionel Trilling, *Sincerity and Authenticity* (Cambridge, MA: Harvard University Press, 1971), ch. 2; James Schmidt, 'The Fool's Truth: Diderot, Goethe, and Hegel', *Journal of the History of Ideas*, 57: 4 (October 1996), pp. 625–44.

35. Denis Diderot, *Le Neveu de Rameau*, ed. Jean Fabre (Geneva: Librairie Droz, 1963), p. 90: 'c'est ce que nous apellons especes, de toutes les epithets la plus

Diderot's *Rameau's Nephew* takes the form of a satirical dialogue conducted between two characters, Moi and Lui, representing a Philosopher and the Nephew of the great composer. Goethe saw the book as Diderot's revenge on his enemies: figures such as Charles Palissot de Montenoy who sought to ridicule the Enlightenment venture that culminated in the *Encyclopedia*. In Palissot's comedy *Les Philosophes*, staged in 1760, Diderot and his associates had been parodied and mocked. In response, Diderot derided his opponents in turn, accusing them of venting their resentment on talented rivals and exposing their base motives in the process. They knew their own shortcomings, Diderot insisted, hiding their corruption for the sake of appearances. Diderot strove, as Goethe saw it, 'to represent his literary enemies together [...] as a bunch of hypocrites and flatterers'.[36] At the same time, Diderot passed judgement on the *querelle des bouffons*, defending Italian opera against the mannerism of French composers, exemplified by the elder Rameau.[37] This opened the way to a discussion of taste in general, and consequently to an examination of the world of fashion. That led to reflection on social aspiration, lifting the lid on an ugly universe of winners and losers brimming with attendant rivalries and resentments. Patrons and

---

redoutable, parce qu'elle marque la mediocrité, et le dernier degré du mespris'. On *espèce*, see also ibid., p. 267. For the English I have used Denis Diderot, *Rameau's Nephew and D'Alembert's Dream*, trans. Leonard Tancock (London: Penguin, 1966), p. 108 (translation modified).

36. J. W. Goethe, *Rameaus Neffe: Ein Dialog von Diderot* (1805), in *Sämtliche Werke: Briefe, Tagebücher und Gespräche*, vol. 11: *Leben des Benvenuto Cellini; Übersetzungen 1*, ed. Hans-Georg Dewitz and Wolfgang Proß (Frankfurt am Main: Deutscher Klassiker Verlag, 1998), p. 788.

37. For context, see Robert Wokler, 'Rousseau on Rameau and Revolution', in *Rousseau, the Age of Enlightenment, and their Legacies* (Princeton, NJ: Princeton University Press, 2012).

protégés were condemned to play the game of culture, striving to advance their cachet by means of mutual exploitation. Assorted enlightened attitudes were exposed in the dialogue. The value of genius, the utility of philosophy, the progress of society, the salience of virtue and even the cosmic structure of rewards were called into doubt. Throughout, the source of suspicion is not the 'honest' figure of Moi, but the unsettled and unsettling character of Lui—the nobody whose only claim to importance is his ability and willingness to milk the system. Looking back from Hegel's vantage point as the French armies overran Europe, Lui seemed to unmask the divisiveness that had led to acrimony and Revolution.

As far as Hegel was concerned, the character of Moi was straining to depict the world as ultimately justifiable.[38] From his angle, the pursuit of virtue and the cultivation of talent would ultimately lead to happiness. By the same token, as Moi argued in quasi-Mandevillian language, the wisdom of nature would reconcile self-interested vices with long-term benefits.[39] In opposition to this, it was Lui who stood these expectations on their head, painting a picture of an inverted (*verkehrt*) world in which interpersonal deception reigned while nefarious personalities prospered.[40] The Parisian society in which Lui

38. Hegel, *Phenomenology*, §521.

39. Diderot, *Rameau's Nephew*, p. 42. For the relevance of Mandeville, see E. J. Hundert, 'A Satire of Self-Disclosure: From Hegel Through Rameau to the Augustans', *Journal of the History of Ideas*, 47: 3 (April–June 1986), pp. 235–48. It is claimed by the editors in G.W.F. Hegel, *Phänomenologie des Geistes*, ed. Hans-Friedrich Wessels and Heinrich Clairmont (Hamburg: Felix Meiner Verlag, 1988), p. 603n, that Hegel has in mind the naturally orchestrated balance between good and evil as presented in J. B. Robinet, *De la nature*, 5 vols (Amsterdam: 1761–68), 1, p. 67. For Hegel's interest in Robinet, see Hegel, *History of Philosophy* (Haldane and Simson), 3, pp. 394ff.

40. Hegel, *Phenomenology*, §522.

longed to gain some status—to be 'somebody'—was one of all-round mendacity and desperation.[41] Every member was on the make. Diderot presents life as a process of jockeying for 'position' by resort to the arts of subterfuge and mimicry.[42] The apparent desire for intellectual achievement was in truth a bid for comparative distinction whose terms were governed by the tyranny of wealth. Hegel contrasted this arrangement with the empire of right under the Romans. In the latter case, the personality of the imperial subject was subordinated to supreme authority, yet power was remote and one could lead an 'atomic' existence.[43] By comparison, in the world of culture under unlimited monarchy, dependence was immediate, stratified and all-pervasive.[44] The 'sociable man', Rousseau claimed—in the work of his that he believed appealed to Diderot most—always lived 'outside of himself', subject to the opinion of others.[45] By extension, social relations in eighteenth-century France were held together by reciprocal ties of service extending from the court to every branch of society, including the roles, as listed by Diderot, of 'sovereign, minister, financier, magistrate, soldier, writer, lawyer, attorney, merchant, banker, artisan, singing master, dancing-master'. Benefaction operated as a form of vengeance, while flattery, fawning, hypocrisy and parasitism became

41. On being somebody see Hegel, *Philosophy of Right*, §207A. Cf. Hegel, *First Philosophy of Right*, §107.

42. Diderot, *Rameau's Nephew*, p. 53.

43. On Roman 'atomicity' (*Punktualität*), see Hegel, *Phenomenology*, §482.

44. Ibid., §517.

45. Rousseau, *Discours sur l'inégalité*, p. 193; Jean-Jacques Rousseau, *The Confessions and Correspondence, including the Letters to Malesherbes*, ed. Christopher Kelly, Roger D. Masters and Peter G. Stillman, trans. Kelly (Hanover, NH: University Press of New England, 1995), p. 326. Cf. Hegel, *Phenomenology*, §517: 'it sees itself outside itself and belonging to another'.

standard practice. This ugly pantomime embraced every division of society, all the way from the crown to the 'jeweller, furnisher, laundry-woman, swindler, chamber-maid, cook, [and] harness-maker'.[46]

Reflecting on the world of culture under the French monarchy, Montesquieu wrote that politeness stemmed from the 'desire to distinguish oneself'.[47] For Voltaire, this ambition extended under the reign of Louis XIV from the *palais* to the *bourg*. It soon permeated all ranks, from the stock exchange to the petty retailer.[48] The result, Hegel believed, was a way of life that betrayed its own ideals. This predicament gave rise to a riven consciousness, divided between a disenchanted secular existence and the promise held out by faith. Given this disjuncture, society was not happily anchored in either vision, and so generated competing 'languages' of evaluation—antagonistic ideologies responding to prevailing realities.[49] From one angle, the state appeared as a source of value and the common good. From another, it was experienced as onerous and oppressive. The same fate befell attitudes to wealth, on one side castigated as compromising autonomy, on the other approved as a means of universal enjoyment.[50] In Hegel's narrative these diverse viewpoints promoted opposing positions, the 'noble' verses the 'base' consciousness—the one disposed to reverence, the other to secret malice.[51] Hegel regarded these attitudes as having a

46. Diderot, *Rameau's Nephew*, pp. 61, 63.

47. Charles-Louis de Secondat, baron de Montesquieu, *The Spirit of the Laws* (1748), ed. and trans. Anne M. Cohler, Basia Carolyn Miller and Harold Samuel Stone (Cambridge: Cambridge University Press, 1989), p. 32.

48. Voltaire, *Le Siècle de Louis XIV*, 2, pp. 138–41.

49. Hegel, *Phenomenology*, §510.

50. Ibid., §497.

51. Ibid., §500.

complex history rooted in the struggle between crown and estates, culminating in the emergence of a strong monarchical executive and a nobility that squandered its substance in exchange for offices and cutting a figure at court.[52]

While in the seventeenth-century the thirst for honour at Versailles spawned the febrile world of envy and aspiration advertised in La Rochefoucauld, gradually such conduct became a social norm under which, in Diderot's words, 'all classes prey[ed] on each other'.[53] This induced a feeling of abjection further down the chain, as the need for 'crawling, cringing and prostituting' oneself spread.[54] Yet, as Hegel saw, notwithstanding his abasement, it was with Lui that the future was deemed to lie. *Rameau's Nephew* concludes with Lui's declaration: 'He laughs best who laughs last.'[55] Hegel took this to mean that, for all his degradation, Lui retained the inward spirit of rebellion lodged in his sense of personal dignity.[56] It followed that, in the alienated world of culture, it was possible for the degraded self to transcend its circumstances insofar as it learned to deplore its condition and implicitly discover its own worth. As a consequence, deference would develop into outrage (*Empörung*) at the sheer presumption exhibited by holders of power. In this process, fragmented (*zerissen*) consciousness would discover its freedom in rejecting conditions that led to its own depravity (*Verworfenheit*). Arrogance disposed the powerful to overlook this 'inner rebellion of the other [. . .] the casting-off of all

52. Ibid., §§502–16.

53. Diderot, *Rameau's Nephew*, p. 63.

54. Ibid. p. 123.

55. Ibid., p. 125

56. Hegel, *Phenomenology*, §525. The verdict is based on Diderot, *Rameau's Nephew*, p. 48.

fetters'.[57] Yet in this silent resistance lay the hope of reconciliation. Diderot had invoked the character of Diogenes to exemplify the spirit of renunciation in the face of greed and self-regard.[58] Yet Hegel, like Lui, rejected this impulse to withdraw from the present state of the world. Diogenes's choice of rigid austerity as a means of escaping the 'vanity of all things' was a product of his own conceit. It made no sense to accept being in the world whilst pretending to be magically outside it. Hegel further claimed that a Rousseauesque nostalgia for the 'simplicity of the natural heart' was no less a repudiation of spirit. [59] The perversity of society could not constructively be dissolved by looking backwards or beyond existence.

III

A notable feature of polite society depicted by Diderot is the decline of birth as the dominant social value in the eighteenth century.[60] Hegel promptly fastened onto this intuition. Modern culture had erased categorical differences, he thought. Independent actors (the figure of the 'proud vassal', in Hegel's nomenclature) gradually disappeared from the scene as competitors in the marketplace of social esteem coordinated their ambitions around shared objectives.[61] Distinctions still mattered, but these were

57. Ibid., §519,

58. Diderot, Rameau's Nephew, pp. 122–23. On Diogenes, cf. Hegel, Philosophy of Right, §195A.

59. Hegel, Phenomenology, §§525–26. Cf. Hegel, History of Philosophy (Haldane and Simson), 3, p. 383.

60. Diderot, Rameau's Nephew, p. 116.

61. Hegel, Phenomenology, §505. The translation here follows G.W.F Hegel, The Phenomenology of Spirit, trans. Terry Pinkard (Cambridge: Cambridge University Press, 2018), §504.

increasingly based on economic and cultural preeminence rather than the advantages conferred by entrenched legal privilege. For this very reason, residual entitlements became peculiarly galling. A softer ascendancy prevailed, rooted in the kind of achievements that won applause in Parisian salons. Talent rather than heredity was paramount. In the worlds of music and the republic of letters— the 'spiritual animal kingdom', as Hegel described it—'Genius' trumped ancestry. Under these circumstances, the spectrum of accomplishment ran from the exceptional to the mediocre. Yet still this arrangement was haunted by the inkling that the resulting hierarchies were in any case fraudulent. Differences now were simply 'quantitative', if they had any credibility at all.[62]

As Hegel saw it, in this environment of vain distinctions, rival approaches to intellectual authority confronted one another: on one side stood 'faith' (*Glaube*) and on the other 'insight' (*Einsicht*).[63] Unlike the unhappy consciousness of early Christianity, modern faith wielded secular power even as it pined after its own thought-world projected into the 'beyond'. Unlike in Stoicism, this longing found expression in a 'flight' into a fictional yet imaginatively rich realm, as depicted in the lavish religious art works of early modern Europe.[64] Despite this wealth in terms of aesthetic representation, the true object of faith remained obscure—at once remote and incomprehensible.[65]

---

62. Hegel, *Phenomenology*, §537. On the spiritual animal kingdom more generally, see ibid., §§397–418.

63. This antithesis was already the subject of G.W.F. Hegel, *Faith and Knowledge* (1802), ed. and trans. Walter Cerf and H. S. Harris (New York: State University of New York Press, 1977).

64. Hegel, *Phenomenology*, §§527–28.

65. Ibid., §552. Cf. G.W.F. Hegel, *History of Philosophy*, 1825–6, 2, p. 72: 'Art flourished in the Catholic church, but when freethinking came on the scene the church was quite unable to accommodate it and parted company with it.'

Reason or 'insight', by comparison, placed value in the 'hither' sphere.[66] Yet what it prized was the activity of self-consciousness itself in seeking to extirpate error. Reason operated by means of conceptual negation directed against the principles advocated by faith. It had no content other than the material it sought to reject: it endeavoured to eliminate 'every objective essence supposedly standing over against consciousness'.[67] Whereas faith aimed at an immaculate morality transcending the vanity that governed this vale of tears, insight cherished purity of intention in opposition to the corrupt practices it associated with positive religion.[68] However, the confrontation was marked by mutual misunderstanding, not least since reason was determined to downgrade religion without comprehending what gave rise to its characteristic attitudes.

Whilst faith was initially happy to pursue its own tranquil course, insight was motivated to contend with its assumptions. In this spirit, reason aimed to challenge all aspects of religious belief. First, it parodied Christianity's conception of the divinity by equating its idea of God with representational images—crucifixes in wood or stone or the wafer of the host.[69] Next, it sought to expose the grounds of belief, not least by collapsing their plausibility into the 'contingent events' of

---

66. Hegel, *Phenomenology*, §567. Friedrich Jacobi dubbed Spinozistic reason 'insight' in *Concerning the Doctrine of Spinoza in Letters to Herr Moses Mendelssohn* (1785), in Jacobi, *The Main Philosophical Writings and the Novel 'Allwill'*, ed. and trans. George di Giovanni (Montreal-Kingston: McGill-Queen's University Press, 1994), p. 190. For the uptake of the term, see Jeffrey Reid, 'Insight and the Enlightenment: Why *Einsicht* in Chapter Six of Hegel's *Phenomenology of Spirit?*', *Hegel Bulletin*, 40: 2 (2016), pp. 175–97.

67. Hegel, *Phenomenology*, §529.

68. Ibid., §§534, 538.

69. Ibid., §552.

biblical revelation.[70] Finally, reason denounced the ethical import of faith by undermining its forms of worship and service, above all its attempts to bring about salvation by token gestures such as abstinence or charity.[71] In general, insight castigated religious conviction as a mental figment whilst refusing to examine the source of its commitments. The *sheer yearning* that drove the Christian religion was left unexplained and unexplored.[72] Yet despite their divergence, insight and faith shared basic tenets of rational procedure, enabling reason to get a foothold inside the enemy camp. This was secured by means of publicity and proselytism. Philosophy appealed to public opinion over the heads of the ecclesiastical authorities and the power of the state. The critical spirit extended itself by insinuation rather than violence: 'the communication of pure insight is comparable to a quiet expansion [*ruhigen Ausdehnung*] or to the *diffusion* of, say, a perfume in the unresisting atmosphere. It is a penetrating infection which does not make itself noticeable beforehand.' It is this process of dissemination that Hegel termed 'enlightenment'. He cited *Rameau's Nephew* on the subtle ascent of Christianity as propagated by missionaries in China: on the back of incremental infiltration, suddenly, '*one fine morning*', the old 'idol' crashes to the ground.[73] In this vein, enlightenment helped to trigger revolution.

Yet it also needs to be borne in mind that philosophy, for Hegel, was not by any stretch the exclusive cause of this process of transformation. Enlightenment, instead, was partly

70. Ibid., §554.
71. Ibid., §§569–71.
72. Ibid., §573.
73. Diderot, *Rameau's Nephew*, pp. 100–101; Hegel, *Phenomenology*, §545 (translation modified).

symptomatic. The roots of the 'crash'—of the Revolution—lay deeper, in cumulative normative shifts. Crucial to this process was the passage of society from the culture of honour to the value of utility, from interpersonal *amour-propre* to the impersonal market. In Hegel's mind, the atheism and deism that came to prominence in the period alike endorsed the ascendancy of 'useful reciprocity'. Even orthodox religion came to base itself on a vision of the world as a 'garden' planted for humanity's benefit. The bonds of social life, much like the structure of the universe, were presumed to be held together by utilitarian exchange.[74] This conception became central to enlightenment, which helped to legitimise a form of value that had begun to establish itself. Philosophy, Hegel believed, is merely one aspect of a larger 'whole'. At the same time, its role as a determinant of historical change was circumstantially variable. For the Greeks, as Hegel put it, philosophy had come 'too late': it made its entrance when the substance of Athenian ethical life faced dissolution. Its practitioners, accordingly, 'withdrew from the affairs of the state'.[75] Yet with the Enlightenment it acquired a more directly formative significance and focused its energy, at least in France, on social and political renewal. For this reason, Hegel could argue that the Revolution received its first 'stimulus' (*Anregung*) from philosophy.[76] In an age when thought mattered, enlightenment could prove decisive. Nonetheless, although philosophy made a difference, it did not determine the shape of the future. In fact, its impact in the French context was largely destructive, since it misconceived its own function. It mistook

---

74. Ibid., §§556, 559–62, 580–81.

75. Hegel, *History of Philosophy, 1825–6*, 3, pp. 66, 68–69. Cf. Hegel, *Philosophy of Right*, 'Preface', p. 23, on the belatedness of philosophy in relation to politics.

76. Hegel, *Philosophie der Weltgeschichte: 1830/31*, p. 1560.

its abstraction from prevailing circumstances for practical leverage. Philosophy, to be effective, needs to work with the grain of
history. However, in France it became a vehicle for angry opposition, bellowing its dissent into the void.

Hegel's style of argumentation traded in large, agglomerat-
ing categories—'culture'; 'faith'; 'enlightenment'. Yet he perfectly appreciated the more intricate reality that underlay these
ideal types. Enlightenment itself was no exception: inside the
generic concept, he often adopted a more specific usage. In the
narrower sense he associated *Aufklärung* with the *Popularphi-
losophie* that prospered in Germany between the heyday of
Wolffianism and the arrival of the mature Kant. Its watchwords
were 'sound reason' (*gesunde Vernunft*) and 'common sense'
(*allgemeiner gesunder Menschenverstand*), and its adherents included figures such as Garve, Feder, Weishaupt, Eberhard and
Nicolai. Some directed their fire against positive religion,
against both the tenets of revelation and ecclesiastical structures.[77] Hegel found aspects of the same critical disposition in
Britain and France as well, yet he held the impact of 'insight'
in all three countries to be different. In Britain, for instance,
not least under Scottish influence, the conclusions of philosophy apparently reinforced the power of custom in human affairs. The Germans, for their part, took ultimate value to lie in
the human faculty of self-consciousness, yet this did not result
in burning rage against the establishment. According to Hegel,
only in France did philosophy, now also dubbed 'enlightenment', seek to abolish all religious ideas and every reigning
institution. Ultimately, it was the French Enlightenment that
rebelled against 'the condition of the world as legally established, against the constitution of the state, the administration

77. Hegel, *History of Philosophy, 1825–6*, 3, pp. 160–61, 403–4.

of justice, the mode of government, political authority, and likewise against art'.[78] As Hegel described it, in the place of all these tangible structures there emerged 'the consciousness of perfect liberty'.[79] In the subsection of the *Phenomenology* on 'Absolute Freedom and Terror', this consciousness is identified with the concept of the will as formulated in the political thought of Rousseau.

IV

Hegel's argument contributed to the development of a debate about Rousseau's role in the course that the French Revolution took.[80] Discussion, however, has long been confused, since Hegel's argument was never that Rousseau caused the Revolution, nor even that he influenced some of its main protagonists. His point, instead, was that a conception of legitimacy, having crystallised in Rousseau, played a vital part in subsequent thinking about politics. The writings of Rousseau, like those of Kant, marked a reorientation in fundamental values. For Hegel this amounted to a profound intellectual sea-change. In the passage from Hobbes and Pufendorf to the thought of Rousseau and its

78. Hegel, *History of Philosophy* (Haldane and Simson), 3, pp. 358–60, 384.

79. Ibid., p. 480.

80. A range of reflection on the controversy can be found in Jean Hyppolite, 'La Signification de la Révolution française dans la *Phénoménologie* de Hegel', *Revue philosophique de la France et de l'étranger*, 128: 9/12 (September–October and November–December 1939), pp. 321–52; Alfred Stern, 'Hegel et les idées de 1789', ibid., pp. 353–63; Robert Wokler, 'Contextualizing Hegel's Phenomenology of the French Revolution and the Terror', *Political Theory*, 26: 1 (February 1998), pp. 33–55; Robert Stern, *Hegel and the 'Phenomenology of Spirit'* (London: Routledge, 2002), pp. 179–90; and Reidar Maliks, 'Echoes of Revolution: Hegel's Debt to the German Burkeans', in James A. Clarke and Gabriel Gottlieb, eds, *Practical Philosophy from Kant to Hegel* (Cambridge: Cambridge University Press, 2021).

German reception, the regulative role of 'self-interest' in moral philosophy was challenged. The principle of utility was replaced by the norm of freedom as the guiding criterion of practical judgement. An ideal of liberty was now celebrated as the distinguishing characteristic of humanity.[81] Freedom here was not that of self-interested agents protected by government; it was the liberty of the self-conscious will regarded as the source of all moral and political value. Individuals no longer saw themselves as maximising an objective standard utility. Instead, each self-governing consciousness determined its own 'purpose'. The self no longer appeared as a passive instrument within a nexus of reciprocal service but as the locus of inviolable rights founded on the intrinsic worth of the self-determining will. The actual Revolution emerged from this 'inner' revolution.[82] As Hegel saw it, the political expression of the sanctity of the will took the form of a commitment to democratic sovereignty in Rousseau. Under this form of social contract, citizens would be subject to their own collective authority whilst retaining their full freedom.[83] It was not the details of Rousseau's doctrine that determined the trajectory of the Revolution, but the idea that the purely abstract will was entitled to unmediated practical expression. For this 'universal' self, the 'world is [. . .] quite simply its will'.[84]

---

81. Hegel, *History of Philosophy* (Haldane and Simson), 3, p. 401.

82. Hegel, *Phenomenology*, §§582–83. Hegel's word here is *Umwälzung* (upheaval) rather than *Revolution*.

83. Hegel, *History of Philosophy* (Haldane and Simson), 3, pp. 401–2, explores Rousseau's famous account of the social contract in *Du contrat social* (1762), in *Oeuvres complètes*, 3, p. 360, as a 'form of association' under which one is absolutely obedient yet still morally free ('aussi libre qu'auparavant').

84. Hegel, *Phenomenology*, §584; Cf. Hegel, *Philosophy of Right*, §5; Hegel, 'Die "Rechtsphilosophie" von 1820', pp. 694–95.

Hegel did not claim that the main protagonists of the Revolution sought diligently to apply Rousseau's precise conception to the circumstances of France, but that they variously strove to impose the idea of equal freedom on the structures of the modern state. Wilful attempts to fit such a formal ideal of autonomy with the material conditions of political life led ultimately to conflict. Rousseau had argued in his *Social Contract* that while power could be delegated on terms to a deputy, or that government could execute the business of the state, the legislative will of the people could never be legitimately transferred: 'power can indeed be transferred, but not will'.[85] Such transference, including the subordination of a minority to the majority, amounted for Rousseau to a form of expropriation, an alienation of the will.[86] Hegel believed that such a vision of absolute freedom bridled at every form of dependence. For Rousseau it meant specifically that sovereignty could be neither represented nor divided, while for others it meant more generally that the state should realise equality. Under political conditions which presupposed a complex division of labour, and thus interlocking systems of inequality, the demand for equality was in Hegel's eyes quixotic. Diverse responses to this conundrum—in Sieyès, Condorcet and Robespierre, for example—could only approximate to the ideal in various ways. None of these attempts had happy consequences, in Hegel's view, and in the Jacobin case the impact was devastating. However, according to Hegel, Jacobinism was not solely responsible for dismembering social and political ties and plunging the French polity into civil strife.

---

85. Rousseau, *Du contrat social*, p. 368. Hegel's summary of Rousseau's point here at *Phenomenology* §588 states that where the will is 'represented' (*vertreten*), it 'is not'.

86. Rousseau, *Du contrat social*, p. 359, a passage singled out for comment by Hegel in *History of Philosophy* (Haldane and Simson), 3, p. 402.

We have noted already that as early as 1794, Hegel had condemned the 'complete ignominy' of the Robespierre faction.[87] Yet it is a mistake to conclude that he favoured the measures of any other party. For instance, nothing in his writings serves to buttress the Girondins, and he was scathing about the incompetence of Sieyès.[88] From the beginning, he thought, the Revolution had been misconceived. Hegel's student Eduard Gans similarly concluded that the Terror was not some kind of deviant development, but a linear consequence of the original upheaval.[89] Likewise, Hegel was not just critical of the republican constitution of Year I: he also thought that arrangements under the National Assembly had been skewed.[90] He considered the social and political ideas of leading protagonists to have been no less disjointed. Already in the early months of 1789, the validity of distinctions among orders in the state were being rejected, not least by Sieyès.[91] Others, such as Condorcet, came to repudiate mixed government as a corruption of popular power.[92] For his part, Robespierre cast doubt on the legitimacy of representation by regarding rightful authority as mandated by a virtuous citizenry.[93] As Hegel later explained, cumulatively 'all differences of talents and authority' were uprooted with

87. Hegel to Schelling, 24 December 1794, *Hegels Briefe*, 1, p. 12.

88. G.W.F. Hegel, 'On the English Reform Bill' (1831), in *Hegel: Political Writings*, p. 261.

89. Eduard Gans, *Naturrecht und Universalrechtsgeschichte*, ed. Manfred Riedel (Stuttgart: Klett-Cotta, 1981), p. 48.

90. Hegel, *Philosophie der Weltgeschichte: 1830/31*, pp. 1564–65.

91. Sieyès, *What Is the Third Estate?*, pp. 95–103.

92. See the *Plan de Constitution présenté à la Convention nationale les 15 et 16 février 1793, l'an II de la République* (Paris: De L'Imprimerie nationale, 1793), Titre 1, Articles 25–28, which Condorcet helped to draft.

93. See Lucien Jaume, *Le Discours jacobin et la démocratie* (Paris: Fayard, 1989), pp. 389ff; Istvan Hont, *Jealousy of Trade: International Competition and the*

fanatical zeal.[94] Under an assortment of ideological pressures, a whole array of social and political institutions was spurned, beginning with the dissolution of the Estates General between 28 May and 17 June 1789. The principle of social rank was renounced and any corresponding division of political power rebuffed in favour of the isomorphic rights of all citizens. According to Hegel, '[t]he undivided substance of absolute freedom ascends the throne of the world without any power being able to offer resistance to it.'[95]

Hegel believed that the will of the individual in the era of the Revolution, licensed by Rousseau's conception of the self, was encouraged to regard itself as comprehensively authoritative. It shed its singularity and constructed itself as normative. It relinquished all aspects of its social and corporate identity, ignored its station and discarded its roles: 'each singular consciousness raises itself out of its allotted sphere, and no longer finds its essence and its labour within its particular order [*Masse*]'.[96] Even its deity was shorn of all distinguishing characteristics: it became, as Hegel put it, a 'predicateless absolute' or, in Robespierre's phrase, which Hegel cited, an *être suprême*.[97] Grounded on its own empty universality, consciousness assumed the right to determine the shape of public life for all. However, having erased the particularities of social existence, it lacked the means of constructive collaboration; and, having jettisoned all countervailing branches of government, it could only act despotically: 'the universal will is only an *actual* will in a Self that is

---

Nation-State in Historical Perspective (Cambridge, MA: Harvard University Press, 2005), pp. 488–92.

94. Hegel, *Philosophy of Right*, §5A.
95. Hegel, *Phenomenology*, §585.
96. Ibid. (translation modified).
97. Ibid., §§577, 586.

One'. The natural constitutional form of absolute freedom was tyranny—'pure terrible domination', as Hegel had previously described it—confronting the world in an attitude of 'fury' (*Furie*).[98] In a society populated by opposing interests, the will to universality directly confronted an infinity of dissenting personalities. Hegel's use of the term 'personality' was deliberate: individuals were pitted against one another as rights-bearing aspirants to power. Their struggle fast became a zero-sum contest. Authority, claiming absolute right, saw only resistance in the independent rights of citizens. The programme of political justice embarked upon under the National Assembly deteriorated into the violence of the Jacobin Terror.

Like the popular mood under the Roman Empire, the French Revolution sunk into a 'mournful' frame of mind.[99] Adversarial claims to rights were staked in the absence of social cohesion or an agreed framework of morality. Atomic individualism ensured that while votes might be counted, unity of purpose could not be achieved. At the time of the Convention Assembly, Hegel remarked, 'Tyranny, Despotism raised its voice under the mask of Freedom and Equality'.[100] Under the Romans, he thought, the abstract personality of the property-owning subject eked out a 'soulless' existence cut off from public life. The isolated ego was overwhelmed by the distant powers of sovereignty and fate.[101] However, in France under the Revolution, the members of a still more fragmented society struggled against one another to seize control of the institutions of government.

98. Ibid., §589; Hegel, *Jenaer Systementwürfe 3*, p. 236: 'reine entsetzliche Herrschaft'. Cf. Hegel, *Philosophy of Right*, §5R.

99. Hegel, *Philosophie der Geschichte*, p. 339.

100. Ibid., p. 312.

101. Ibid., pp. 384–85.

Suspicion and recrimination mounted in a society that had already lost its metaphysical bearings. Under the sway of a detached and characterless Supreme Being, the meaninglessness of existence came home to roost, and so death itself lost all potential value. The spectacle of murder staged by Roman gladiatorial circuses was described by Hegel in his *Philosophy of World History* as a pageant of 'cold negativity'.[102] In France, as he observed in the *Phenomenology*, the same display of pointless sacrifice was unleashed upon the citizens at large. The rote drownings and guillotining of the Revolutionary Terror gave rise, in Hegel's memorable description, to 'the coldest, most indifferent of all deaths, with no more significance than chopping through a head of cabbage or a gulp of water'.[103]

Jacobin government, pretending to universality, was in practice involved in the partial exercise of power. Despite its appeal to the common good, it was in truth no more than a '*victorious faction*'.[104] Partisan government deployed its resources against every incipient ('unactual') challenge. Such challenges, often being latent, were only revealed by their intentions. The hidden will of presumed opponents fell under heavy suspicion. Hoarders, plotters and foes of the republic generated misgivings. To be suspect, in effect, was to be liable. The ordinary virtues were found to fall short of patriotic duty. Any show of human frailty could be construed as a sign of treachery. Rights claimed by adversaries were exposed as covert interests; public spiritedness was unveiled as self-regard. Faced with a rising tide of suspect vices, the wielders of executive power conducted affairs by condemning increasing numbers of enemies. Scores of thousands

102. Ibid., p. 357.
103. Hegel, *Phenomenology*, §590 (translation modified).
104. Ibid., §591.

perished in public executions or died in prison.[105] Punishment was less a response to actual deeds than revenge on hypothetical intentions. Given the inaccessibility—the 'intangibility'— of evidence of guilt, the souls of opponents could never be cleansed. Culpability, therefore, could only be purged by annihilating the source of sin, human life itself.[106] The conduct of government became an exercise in ruthless retribution. The macabre business of the Revolutionary Tribunal was endlessly repeated. Much like the case of early modern witch trials, Hegel later remarked, 'mere disposition, unaccompanied by any overt act or expression, was made an object of punishment'.[107] The fury of the Revolution could be usefully compared and contrasted with the cycle of vengeance that Hegel associated with the Erinyes (Furies) of Aeschylus's *Oresteia*.[108] In the latter case, tit-for-tat retaliation was the condition of life pre-existing the institution of justice: prior to civilisation—before 'magistrates and laws'—'revenge is undying', Hegel argued.[109] However, with the activities of the Committee of Public Safety in 1793–94, the spirit of vengeance came to characterise public administration itself.

In the French case, moreover, the spiral of violence was not interminable. There was an intensification of repression between 11 March 1793 and the infamous Law of 22 Prairial (10 June 1794), but then came an end to the reign of terror after 9 Thermidor (27 July 1794). As with the master–slave dialectic,

---

105. Donald Greer, *The Incidence of the Terror during the French Revolution: A Statistical Interpretation* (Cambridge, MA: Harvard University Press, 1935).

106. Hegel, *Phenomenology*, §592.

107. Hegel, *Philosophie der Geschichte*, p. 507.

108. On justice and vengeance in the *Oresteia*, see Hegel, *Philosophy of Right*, §101A.

109. Ibid., §§102A, 220.

ABSOLUTE FREEDOM AND TERROR 161

so also here the experience of complete terror proved edifying. Once more, the 'fear of death'—the 'absolute master'—marked the beginning of wisdom.[110] With the return of primordial fear and subjection, the experience of the Revolution might have been expected to culminate in repetition. However, in the event, an abysmal cycle was avoided. There would be no repeat journey from 'ethical life' through 'culture' and 'enlightenment' to 'revolution' again.[111] Consciousness instead plotted a forward course, the historical equivalent of the conceptual leap from 'Abstract Right' to 'Morality' as laid out in the *Philosophy of Right*. The 'dreadful tyranny', as Hegel stated in the final lecture of his *Philosophy of History*, 'necessarily had to pass'.[112] Sentiments, interests, bonds and loyalties inevitably reasserted themselves as preferable to purely abstract justice which only led to death. Under the Directory, the campaign against the clergy and royalists was relaxed. Nonetheless, mistrust did not immediately abate. Equally, some of the constitutional problems which afflicted the Legislative Assembly were carried over into the Directory. Hegel noted that government by committee remained overly dependent on the chambers of deputies.[113] A crisis of the constitution followed, opening another opportunity for change. Napoleon seized the moment. For all his reputed admiration of Bonaparte, Hegel's verdict was in fact withering: 'never did the impotence of victory appear in a clearer light than then'.[114] Stability had been restored to France, but the Revolution had ended in failure. The way forward, Hegel concluded,

---

110. Ibid., §593. Cf. ibid., §197.
111. Ibid., §594.
112. Hegel, *Philosophie der Weltgeschichte: 1830/31*, p. 1565.
113. Ibid., pp. 1565–66.
114. Ibid., p. 1566.

lay in Protestant Europe.[115] In the case of Germany a programme of political reform had begun with improvements in religion and morality rather than the resort to bloodshed. Under Kant's influence, spirit advanced beyond mere personality and embarked on the construction of moral subjectivity, on the discovery of the universal will as a source of normativity, rather than of all-consuming destruction.

115. Hegel, *Phenomenology*, §595.

6

Revolution and the Modern Constitutional State

THE SEVENTEEN PARAGRAPHS that make up the subsection on 'Absolute Freedom and Terror' in the *Phenomenology* provide a schematic analysis of the fate of political rights between Rousseau's *Social Contract* and the immediate aftermath of Robespierre. Yet Hegel's larger point was that the future did not lie with the Revolution. It was true, he recognised, that legislation in France after 1789 helped to dismantle the system of legal privilege that inspired resentment across the population. However, it was also the case that privileges attached to birth had been progressively undermined as feudalism declined over the previous centuries in many parts of Europe. Moreover, the older regime of 'particularity', under which social distinctions undermined the principle of equality, had likewise been challenged by reforms introduced into Prussia under Frederick the Great. The French monarchy had no monopoly on social and political change.

In his 1831 lectures on the philosophy of world history, Hegel singled out the Prussian king as having transformed the foundations of his state by substituting the principle of civil rights for a system of 'private' exemptions which had defined the traditional body of law. Privileges were gradually subordinated to 'universal' norms as Frederick prioritised the national good (*das Beste seines Staats*), which became the standard against which legislation was to be measured.[1] Indeed, according to Hegel, for this philosopher-king, the precedence of the common good over partial interests was the very definition of enlightenment (*la lumière* [*sic*]) itself.[2] Enlightenment promoted institutions which reason rather than custom prescribed. Hegel had in mind the codification of Prussian laws, inaugurated by Frederick the Great in 1780, and finally promulgated under his successor in 1794 as the Prussian Civil Code. Under the Code, provincial interests were subordinated to the national interest. The intention was to render the will of the state preeminent over the traditional entitlements of the Prussian nobility. However, from Hegel's point of view, the aims of the Code were limited in scope, and its achievements were in any case incomplete. In many ways the new provisions merely entrenched existing agrarian structures by incorporating them into written statutes supposedly sanctioned by natural law.[3]

Yet despite their inadequacy from the perspective of a later generation, Hegel still regarded Frederick's reforms as an

1. G.W.F. Hegel, *Vorlesungen über die Philosophie der Weltgeschichte 2: Nachschriften zum Kolleg des Wintersemesters 1824/25*, ed. Walter Jaeschke and Rebecca Paimann (*Gesammelte Werke 27.2*) (Hamburg: Felix Meiner Verlag, 2019), p. 783; G.W.F. Hegel, *Vorlesungen über die Philosophie der Weltgeschichte 3: Nachschriften zum Kolleg des Wintersemesters 1826/27*, ed. Walter Jaeschke (*Gesammelte Werke 27.3*) (Hamburg: Felix Meiner Verlag, 2019), p. 1145; Hegel, *Philosophie der Weltgeschichte: 1830/31*, p. 1557.

2. Hegel, *Philosophie der Weltgeschichte: 1830/31*, p. 1557n.

3. Reinhart Koselleck, *Preussen Zwischen Reform und Revolution: Allgemeines Landrecht, Verwaltung und Soziale Bewegung von 1791 bis 1848* (Stuttgart: Ernst Klett Verlag, 1967), pp. 38ff.

important milestone in the period. He believed that it made no sense lamenting the failure to go further, when the circumstances of the times limited everyone's horizons. There was, for instance, little demand for representative institutions in the period.[4] More comprehensive schemes for renewal were developed after 1807 under the influence of leading ministerial figures such as Baron vom Stein and Karl August von Hardenberg. Naturally, Hegel paid close attention to these projects for improvement, including plans for the overhaul of land ownership, the education system, the constitution and the military establishment. Early in the reform period serfdom was abolished, a free market in land created and the right to choose one's occupation introduced. Transformative change had been brought about by bureaucratic fiat.[5]

Hegel viewed these developments with the history of Württemberg in mind, where centralised authority had long been offset by representative organs of state. Furthermore, at the Congress of Vienna in 1815, in accordance with Article 13 of the Landständische Verfassung, a commitment to the redesign of the kingdom's constitution had been made.[6] Hegel plainly endorsed the legitimacy of a representative regime appropriately structured under a constitutional monarchy. More

4. Hegel, *History of Philosophy* (Haldane and Simson), 3, p. 391.

5. Walter Simon, *The Failure of the Prussian Reform Movement, 1807–1819* (Ithaca, NY: Cornell University Press, 1955), pp. 6–37; Friedrich Meinecke, *The Age of German Liberation, 1795–1815* (Berkeley, CA: University of California Press, 1977), pp. 69–101; James J. Sheehan, *German History, 1770–1866* (Oxford: Oxford University Press, 1989), pp. 294–310; Matthew Levinger, 'The Prussian Reform Movement and the Rise of Enlightened Nationalism', in Philip G. Dwyer, ed., *The Rise of Prussia, 1700–1830* (Edinburgh: Pearson, 2000); Clark, *Iron Kingdom*, pp. 320–38.

6. On the importance of Württemberg in shaping Hegel's constitutional views, see Elias Buchetmann, *Hegel and the Representative Constitution* (Cambridge: Cambridge University Press, 2023), ch. 1.

generally, he also supported the adoption of legal codes. In this he opposed the leaders of the historical school of law, loudly denouncing Savigny's campaign against codification.[7] It had recently been denied, he noted in the *Philosophy of Right*, 'that nations have a vocation to legislate'.[8] For Hegel, this denial was regressive on two counts: first, it underestimated the intelligence of the people; and second, it justified every provision already in operation.[9] Opposing this implicit attachment to established customs, as well as the arcana of professional jurisprudence, Hegel thought that reasoning from principles was a positive development.[10] However, the approach adopted in France had been fundamentally flawed. As Hegel would convey the point after his arrival in Heidelberg, every constitutional structure in France had been fundamentally defective.[11]

The misstep in French political thinking was immediately evident after the establishment of the National Assembly in June 1789. French innovation was merely the most dazzling example of a wider tendency in the age to place politics on a constitutional footing. With the rise of the modern state, debate about its constituent powers became commonplace, and with that a range of controversies about 'articulated' constitutions

7. For the context and substance of Savigny's position, see Charlotte Johann, 'Friedrich Carl von Savigny and the Politics of Legal Pluralism in Germany, ca. 1810–1847', PhD thesis, University of Cambridge, 2021.

8. This was a reference to Friedrich Carl von Savigny, *Vom Beruf unsrer Zeit für Gesetzgebung und Rechtswissenschaft* (Heidelberg: Mohr and Zimmer, 1814), itself a response to Anton Friedrich Justus Thibaut, *Über die Notwendigkeit eines allgemeinen bürgerlichen Rechts für Deutschland* (Heidelberg: Mohr and Zimmer, 1814).

9. Hegel, *Philosophy of Right*, §211R.

10. On the use of specialised knowledge, including judicial technicalities, to bamboozle and exploit the population, see ibid., §279R.

11. Hegel, *First Philosophy of Right*, §133A.

spread.[12] The question was how the components of a given regime best fitted together while an appropriate division of functions along with the unity of the state were both respected. In the sixteenth and seventeenth centuries, wrangling over the issue led to turmoil. More recently in France, a 'terrifying' sequence of mishaps stood as a warning against precipitous and ill-considered statecraft. As Hegel argued in a review of the recent proceedings of the Württemberg assembly, published in 1817 in response to proposals for constitutional reform, in the previous quarter-century since the advent of the French Revolution the course of events had given rise to a litany of misbegotten constitutional theories as well as misguided ideas about the content of the law.[13] The most conspicuous mismanagement involved a confusion of roles between legislative and executive power.

Whilst Hegel backed the notion that political judgement should be based on principles—as opposed to just precedent or positive feelings—he was still critical of the idea that a constitution might be invented. Nonetheless, he deplored the claims advanced by Ludwig von Haller to the effect that right could be grounded on authority, which in practice meant that justice was no more than a question of power.[14] Likewise, he repudiated the cult of sensibility, which he associated with Friedrich Schleiermacher as well as Jakob Fries. Their approach, he contended, based moral approval on the strength of

12. Hegel, *Proceedings of the Estates of Württemberg*, p. 34.

13. Ibid., p. 65.

14. Hegel, *Philosophy of Right*, §258R, commenting on Ludwig von Haller, *Restauration der Staats-Wissenschaft, oder Theorie des natürlich-geselligen Zustands, der Chimäre des künstlich-bürgerlichen entgegengesezt*, 6 vols (Winterthur: Steinerischen Buchhandlung, 1816–34), 1, pp. 342ff.

sentiment.[15] This led Hegel to place the individual will at the centre of his political philosophy, understanding this as subject to rational determination, and consequently as a matter for conceptual evaluation. This implied that Rousseau and Kant, tracing moral value to individual autonomy, had supplied the foundations for a properly justified conception of legitimacy.[16]

At the same time, as Hegel repeatedly argued, revolutionary conceptions of the will lacked substance. This amounted to claiming that the new resort to 'abstract' volition involved an inadequate conception of the moral and political world.[17] As a consequence, moral standards were separated from ethical life (*Sittlichkeit*). Equally, intention was problematically divorced from action, morality from wider social relations, and society from public administration and the state. To repair this damage, Hegel strove to integrate individual conscience with practical life understood in interconnected, holistic terms. The question of 'right' was not restricted to contractual and moral relations, but also involved economic and institutional arrangements. Practical judgement, therefore, had to be inclusively contextual. It should begin with actual conditions as these currently presented themselves. It made no sense to start by reinventing an alternative world, which by definition lacked tangible reality. In the same vein, Hegel believed that constitutional design should begin with how things were. A given constitution simply 'is', Hegel

15. Hegel, *Philosophy of Right*, 'Preface', pp. 11, 20–22. See also ibid., §2R. Hegel took such ideas to have been expressed in Friedrich Schleiermacher, *Über die Religion: Reden an die Gebildeten unter ihren Verächtern* (Berlin: Unger, 1799) and Jakob Fries, *Von deutschem Bund und deutscher Staatsverfassung: allgemeine staatrechtliche Ansichten* (Heidelberg: Mohr and Winter, 1816).

16. Hegel, *Philosophy of Right*, §258R.

17. Robert Pippin, *Hegel's Practical Philosophy: Rational Agency as Ethical Life* (Cambridge: Cambridge University Press, 2008).

insisted. Beyond that, as it develops, it 'becomes'.[18] However, it is never spontaneously made, not even by the legislature. The legislative branch is in fact a part of a larger whole, which can be reformed or left to evolve, but cannot be engineered *ab initio*.

II

The French Revolution had evidently violated this principle. Its protagonists strove to revise the form of the state 'from first principles and purely in terms of *thought*'. Still more radically, they sought to 'overthrow' all exiting conditions 'for the first time [. . .] in human history'. Driven by fanaticism, they 'turned the attempt into the most terrible and drastic event'.[19] As Hegel presented it, fanaticism, which historically had been associated with religious delirium, had assumed a new ideological form centred on the political world.[20] The problem for Hegel was not that politics should be based on principles, but that these principles were abstracted from historical circumstances. This implied a flight from 'actuality'; a withdrawal into the purity of moral intentions, from where evil ironically could be generated. Extreme admiration for the untainted will was liable to self-conceit. Equally, a principled commitment to universal norms habitually slid into the adoption of arbitrary preferences. At that point, self-interest tended to masquerade as principle.[21] In other words, morality was exposed to self-corruption. For this reason, whilst 'the moral point of view' was one of the great

18. Hegel, *Philosophy of Right*, §298A.
19. Ibid., §258R.
20. On fanaticism, see ibid., §270R.
21. Ibid., §139.

accomplishments of the modern world, it also posed exceptional dangers.[22] It enabled hypocrisy to flourish in the guise of
conscience.[23] The revolt of this worldview against the prevailing
state of things aimed at expanding its powers at the expense of
existing restraints. Revolutionary zeal imposed itself indiscrimi-
nately on the current order, often with devastating results. This
included the goal of constitutional renovation at the outset of
the Revolution.

In the *Philosophy of Right* Hegel proclaimed that when
'people say they want to be free, this means primarily that they
want to be free in an abstract sense, and every determination
and division [*Gliederung*] within the state is regarded as a limitation of that freedom.'[24] In this spirit, after the creation of
what became known as the National Constituent Assembly on
17 June 1789, the legislative power of France was pitted against
the executive. Each branch strove, in Hegel's words, for 'self-
sufficiency'. Pursuing this course, both powers were headed
inadvertently toward 'the destruction of the state.'[25] Montesquieu had been right, Hegel argued, in proposing that the elements of a constitution should form a 'totality.'[26] The alternative,
which came to pass in France, was that the agents of the national will would conflict, leading to the subordination of one
to the other, or descent into an irresolvable struggle.

Ideally, the branches of government should comprise dependent moments within a harmonious whole. In practice, for
Hegel this meant that the discrete functions of legislative,

---

22. Ibid. Cf. Hegel, *Phenomenology*, §§599ff.

23. Hegel, *Philosophy of Right*, §140.

24. Ibid., §149A.

25. Ibid., §272R.

26. Ibid., §§3R, 261R. Cf. ibid., §278R. Cf. Hegel, *Lectures on the Philosophy of World History, Introduction*, pp. 22, 102.

executive and princely power should be carefully differentiated. Yet they should also be made to cohere organically. The state was not an aggregation of elements, but a union of parts.[27] This required effective coordination between the levers of power. Ancient states were held together by substantial sentiment, or public virtue: a common will was sustained by patriotic 'dispositions'.[28] By comparison, the modern state was premised on 'the principle of subjectivity'.[29] Authority had to win the allegiance of free consciousness. Unlike among the Spartans or the Romans, 'universality'—or the common good—could not override 'particularity': 'The essence of the modern state is that the universal should be linked with the complete freedom of particularity [Besonderheit] and the well-being of individuals'.[30] This could only be brought about by constitutional coordination. Government could not be conducted between mutually hostile parties.[31] Yet immediately after the abolition of the Estates General in France, the Assembly and the monarchy were animated by suspicion. Either side aimed to subvert the function of the other, promptly leading to mistrust and recrimination.

In the *Philosophy of History* Hegel laid out the principal elements of a modern state. These included the substance of the laws, directed to maintaining both right and welfare; the form of administration, which determined the mechanisms of decision-making; and national sentiment, which guaranteed allegiance.[32] It was soon found that the French state failed to

27. Hegel, *Philosophy of Right*, §§258R, 276.
28. Ibid., §260.
29. Ibid., §§273R, 124R.
30. Ibid., §260. Cf. ibid., §261A.
31. Ibid., §301A.
32. Hegel, *Philosophie der Weltgeschichte: 1830/31*, pp. 1562–63.

guarantee justice and the common good, since the business of decision-making could not be formally agreed. On the one hand, in a monarchy, the crown should execute. On the other, under a free regime, the people should have a role. Yet the branches of government, as they pursued reform, failed to allocate the respective tasks. In addition, there was contention over the meaning of the 'people'. In the first place, the 'many' meant 'all'. But in practice the multitude had to be governed by the 'few'. Inevitably, the governing minority aroused suspicion. Wariness spread through the population, undermining public allegiance among the citizen body.[33] According to Hegel, for any polity to function, administrators had to internalise a 'sense of the state', while the people at large had to exhibit a rational esteem for its proceedings.[34] In the French case these conditions were sorely wanting.

The Assembly was not content simply to legislate; instead, it aspired to govern. It extended its remit from establishing rights to managing finances and the budget. Before long, parties multiplied in the legislature. Opposing factions increased misgivings; distrust pervaded all organs of government.[35] Elections became mechanical and voters grew apathetic.[36] Charges of betrayal mounted in the chamber as well as out of doors. The Terror followed, when being under suspicion (*Verdacht*) itself became a crime (*Verbrechen*).[37] Although government returned in 1795 under the Directory, confusion still reigned, and atomisation spread. 'French abstractions' concerning 'number and

---

33. Ibid., pp. 1563–64.

34. Hegel, *Proceedings of the Estates of Württemberg*, p. 43.

35. Hegel, *Philosophie der Weltgeschichte: 1830/31*, p. 1565.

36. Hegel, *Proceedings of the Estates of Württemberg*, p. 48.

37. Hegel, *Philosophie der Weltgeschichte: 1830/31*, pp. 1565, 1565n.

quanta of wealth' determined the eligibility to vote. Accordingly, under the influence of 'democratic formlessness', politics was disconnected from society at large.[38] In addition, the executive proved weak and could not manage the Councils. Napoleon's coup of 1799 finally resolved the power vacuum in government, although at the cost of severing administration from popular allegiance. As Napoleon conquered Europe, he diffused liberal reforms across the continent. Progressive legal provisions conflicted with public opinion. The situation that followed in Spain encapsulated the resulting problem: the population revolted against 'rational' institutions.[39] It therefore came to pass that nationality and religion challenged empty forms of constitutionalism under which society was directly subject to ministerial control.[40] The Restoration, along with the constitutional Charter of 1814, promised to reconcile the government with the populace. Yet party spirit persisted under the restored monarchy. Looking back in the months before his death over developments since the French Revolution, Hegel described the fallout from 1789 as having left a trail of turbulence and confusion: 'disturbances and ferment continue to persist'.[41]

While the Revolution failed in France, it succeeded in spreading itself abroad. But here its record was similarly erratic. The apparatus of 'liberalism' was planted across Europe, though without reconciling popular sentiment to the new procedures.

38. Hegel, *Proceedings of the Estates of Württemberg*, pp. 48–49; Hegel, *Philosophy of Right*, §290A.

39. Hegel, *Philosophy of Right*, §274A. Cf. G.W.F. Hegel, 'Nachschrift Rudolf Ringier (Wintersemester 1819/20)', in *Vorlesungen über die Philosophie des Rechts 1: Kollegien der Jahre 1817/18, 1818/19, 1819/20*, ed. Dirk Felgenhauer (*Gesammelte Werke* 26.1) (Hamburg: Felix Meiner Verlag, 2014), p. 530.

40. Hegel, *Philosophy of Right*, §290A.

41. Hegel, *Philosophie der Weltgeschichte: 1830/31*, p. 1567.

The dissemination of formal rights failed to awaken active consent in Piedmont, Rome, Spain or Naples.[42] Over a thirty-year period succeeding the French Revolution, each of these Catholic territories, along with Portugal and Ireland, had been shaken by violent insurrection.[43] The situation was happier in the remaining Protestant states. Austrian dependencies continued to be oppressed by serfdom and coercion.[44] For its part, Britain avoided the pitfalls of centralisation; however its property relations were still mired in the residues of feudalism. More positively, the British left some initiative to subordinate jurisdictions while also ensuring the effectiveness of executive power. On top of this, the constitution reliably reproduced a class of effective statesmen devoted to the affairs of government.[45] Hegel contrasted these arrangements with the situation in Germany. This, of course, included a variety of regime forms. Hegel was mostly interested in Württemberg and Prussia. What he prized was the modernisation of the system of property and the existence of a ruling class of officials.[46]

These achievements were the product of a gradual transition from feudal governance (*Feudalherrschaft*) to constitutional monarchy. As we have seen, this development was charted under the rubric of *Bildung* in the 'Spirit' section of the *Phenomenology*. But its details were further elaborated in the *Philosophy of History*. There the change was presented in terms of the 'breaking' of arbitrary will (*Wilkür*) among competing lords

42. Hegel, *Philosophie der Weltgeschichte: 1824/25*, p. 784; Hegel, *Philosophie der Weltgeschichte: 1826/27*, p. 1146; Hegel, *Philosophie der Weltgeschichte: 1830/31*, p. 1567n.
43. Hegel, 'Vorlesungsnachschrift, K. G. v. Griesheim, 1824–5', p. 650.
44. Hegel, *Philosophie der Weltgeschichte: 1830/31*, p. 1568.
45. Ibid., pp. 1568–69.
46. Ibid., p. 1569.

and vassals. This led to the concentration, or 'unification', of power. By this Hegel meant the emergence of supreme authority vested in the state, under which 'particular' exemptions were eliminated. Members of the state came to enjoy universal rights. Under the feudal order, what he termed the 'dynastic' principle reigned.[47] Obligations were immediately personal, and their enforcement depended on either patronage or violence, never duty based on general norms. The arbitrariness of feudal entitlements produced a stark confrontation between lord (*Herr*) and serf (*Knecht*)—a subordination of slave to master in the absence of principled accommodation. It was characterised by struggle instead of a system of obligations, and so yielded what Hegel called a 'polyarchy'.[48] Rival contestants were motivated by 'honour' instead of serving public utility.[49] Modern monarchy sublated this anarchical combination of forces. Vassalage gave way to distinct 'orders' in the state, which came together to form a constitutional settlement. Estates and corporations prospered without pulling the regime apart.[50] Equally, serfdom and domination were replaced by regular government dedicated to the maintenance of generalised rights and standards. During that process, state officials took the place of competing dynasts. Altogether, these alterations promoted a shared allegiance to the public weal.[51] Over time, the state appeared as a properly universal authority, displacing the older structure of

---

47. Ibid., p. 1515.

48. Ibid., p. 1516.

49. Hegel, *Philosophy of Right*, §273R.

50. For a modern interpretation of the process, see F. L. Carsten, *Princes and Parliaments in German: From the Fifteenth to the Eighteenth Century* (Oxford: Clarendon Press, 1959).

51. Hegel, *Philosophie der Weltgeschichte: 1830/31*, pp. 1516–17.

'contractual' principalities.[52] While under feudal conditions each territory might exercise external sovereignty, internally competing powers rendered the polity an 'aggregate' rather than an integrated organism.[53]

III

For Hegel, the passage from feudal to constitutional monarchy was one of the great achievements of European history. While that development was based upon the consolidation of a powerful executive drawing together the elements of society into a state, it also presupposed the emergence of civil society (*bürgerliche Gesellschaft*). 'The creation of civil society', Hegel announced in the *Philosophy of Right*, 'belongs to the modern world.'[54] In Hegelian taxonomy, civil society was distinguished from 'society' and from 'the state' as both had been theorised in the traditions of natural law.[55] The category did not simply refer to a natural association prior to the institution of government. Neither was it equivalent to what Hegel thought of as the higher, or more fully integrated, sphere of political society. It denoted commercial interaction secured by a system of laws, or needs-based relations constrained by judicial regulations. Since ancient societies were supported by slave economies with communities differentiated into political (*polis*) and family (*oikos*) life, there was no classical equivalent to civil society. Equally, civil society was contrasted by Hegel with the more capricious

---

52. Hegel, *Philosophy of Right*, §§75R, 75A, 258R. Cf. Hegel, *First Philosophy of Right*, §33A.

53. Hegel, *Philosophy of Right*, §278R.

54. Ibid., §182A.

55. Ibid., §33A.

forms of social exchange which he took to be typical of the feudal system. For instance, neither the hospitality, the deference, nor the personal fidelity characteristic of vassalage were features of specifically civil society. Under *bürgerliche Gesellschaft*, members pursued their own ends freely, and the goals they aimed at served particular interests. With that purpose in view, each individual satisfied their desires by relying on others as means to that objective. Individual gratification was 'mediated' by the form of 'universality'.[56] Self-interested actors stood in a relation of interdependence with others. This interdependence had to be distinguished from fealty since it was conducted in terms of individual rights based on property and contract and enforced through punishment.

The appearance of civil society was connected with the rise of the citizen, or the *Bürger* in the sense of *bourgeois* rather than *citoyen*.[57] This social type was first produced by the medieval towns which subsisted in the midst of a feudal countryside. The role of the towns in the development of modern liberty was a theme explored in philosophical histories stretching from Adam Smith to François Guizot. Hegel certainly drew on the relevant Scottish sources.[58] So too, of course, did Guizot, for whom Europe was in part a product of the enduring municipal spirit which the Roman Empire had bequeathed to the succeeding era.[59] In the third book of the *Wealth of Nations*, Smith associated modern freedom with the rise of commerce and

56. Ibid., §§182, 182A, 183 and 185

57. Ibid., §190R. Cf. Hegel, *First Philosophy of Right*, §§72A, 89A.

58. Waszek, *Hegel's Account of 'Civil Society'*; Gareth Stedman Jones, 'Hegel and the Economics of Civil Society', in Sudipta Kaviraj and Sunil Khilnani, eds, *Civil Society: History and Possibilities* (Cambridge: Cambridge University Press, 2001).

59. François Guizot, *The History of Civilization in Europe* (1828), ed. Larry Siedentop, trans. William Hazlitt (London: Penguin, 1997), p. 37.

manufactures. He went on to ascribe this insight to David Hume, who had canvassed the thesis in his *Essays* as well as his *History of England*.[60] Smith connected the argument to the history of European cities as they revived after the collapse of Roman power. The inhabitants of towns and cities, although at first subject to exploitation, gradually carved out a measure of autonomy from the surrounding area.[61] So-called 'free-burghers', liberated from the arbitrary impositions of barons, created orderly conditions under which commerce could prosper. Over time, the institutions of municipal government took root, further guaranteeing the security of rights, which again favoured the pursuit of commerce. Following James Steuart, Adam Ferguson, John Millar and William Robertson, Hegel addressed this subject in his *Philosophy of History*.[62] Like the church, Hegel contended, cities emerged as part of a reaction against feudal exploitation, facilitating the establishment of 'right' (*Recht*) in the midst of 'wrong' (*Unrecht*).[63]

The principle of 'free possession', which had prospered before the consolidation of feudalism, emerged again in cities

---

60. David Hume, 'Of Refinement in the Arts' (1752: 'Of Luxury'), in *Essays Moral, Political, and Literary*, ed. Eugene F. Miller (Indianapolis: Liberty Fund, 1985); David Hume, *The History of England*, 6 vols (Indianapolis: Liberty Fund, 1983), 4, pp. 374ff.

61. Adam Smith, *An Inquiry into the Nature and Causes of the Wealth of Nations* (1776), ed. R. H. Campbell and A. S. Skinner, 2 vols (Indianapolis: Liberty Classics, 1976), 1, p. 399. Cf. Hegel, *Philosophie der Weltgeschichte: 1830/31*, pp. 1498–99.

62. See James Steuart, *An Inquiry into the Principles of Political Oeconomy* (1767), ed. A. S. Skinner, 2 vols (Chicago: Chicago University Press, 1966), 1, p. 249; 2, p. xiii; Adam Ferguson, *An Essay on the History of Civil Society* (1767), ed. Fania Oz-Salzberger (Cambridge: Cambridge University Press, 1995), p. 139; John Millar, *The Origin of the Distinction of Ranks* (1767), ed. Aaron Garrett (Indianapolis: Liberty Fund, 2006), pp. 220ff., 326ff.; William Robertson, *The History of the Reign of Charles V* (1769), 3 vols (Philadelphia: Robert Bell, 1771), 1, pp. 28ff.

63. Hegel, *Philosophie der Weltgeschichte: 1830/31*, p. 1498.

created in the feudal era: 'The essence of freedom and order has therefore arisen mainly in towns.'[64] This ultimately led to the formation of early modern republics—in Italy, Switzerland, the Netherlands, Germany and France.[65] But the resulting 'republican' norms, which secured justice under regulated governments, came to characterise early modern monarchies as well. By degrees, bourgeois—or *bürgerliche*—societies were formed. Under their influence, subjectivity in all its dimensions dominated custom.[66] The impact of this principle was felt in various domains—including contractual relations, moral ideas, professional life and the family.

Civil society was not the cause of each of these phenomena, but under its shadow they were able to extend themselves. Conceptually, association in accordance with the norms of *bürgerliche Gesellschaft* was distinct from strictly moral behaviour. The former, Hegel argued, represented a 'negative' form of freedom, while the latter was essentially 'positive': the one referred to the enjoyment of personal rights, the other covered duties towards others.[67] Nonetheless, modern moral ideas flourished in the same context in which civil society rose to power. Both presupposed the idea of free subjectivity, against which all objective standards were measured.[68] This meant that the conditions under which civil freedoms prospered coincided with those under which modern attitudes to responsibility thrived. The character of Oedipus, who typified ancient ideas

64. Hegel, *Philosophy of Right*, §204A.

65. Hegel, *Philosophie der Weltgeschichte: 1830/31*, pp. 1499, 1501. Cf. Smith, *Wealth of Nations*, 1, p. 403.

66. Hegel, *Philosophy of Right*, 'Preface', pp. 13–14n.

67. Ibid., §112A. The literature on this distinction usually betrays an ignorance of its Hegelian origins.

68. Ibid., 'Preface', p. 20.

of liability, became inconceivable after the modern conception of guilt had been established.[69] For the moderns, responsibility was connected to an agent's goal in acting. For this reason, civil negligence had become an expanding area of jurisprudence. To use Hegel's chosen example, an arsonist is answerable not only for their intention (*Absicht*), but also for the ramifying consequences following from their purpose (*Vorsatz*): '"The stone belongs to the devil when it leaves the hand that threw it."'[70]

Among the most conspicuous features of modern history was the gradual unburdening of 'personality' during the progress of European social development. Hegel tackled this theme under the rubric of the 'right of persons', referring to the entitlement to property and contractual relations.[71] The polar opposite of personality was slavery—the 'alienation of personality'—which constituted an unsurpassed abomination in world history.[72] Hegel wrote, 'It is only because I am alive as a free entity within my body that this living existence [*Dasein*] may not be misused as a beast of burden.'[73] A proper understanding of this principle meant that ownership had to be '*free and complete*'.[74] Hegel used this insight to criticise confused ideas about property which he associated at once with Roman jurisprudence, all forms of communalism, feudal relations and the Kantian conception of rights. The 'person', as Hegel saw it, had to be freed from status relations, and differentiated from membership of a family.[75] At the same time, he contrasted

69. Ibid., §118R.
70. Ibid., §119A.
71. Ibid., §40.
72. Ibid., §66R.
73. Ibid., §48R.
74. Ibid., §62.
75. Ibid., §§40, 43R.

personality with the feudal notion of dependence. Partial and divided property—estates in fief, usufructs and entails—were all corruptions of the notion of unfettered ownership.[76] Under contemporary Prussian reforms, limitations of the kind were 'for the most part disappearing'.[77] Modernity was liberating the rights-bearing personality. This laid the foundations for the current conception of a professional vocation along with the institution of the conjugal family.

This meant that the conditions which yielded the rise of inalienable and imprescriptible rights likewise freed the individual from predetermined social roles. In broad terms, this shift differentiated eastern from western societies as well as the ancient from the modern world—schematically, Sparta and India from Germany and France.[78] In the latter cases, allocation to estates was not rigidly prescribed. At least, the process was not determined by nature. Nonetheless, as Hegel noted in 1817, a culture of separation still pervaded the Prussian nobility, just as it had the Roman patriciate.[79] Even so, although social position in modern Europe was partly governed by chance, it included a major element of 'subjective particularity'.[80] The pursuit of a trade or entry into a profession now involved the element of choice. Free choice likewise shaped the institution of the modern family: 'In modern times [. . .] the subjective origin [of marriage], the state of being in love, is regarded as the only important factor.'[81] Marriage, to be sure, was not a contract, since at root it was not an agreement between self-interested

76. Ibid., §§46R 62R,
77. Ibid., §63A.
78. Ibid., §206R.
79. Hegel, *First Philosophy of Right*, §106A.
80. Hegel, *Philosophy of Right*, §206.
81. Ibid., §162A.

parties.[82] Individuality was superseded in a more substantial union. Commonly in the past, marriage had been a matter for parents to decide. More recently the element of reciprocal love based on 'the subjective principle of the modern world' had come to predominate. The change was reflected in numerous departments of culture: 'love, or being in love, is for the most part the object of our comedies and tragedies.'[83] Yet Hegel also believed that this subjective aspect was not equivalent to whim or 'arbitrary' desire.[84] The sexual appetite, he conceded, was satisfied in marriage, but the institution was not just a means of mutual use or gratification.

Hegel thought that this more functional sense was implicit in the ideal of sexual love depicted in Schlegel's 1799 novel *Lucinde*, based on his affair with Dorothea Veit, the daughter of Moses Mendelssohn.[85] There, sexual relations were centred on the transient expression of passion. External recognition was seen as a betrayal of its intensity. However, for Hegel, marriage served a more enduring purpose, which included rearing children. Nonetheless, at the same time, the modern family had to be distinguished from the notion of lineage. In its modern guise, the value of the family was particularised in its present members, instead of in the idea of the *stirps* or the *gens* whereby the family was submerged in the attachment to posterity. Under feudalism, with inheritance hemmed in by primogeniture and entails, this more ancestral conception had become widespread. The *splendor familiae*—the family line and its

82. Ibid., §75R, where Hegel is criticising the views of Kant.

83. Hegel, *First Philosophy of Right*, §76A. Cf. Hegel, 'Vorlesungsnachschrift, K. G. v. Griesheim, 1824–5', p. 433.

84. Hegel, *Philosophy of Right*, §§161A, 162, 162R, 162A, 163, 163A.

85. Ibid., §164A.

renown—outshone the nuclear unit characteristic of modern times.[86] Altogether, contemporary society, with its moral attitudes, its system of property, its forms of work and family life, was not the product of a single revolutionary explosion, but an expression of a general transformation in which subjectivity achieved preeminent status.

IV

By now it should be clear that, for Hegel, subjectivity defined the modern world. This was expressed in the refinement of rights, the keenness of conscience and the practices of ethical life. Subjectivity shaped attitudes to vocational roles and the outlook on marriage. It also changed the principles determining selection to office. It corroded the idea of estate-based entitlement to rule. Aptitude rather than status became a qualification for government: '[a]bility, skill, and character' were increasingly decisive for access to occupations, including administration and political representation.[87] Hegel was unstinting in drawing out the implications: 'Individuals are not destined by birth or personal nature to hold particular office.'[88] On the contrary, knowledge and competence were key. This created opportunities for the cultivated middle class (*Mittelstand*).[89] In Hegel's view, a university-trained bureaucratic elite was an essential component of the modern state. Officials had to be safeguarded against influence and dependence. Once supported in this way, they were in a position to focus on the

86. Ibid., §§170R, 180R.
87. Ibid., §277A.
88. Ibid., §291.
89. Ibid., §297A.

universal aspects of affairs. By this means, the norms of public duty could replace arbitrary authority; the civil servant succeeded the 'errant' administrator.[90]

Nonetheless, while Hegel thought that education and integrity were indispensable to impersonal rule, he also believed that the sacredness of the individual had to be symbolised in the state by placing a princely figure at its head. The purpose of the monarch was to crystallise the image of leadership in a single person. Hegel insisted that legislation had to address the universal interest, but he was also committed to retaining a token of discretion to express the value of subjectivity in modern life. For this reason, he argued that the existence of a monarchical head under a constitutional system—exercising the final 'I will' in the political process—constituted 'the great difference between [the] ancient and modern worlds'.[91] This epochal difference was manifested in many other domains. In addition to individuality being symbolised by the prince, subjectivity was further evident in every aspect of culture. Modern art, philosophy and religion all gave expression to this reigning principle. Each instance signalled the decline of arbitrary dependence. However, for all its capacity to transform, Hegel recognised that subjectivity was also destabilising. Nowhere was this more obvious than in the circulation of opinion: 'Public opinion has always played a role, but in the age of subjectivity it plays a powerful role.'[92] It followed for Hegel that, given its whimsical nature and its connection to the people, opinion deserved to be both 'respected' and 'despised'. Reflecting on the proliferation of print media since the French Revolution, Hegel observed how every kind of

90. Ibid., §§294A, 297.
91. Ibid., §279R.
92. Ibid., §316A.

ignorance, falsity, prejudice, criticism and alarm bodied forth in numerous organs of public commentary.[93] Ultimately, newspapers and pamphlets articulated the attitudes of the people, but they did so in a wildly disorganised fashion which often proved counterproductive. The masses, Hegel concluded, were capable of self-deception.[94] Popular preferences therefore needed to be processed and digested. It was the job of the constitution to ensure that this could happen.[95]

This meant that, for Hegel, popular opinion ought to be channelled through the mechanisms of constitutional government. Sentiments needed to be distilled. To achieve that, circumspection, reflection and deliberation were necessary. Hegel considered this an urgent matter under specifically modern conditions. In those circumstances, pervasive self-interest and steep inequalities needed to be reconciled. This objective had to be pursued against a particular background: equality had become the mantra of modern politics. Hegel believed that the slogan masked enormous differences. In effect, this meant that the word was an empty and misleading term. It was quite correct, Hegel argued, that from the vantage point of abstract right each person was on a par with their fellow comrades and competitors. Yet this perspective disregarded the individual's social position: 'Equality, in this case, can only be the equality of abstract persons as such, which thus *excludes* everything to do with possessions, this *basis of inequality*.'[96] The goal of levelling was certainly an understandable wish, but a moral wish was no

93. For a modern overview, see Hugh Gough, *The Newspaper Press in the French Revolution* (London: Routledge, 1988).

94. Hegel, *Philosophy of Right*, §§317, 317R, 318.

95. For a fuller account of Hegel's constitutional theory, see Buchetmann, *Hegel and the Representative Constitution*, passim.

96. Hegel, *Philosophy of Right*, §49R.

more than a baseless aspiration. Inequalities spontaneously emerged in social life. Consequently, the only parity that could be guaranteed in terms of rights was the equal entitlement to property.[97] However, it was exactly this principle that yielded immense disparities in civil society. Modern economic relations multiplied desires and their satisfaction. Needs were dominated by the 'opinion' of needs, which meant that specialised luxuries became ever more necessary. Skills, desires and commodities were increasingly refined. The craving for a 'comfortable' life gave rise to inexhaustible improvements.[98] As luxury spread, the diversity of fortunes expanded, and poverty became a systemic problem. The relative proximity of rich and poor, observable among the more frugal societies of the ancients, gave way to 'boundless extravagance' and dispiriting 'deprivation.'[99] The resulting struggle had to be moderated and conducted toward the common good.

Progress in this direction was both a social and political task. Social improvement fell to public administration or, in Hegel's language, to the activities of 'police'. Public works and economic regulations came within the ambit of this police function. Fire safety measures, street-lighting, the price of necessities and public health were likewise part of its remit.[100] So also were questions of individual welfare. This Hegelian concession was a massive departure from Kant. Civil society was charged with indemnifying rights, but also with promoting well-being. The system of right, Hegel insisted, could result in harm.[101] Markets

97. Ibid., §49A.

98. Ibid., §§190, 190R, 190A, 191, 191A

99. Ibid., §185A.

100. Ibid., §236A. Cf. G.W.F. Hegel, *Philosophie des Rechts: Die Vorlesung von 1819/20*, ed. Dieter Henrich (Frankfurt am Main: Suhrkamp, 1983), p. 187.

101. Hegel, *Philosophy of Right*, §232.

needed security to ensure property and prosperity, yet their interests should be subordinated to public utility. It followed that adverse effects stood in need of correction. Hegel was clear that this should be a matter not for charitable donations, but for impersonal public oversight.[102] Equally, corporations could play a role in protecting against hardship.[103] Even so, poverty was a concern for civil society in general: 'I have a right to demand that [...] my particular welfare should be promoted.'[104] The economy stood over its participants as an 'immense power'.[105] As a result, individual agents dependent on its opportunities had claims on its resources. Redress would never eliminate inequality, but at least poverty could plead injustice.

In the midst of an elaborate division of labour together with ineliminable social differences, Hegel thought that politics should play an integrating role. However, attempts since the French Revolution had largely failed in the endeavour. This started with a sort of bogus return to the ancients. That included imposing the language of Greek political ideas on the edifice of the modern state. Debate revolved around the merits of democracy and aristocracy, as if these concepts had any purchase on existing conditions. Ancient political communities exhibited what Hegel termed 'substantial' unity.[106] Political coherence was based on patriotic allegiance. The resulting cohesion was embodied in the 'many' or the 'few', giving rise to democracy or aristocracy. In either case consensus was enabled by public virtue, or the active desire to serve the common good.

102. Ibid., §242A.
103. Ibid., §253R.
104. Ibid., §229.
105. Ibid., §238A.
106. Ibid., §273R.

This desire was absent in the context of the modern state where 'the forces of developed particularity' were in play.[107] The struggle between competing interests had to be managed through political structures. For this to occur, the relevant branches of government had to perform their appropriate functions.

In the absence of harmony, 'an incipient divergence between public power and private interest' would appear, imperilling the integrity of the state.[108] To offset the threat, legislative and executive power would have to be streamlined, thereby avoiding the great defect in constitutional organisation that maimed the French Revolution from the start.[109] To begin with, the fallacy in the equation of the *vox populi* with the *vox dei* would have to be exposed. The people were the origin of legitimacy in Hegel, but equally a source of potentially destructive power. To avoid a collision of opinions, and the ensuing political mayhem, effective decision-making would have to be rooted in ministerial judgement, supported by a qualified bureaucracy. However, equally, the actions of the government would have to reflect the preferences represented by an assembly of estates. The insights of delegates were essential for ascertaining the popular will— or, in Hegel's phrase, 'the subjective consciousness of the people'.[110] Representatives should perform a critical function, holding the executive to account. But they should also compose a mediating organ, relaying the attitudes of society. In order to live up to that task, the assembly ought to be populated not by

107. Ibid.
108. Ibid.
109. G.W.F. Hegel, 'Nachschrift Heinrich Gustav Hotho, Wintersemester 1822/23', in *Vorlesungen über die Philosophie des Rechts 2: Nachschriften zu den Kollegien der Jahre 1821/22 und 1822/23*, ed. Klaus Grotsch (*Gesammelte Werke 26.2*) (Hamburg: Felix Meiner Verlag, 2015), p. 1009.
110. Hegel, *Philosophy of Right*, §301A.

an aggregate of delegates, but by deputies from 'circles' of interest organised into corporations. The alternative was the sovereignty of a 'formless mass'—'elemental, irrational, barbarous and terrifying'.[111] For Hegel, the French Revolution had unleashed this brand of malevolent energy. The resulting fallout was not a model for imitation, but a lesson in what to avoid.

111. Ibid., §303R.

PART III

The History of
Political Thought

Introduction

AS WE HAVE SEEN, Hegel aimed to justify constitutional government as a solution to the conflicts of feudal monarchy that
had plagued Europe from roughly the eighth to the seventeenth
century. In broad terms, this development included the impact
of the Reformation as a response to the moral decline of Christianity. The Enlightenment then introduced the spirit of criticism while accelerating the demise of the society of orders and
the advance of a style of politics based on principle. This meant
that merit, competence and accountability replaced entitlement, deference and privilege. The transition, we saw, was the
work of a lengthy struggle, not the product of a single revolutionary episode. In many ways, Hegel's account encapsulated
the basic norms that characterise modern society. His ruling
concepts are now an integral part of contemporary analysis.
In fact, viewed in the round, Hegel's scheme was more nuanced than the garbled imitations that persisted into the following centuries. For this reason, part of the value of Hegel's

contribution to political thought lies in the precision with which he depicted the practical contexts in which any assessment of constitutional monarchy ought to be conducted.

However, equally, the fact is that we no longer live under constitutional monarchies of the kind familiar in the period prior to 1848. To begin with, the expansion of the electoral franchise from the late nineteenth century further altered the shape of modern political organisation. Other important changes were to follow: the relative decline of Europe in international influence, the corresponding loss of overseas empires, the rise and fall of communism, the eruption of National Socialism, and a revolution in relations between the sexes. Nonetheless, Hegel's assumptions have more in common with current beliefs than with the worldviews of the ancients. As he famously put it, modern conditions presupposed that all were free. This marked not only a seismic shift but also an epochal achievement. The recognition of universal humanity separates us categorically from the archaic regimes of the Egyptians and Assyrians, but also from the age of Plato. For Hegel, this raised the question of whether antiquity could in any sense speak for us. He concluded that nostalgia for a departed world was misplaced, and that a renaissance of its values was incoherent. As he argued in 1817, 'there is nothing so irrational as for us to have recourse for our constitutions to those of the Greeks and Romans'.[1] In this vein, he observed that many of the great names of recent history had pined for the classical world out of a craving for better times. Somewhat unfairly, he associated Rousseau with the genre. But the impulse, he concluded,

---

1. G.W.F. Hegel, *Lectures on Natural Right and Political Science: The First Philosophy of Right*, ed. and trans. J. Michael Stewart and Peter C. Hodgson (Oxford: Oxford University Press, 2012), §135A.

was a 'mistake' (*Irrtum*).[2] Hegel accepted the need to understand how earlier civilisations had formed us, but not the view that they should guide us through our own peculiar problems. Related but different issues surround the revival of Hegel himself. In the next chapter, I set out how attempts were made to revitalise his significance, stretching from Wilhelm Dilthey to Georg Lukács. I then show how these efforts at resuscitation were followed by a sudden turnaround. After the Second World War, Hegel's fortunes sharply declined. The ground for disparagement had been laid by Heidegger and the Frankfurt School. Then, substantially under the influence of Karl Popper, Hegel became synonymous with a tyrannical brand of nationalism. In their different ways, both the attempt to revive and the effort to deride raised the question of what was living in the philosopher's surviving corpus. Needless to say, that issue is still with us. As Marx phrased it, 'How do we stand as regards the Hegelian *dialectic*?'[3] By this he meant the overarching Hegelian vision rather than just Hegel's method of proceeding. The question reminds us of the constant need to estimate the differences between prevailing conditions and arrangements in the past. Among other things, political theory is a study in how values become superannuated.

A residue might be just dross, or a significant survival, or even a new fact that wears the appearance of being antiquated. In any event, to play a constructive role in politics a remainder from the past needs to enjoy real currency. If aspirations lose

2. G.W.F. Hegel, *Vorlesungen über die Philosophie der Weltgeschichte*, ed. Georg Lasson, 4 vols (Felix Meiner Verlag, 1923), 3, p. 640.

3. Karl Marx, 'Critique of the Hegelian Dialectic and Philosophy as a Whole', in *Economic and Philosophical Manuscripts of 1844*, in Karl Marx and Friedrich Engels, *Collected Works*, 50 vols (London: Lawrence & Wishart, 1975–2004), 3, p. 327.

their relevance they forfeit their purchase on affairs. Despite this, the aim of reconstituting aspects of ancient societies gained momentum in the decades following the Second World War. In the 1950s, Leo Strauss, Eric Voegelin and Hannah Arendt turned to the classics as a means of recuperating lost value. But these exercises in regeneration did not go unchallenged. In the 1960s the study of the history of political thought was re-energised. At that point, the historicity of canonical thinkers became the norm in interpretation. That approach was spearheaded by what is now called the 'Cambridge School.' Under the influence of J.G.A. Pocock, John Dunn and Quentin Skinner the notion of simply applying traditional theories to current problems was made to look procrustean and naïve. However, the challenge soon rebounded on the proponents of historicism. Having insisted on locating political philosophers in their contexts, the Cantabrigians were asked to justify the pertinence of their findings. In response, the historicists divided into moralists and realists. Once more, relations between philosophy and history became befuddled.

While moralists resorted to the great texts in search of treasure, realists rebelled against the Kantian tradition and its claims to abstract moral truth. What both sides ignored was the Hegelian critique of the moral point of view. In contrast to Adorno and his disciples, for Hegel critique was not a straightforward exercise in negation. The moral outlook adopted a viewpoint outside history: instrumental reasoning was completely severed from normative evaluation. Yet post-Kantian philosophy could not just abolish this integral part of its inheritance. Conscientious dissent needs to be explained instead of fancifully expunged. In Hegel's mind, Kantian morality and the French Revolution were products of the same forces. They were created by a spirit of opposition to a present convicted of malevolence and exploitation. Two responses followed: on the one hand, resistance bred an attitude of blind outrage; on the other, it fostered withdrawal into purity of intention. Both mindsets therefore shunned practical means of improvement. Hegel has no recipe for curing all our woes. Nonetheless, he sat at the beginning of our age and showed that the only antidote to disaffection lay with values actually to hand.

7

Hegel's Plato

JOHN RAWLS DESCRIBED his philosophical method in 1993 as dependent on the study of past 'exemplars' of the discipline. He focused on the outstanding texts of the tradition. The approach he followed involved two rules of thumb. First, he interpreted the relevant works from the thinker's point of view. Second, he assumed the coherence of the body of thought he was trying to reconstruct. In both cases, his aim as an interpreter was to understand rather than contradict. He cited R. G. Collingwood as an inspiration for this procedure. As Collingwood had argued, philosophy did not study one single problem with a range of solutions. Rather, it was concerned with the history of different problems. Yet, while Rawls agreed with Collingwood that past thinkers had posed a series of distinct questions, he also thought that philosophy as a whole addressed a single issue. 'I saw each writer contributing to the development of doctrines supporting democratic thought,' Rawls confided.[1] From this perspective,

1. John Rawls, 'Some Remarks about My Teaching', cited in the 'Editor's Foreword' to *Lectures on the History of Political Philosophy*, ed. Samuel Freeman (Cambridge, MA: Harvard University Press, 2007), p. xiii. Rawls is referring to R. G. Collingwood, *An Autobiography* (Oxford: Clarendon Press, 1939), p. 62.

thinkers built constructively on the ideas of predecessors, progressively leading to a better grasp of basic norms. Philosophy, in this way, could correct what came before. To that extent it was similar to natural science. Even moral philosophy, Rawls assumed, had developed ever better theories. Rousseau, for example, had improved upon Locke.

Rawls indicated that it was Kant who had most clearly formulated this conception. In the *Critique of Pure Reason*, Kant had argued that one could not philosophise in a vacuum. One had to begin with 'certain experiments that come to hand'. By 'experiments' he meant past attempts. Philosophy began as reflection on earlier philosophers. However, this did not mean that latecomers were somehow bound by their forerunners. On the contrary, they moved forward equipped with rational 'principles' that served to confirm or deny the claims of predecessors.[2] Rawls therefore accepted, following Kant, that philosophy was essentially critical in nature. Each generation was in a position to improve on its precursors. Kant himself was committed to a final form of philosophy. In the 'Preface' to the *Metaphysics of Morals*, he conceded that there had been numerous philosophical projects, 'each of which made its contribution to present-day philosophy'. Yet this did not mean there existed a plurality of well-founded systems. There was, Kant argued, 'only one human reason'. Consequently, there was only 'one true system of philosophy from principles', and this was the critical system as adumbrated by Kant. The same idea was applicable to his conception of morality: 'there is', Kant claimed, 'only one virtue and one doctrine of virtue, that

---

2. Immanuel Kant, *Critique of Pure Reason* (1781), ed. and trans. Paul Guyer and Allen W. Wood (Cambridge: Cambridge University Press, 1998), A838/B866.

is, a single system that connects all duties of virtue by one principle'.[3]

Kant had a clear-sighted view of how he could draw upon earlier thinkers whilst improving on the systems they had constructed. For instance, he thought of Plato as an exemplar beyond whom he had advanced. In the *Critique of Pure Reason*, Kant pointed to the 'ideas' developed in Plato's *Republic* as a resource on which he had drawn but also enhanced. He dismissed the common notion presented in Johann Jakob Brucker's authoritative history, the *Historia critica philosophiae*, to the effect that Plato's work was no more than a 'dream of perfection that can have its place only in the idle thinker's brain'.[4] According to Kant, Plato had in truth done philosophy a service by arguing that rulers had to be guided by moral precepts and that philosophers were needed to supply them. Whilst the paternalistic character of Plato's city was remote from the model republic that Kant defended, it was still right that a political system should be based upon an 'archetype' whose validity was not a function of circumstance. The relevant archetype in Kant's case was an 'ideal' under which the freedom of all was compatible with the maximal freedom of each. As Kant saw it, Plato was valuable on account of his insight that ideals were necessary to politics. From this perspective, a norm was not a concept based on experience, but a value that transcended happenstance.[5] Without such values political justice was nothing but a matter of preference.

3. Immanuel Kant, *The Metaphysics of Morals*, ed. Lara Denis, trans. Mary Gregor (Cambridge: Cambridge University Press, 2017), AA 6: 207.

4. Kant, *Critique of Pure Reason*, A316/B371, thinking of Johann Jakob Brucker, *Historia critica philosophiae*, 5 vols (Leipzig: Breitkopf, 1742–44)1, p. 726.

5. Kant, *Critique of Pure Reason*, A317/B373.

It follows that ethical and political judgement for Kant were based on reason. This was not an obscure but a transparent, if vulnerable, faculty. Its conclusions were evident to common understanding.[6] It might take an endless stretch of time to render justice practicable, but its principles as such were always available to pure insight. The problem for moral philosophy was not accessing normative principles, but applying them honestly. Moral corruption was endemic to social relations. A propensity to rationalise conduct in the service of selfish ends was a recognisable part of human behaviour. Nonetheless, the content of the laws of duty was always immediately to hand thanks to the ceaseless prescriptions issued by practical reason.[7] This meant that rational norms could always in some sense be recovered. Kant made use here of the Platonic notion of recollection.[8] In the *Meno*, Socrates declared that 'there is no such thing as teaching [δίδαξις], only recollection [ἀνάμνησις]'.[9] Kant updated Plato's claim to justify his own point. He adopted recollection as another name for philosophy. It became, in effect, a metaphor for rational insight. Yet despite arming himself with a revamped concept of recollection, Kant could not explain why Plato had missed the truth. For Kant, Plato had developed valuable intuitions, yet all of them somehow fell short. He was in a position to recollect justice, yet somehow mistook its substance. Kant could not account for his predecessor's deficiency. As he saw it, Plato might in principle have lighted upon a modern understanding of

6. Immanuel Kant, *Groundwork of the Metaphysics of Morals* (1785), ed. and trans. Mary Gregor and Jens Timmerman (Cambridge: Cambridge University Press, 2012), AA 4: 391.

7. Ibid., 4: 405.

8. Kant, *Critique of Pure Reason*, A313/B370.

9. Plato, *Meno*, 82a1–2.

rights, but inexplicably missed the target and settled for a paternalistic state.

Hegel also believed that '[p]hilosophy can only arise in connection with previous philosophy'.[10] At the same time, he thought that he could better explain the content of Plato's thought, beginning with his conception of recollection. Like Kant, he adapted the idea to his own purposes. For Hegel, to recollect was neither to recall nor to philosophise. Its meaning was to be found in the German word's etymology. *Erinnerung* (remembrance) implies a 'going within oneself', a turning inwards to reflect.[11] For Hegel, this process involved the critical scrutiny of concepts, the subjection of experience to self-wrought standards of judgement. Hegel also thought that this process was dynamic, not static. He believed that every intellectual discovery had its time: 'it would be inept if, in the present day, we sought to make the Platonic philosophy into the philosophy of our own time'.[12] Philosophy was therefore not immediate recollection, but the critical reconstruction of past thought. For that reason, philosophical analysis had to involve historical reasoning too. This put some distance between past and present experience and obliged the investigator to explain the meaning of the divergence between the two. Once more, the role of Plato's *Republic* in the history of philosophy was used to exemplify Hegel's conception of the right procedure. Herder's philosophy of history had helped him formulate his approach by its emphasis on the integrity and specificity of historical

10. G.W.F. Hegel, *Lectures on the History of Philosophy*, ed. and trans. E. S. Haldane and Frances H. Simson, 3 vols (Lincoln, NE: University of Nebraska Press, 1995), 1, pp. 3–4.

11. G.W.F. Hegel, *Lectures on the History of Philosophy, 1825–6*, ed. and trans. Robert F. Brown, 3 vols (Oxford: Oxford University Press, 2006), 1, p. 188.

12. Ibid., pp. 136, 58.

experience.[13] At the same time, Hegel was more reconciled to
the attributes of the modern state. He accepted that there had
been tangible improvements since the Greeks. Modern constitutional monarchy marked a clear advance. Hegel's reading of
Plato should be situated in this context. Like Kant, he rejected
the idea that the *Republic* was a kind of chimera: 'his ideal is not
to be taken in that sense'.[14] This was not because he thought
Plato's ideas were directly enlightening, but because he believed
that his conception of a legitimate polis was rooted in the particularities of Athenian culture.

II

The role of Plato in Hegel's account of the history of philosophy
was so crucial that a synoptic analysis of the *Republic* appeared
in the 'Preface' to the *Philosophy of Right*. Plato's dialogue, Hegel
noted, was standardly seen as a byword for empty idealism,
whereas in fact it was a distillation of the foundations of Greek
ethics. In the same spirit, Eduard Gans had noted in his lectures
on natural right that the shortcomings of the Platonic state were
nothing other than the deficiencies of the Greek polis.[15] Hegel
contended that the genius of Plato lay in his ability to recognise
that the ancient approach, embodied in the notion of ethical
life, was being challenged at the time by an insurgent value embodied in the principle of morality. Hegel's generic term for this

13. Johann Gottfried von Herder, 'This Too a Philosophy for the Formation of
Humanity: A Contribution to Many Contributions of the Century', in *Philosophical
Writings*, ed. and trans. Michael N. Forster (Cambridge: Cambridge University Press,
2002), p. 299.

14. Hegel, *History of Philosophy, 1825–6*, 1, p. 218.

15. Eduard Gans, *Naturrecht und Universalrechtsgeschichte*, ed. Manfred Riedel
(Stuttgart: Klett-Cotta, 1981), p. 34.

principle was 'subjectivity', the idiosyncratic assertion of right based on internal standards of judgement.[16] He saw this quasi-individualism as rooted in the rise of Athenian 'selfishness' (*Selbstsucht*).[17] Since this entailed the destruction of the habitual life of the polis, Plato sought to undermine its force by appeal to 'a *world beyond*' (eines *Jenseitigen*).[18] This appeal would acquire a new significance under the impact of Christianity, but with Plato the search for a criterion that transcended prevailing customs led to the construction of a system of constitutional authority legitimised in terms of a 'higher' pattern. Since in truth this superior norm was nothing other than reason itself, Plato in effect made use of the very precept he wished to challenge. To secure the credibility of ideas of reason, he anchored them in a transcendent order beyond the realm of shadows. The resulting intellectual scheme underpinned his system of philosophical rule. Hegel believed that the system violated a sacred human value: it muffled 'free infinite personality'. However, by implication, Plato also recognised the significance of the value he sought to deny. For this reason, he grasped the decisive importance of the very 'pivot' on which 'the impending world revolution turned'.[19]

The approaching revolution, on Hegel's account, would combine the Roman concept of abstract right with the Christian principle of conscientious morality. Both doctrines were 'implicit' in the Sophistic idea that the human being was the measure

16. Hegel, *History of Philosophy, 1825–6*, 1, p. 121.

17. G.W.F. Hegel, 'Vorlesungsnachschrift, K. G. v. Griesheim, 1824–5', in *Vorlesungen über Rechtsphilosophie, 1818–1831*, ed. Karl-Heinz Ilting, 4 vols (Stuttgart: Frommann-Holzboog, 1973–74), 4, p. 478.

18. G.W.F. Hegel, *Elements of the Philosophy of Right* (1821), ed. Allen W. Wood, trans. H. B. Nisbet (Cambridge: Cambridge University Press, 1991), p. 20.

19. Ibid.

of all things.[20] On Hegel's analysis, this notion was duly absorbed by Socrates, for whom it formed the basis of his theory of morals. Socratic morality strove to find a universal measure among the diversity of opinions. In the process of searching, Socrates gave vent to the Sophistic ideal of subjectivity, further undermining the integrity of unconscious ethical life. It was no longer enough simply to be good; one also had to know, and personally approve, what the good was. The consciousness of morality as such had emerged, triggering a dangerous moment in human history. As Hegel wrote, 'Through the free choice of my deciding for the good I gain the consciousness of my excellence.'[21] With this awareness, the individual sense of duty bordered on moral conceit. According to Hegel's interpretation, Plato at once reflected and challenged this cultural turn. To comprehend the *Republic* was to fathom this shift. By studying the work, we would arrive at a better understanding of ourselves as we figured out the significance of the world revolution that Hegel had identified. Plato now appeared as part of our context, but not identical with our context. Philosophical history could only hope to instruct by appreciating the difference between the two.

Hegel put considerable effort into illuminating Plato's specific context, but also into ascertaining the relationship between the Platonic situation and his own. By Hegel's reckoning, from the Homeric period onwards, a delight in individual self-assertion was an essential characteristic of the Greeks. This was

20. The thesis is associated with Protagoras by Diogenes Laertius, *Lives of Eminent Philosophers*, trans. R. D. Hicks, 2 vols (Cambridge, MA: Harvard University Press, 1925), 2 (Loeb Classical Library 185), pp. 462–63. For Hegel's discussion of it, see his *History of Philosophy, 1825–6*, 1, p. 121.

21. Hegel, *History of Philosophy, 1825–6*, 1, p. 139.

based on an 'exhilarating sense of personality', which manifested itself in the inclination to gain distinction by displaying
one's powers. This tendency explained the attraction to athletic
games as much as the proclivity to idealise the human form
in art.[22] In due course, Hegel thought, this plastic impulse
aligned itself with the democratic constitution of the Athenians. The impulse itself expressed a devotion to freedom—to
independence from labour and need.[23] That commitment was
likewise illustrated by the turn to legislation which appeared in
the age of Solon. The active, dynamic, self-shaping individual
became an integrated part of the community, a citizen dedicated to beauty.[24] Yet while individuality was prized, eccentric-
ity was not. Citizenship was bolstered by the operation of
'virtue'—the principle of democracy, as Montesquieu had argued.[25] Accordingly, the commonwealth enjoyed priority over
particular interests; the individual will of the citizen embodied
the objective will of the state. As Hegel put it in an early version
of his philosophy of spirit, '[t]he Platonic republic is, like the
Lacedaemonian state, [characterised by] this disappearance of
self-knowing individuality'.[26] Under such conditions, abstract
volition did not exist, and autonomy remained under-developed.
For this reason, oracles played an essential role in processes of

22. G.W.F. Hegel, *Vorlesungen über die Philosophie der Weltgeschichte 4: Nachschriften zum Kolleg des Wintersemesters, 1830/31*, ed. Walter Jaeschke (*Gesammelte
Werke* 27.4) (Hamburg: Felix Meiner Verlag, 2020), p. 1350.
23. G.W.F. Hegel, *Vorlesungen über die Philosophie der Weltgeschichte 1: Nachschriften zum Kolleg des Wintersemesters, 1822/23*, ed. Bernadette Collenberg-Plotnikov
(*Gesammelte Werke* 27.1) (Hamburg: Felix Meiner Verlag, 2015), p. 303.
24. Hegel, *Philosophie der Weltgeschichte, 1830/31*, p. 1366.
25. Ibid., p. 1352.
26. G.W.F. Hegel, *Jenaer Systementwürfe 3: Naturphilosophie und Philosophie des
Geistes*, ed. Rolf-Peter Horstmann (Hamburg: Felix Meiner Verlag, 1987), p. 240.

decision-making.[27] Conscience, in the modern sense, had yet to evolve. Hegel's claim was that Plato's republic still represented a moment in history in which duty was synonymous with the demands of public life.

This compatibility, as captured by Plato, presented the substance of ethical life 'in its ideal of *beauty* and *truth*'.[28] The analogy in the *Republic* between the soul and the city perfectly encapsulated this paradigmatic harmony.[29] However, that pleasing fit was compromised in the era of Periclean Athens by the emergent forces of 'subjective freedom' already analysed. Hegel contended that, in reaction, Plato sought to limit the influence of individuality by encroaching upon private property and the family, and assigning roles to the population by courtesy of authority: 'the allocation of individuals to specific estates was left to the rulers'.[30] Hegel argued that in this way Plato made everything, including education, rely upon government. As a result, the coherence of the state depended on public virtue, in contradistinction to the modern emphasis on individual will.[31] Given this contrast, any attempt at a 'renaissance' made no sense to Hegel.[32] The hierarchical classification of types of person that underpinned ancient political organisation—in China, India and Egypt alike—was residually apparent in Plato's

27. Hegel, *Philosophie der Weltgeschichte, 1822/23*, p. 318; Hegel, *Philosophie der Weltgeschichte: 1830/31*, p. 1356.

28. Hegel, *Philosophy of Right*, §185R. Cf. G.W.F. Hegel, 'Die "Rechtsphilosophie" von 1820, mit Hegels Vorlesungsnotizien, 1821–1825', in *Vorlesungen über Rechtsphilosophie, 1818–1831*, 2, p. 635.

29. Hegel, *Philosophie der Weltgeschichte, 1822/23*, p. 351.

30. Hegel, *Philosophy of Right*, §§185R, 206R, 262A.

31. Hegel, *Philosophie der Weltgeschichte, 1830/31*, p. 1564.

32. Hegel was for this reason critical of the Renaissance itself. See Hegel, *History of Philosophy, 1825–6*, 3, pp. 57ff.

theory of the state, according to Hegel. The only difference was that Plato's distinctions were determined by the conscious will of the rulers rather than by nature.[33]

Nonetheless, given the distribution of classes into castes, the ideas of the ancients could not be revived. The Platonic and Aristotelian systems, much like the Stoic and Epicurean schools, could never be simply 're-awoken' (*wiedererweckt werden*).[34] Having said that, neither were they completely dormant. Hegel regarded the history of philosophy as an integral part of the system of philosophy.[35] We had to think in the present, he was suggesting, yet the material that formed the basis for our ideas was derived from the past.[36] Past norms examined through philosophical activity could not be reanimated, but neither was it possible wholly to dispense with them. They were not lifeless deposits, but superseded values.[37] Despite this supersession, they had shaped the course of what followed, and so retained significance as a vibrant element of world culture. Contemporary conditions were not intelligible without a grasp of the historical process that brought them into being.

33. G.W.F. Hegel, *Lectures on the Philosophy of World History: Manuscripts of the Introduction and the Lectures of 1822–3*, ed. and trans. Robert F. Brown and Peter C. Hodgson, with William G. Geuss (Oxford: Clarendon Press, 2011), p. 258.

34. G.W.F. Hegel, *Vorlesungen über die Geschichte der Philosophie 1*, vol. 18 in *Werke*, ed. Eva Moldenhauer and Karl Markus Michel, 21 vols (Frankfurt: Suhrkamp, 1986), p. 65.

35. Hegel, *History of Philosophy, 1825–6*, 1, p. 55.

36. On philosophising with past philosophers, see Robert Pippin, *Hegel's Practical Philosophy: Rational Agency as Ethical Life* (Cambridge: Cambridge University Press, 2008), p. 33n; John McDowell, *Having the World in View: Essays on Kant, Hegel, and Sellars* (Cambridge, MA: Harvard University Press, 2009), p. 3.

37. Hegel, *History of Philosophy, 1825–6*, 1, p. 62.

III

The Platonic state was rooted in Greek ethical life, in whose shadow modern history was still evolving. Yet for Hegel this residual fallout did not justify attempts to resuscitate antiquated values. The job of philosophy was not to rejuvenate the ancient city-state, but to understand the prospects for modern political life. This aspect of Hegel's thought became a focus of twentieth-century debate. Following a renaissance in Hegel studies at the start of the last century, the future of the nation-state became a matter of controversy. Hegel's own political philosophy was drawn into the discussion. This came on the back of existing arguments about the relevance of Hegel to what some saw as a post-rationalist age. It is well known that his teaching spawned opposing strands of Hegelianism as soon as his ideas began to be disseminated.[38] This raised the issue of whether the original doctrine was pertinent to later generations. It posed the question, in Croce's phrase, of what was still 'living' in the philosophy of Hegel.[39] One of the founders, along with Michel Foucault and Gilles Deleuze, of the Philosophy Department at the University of Vincennes argued in 1968 that 'Hegel [. . .] is *our* Plato'.[40] But if the Platonic state was outmoded in Hegel's eyes, it seems right to wonder whether his own ideas are not equally outdated. The Hegel revival began in Germany with Dilthey, Windelband and

38. Jacques D'Hont, 'Hegel et les socialistes', *La Pensée* 157 (May–June 1971), pp. 3–25; John Toews, *Hegelianism: Path to Dialectical Humanism, 1805–1841* (Cambridge: Cambridge University Press, 1980); Douglas Moggach, ed., *The New Hegelians: Politics and Philosophy in the Hegelian School* (Cambridge: Cambridge University Press, 2006).

39. Benedetto Croce, *What Is Living and What Is Dead in the Philosophy of Hegel*, trans. Douglas Ainslie (London: Macmillan, 1915).

40. François Chatelet, *Hegel* (Paris: Éditions du Seuil, 1968), p. 13.

Herman Nohl.[41] It involved relegating Hegel's system of logic to the margins of his philosophy and emphasising an allegedly mystical strain that spoke to current needs. Gans reported Goethe's observation that Hegel's ideas would be subject to continuous modification.[42] By the early twentieth century, the adjustment took the form of separating Hegel's account of objective spirit from its architectonic structure. As Karl Löwith would observe on the eve of the Second World War, the speculative system was jettisoned with the purpose of engineering a refurbishment that would better chime with contemporary life.[43]

Among the most significant contributions to the revival was Dilthey's work on the youthful career of Hegel. This helped to foster the identification of Hegelianism with strands of *Lebensphilosophie*. The early Hegel was taken to have championed the value of multiplicity in unity through the experience of 'life' as an immediate totality.[44] The achievement of Dilthey's book did not only lie in its fresh focus on the philosopher's supposed mystical pantheism, however, but

41. Wilhelm Windelband, 'Die Erneuerung des Hegelianismus' (1910), in *Präludien: Aufsätze und Reden zur Philosophie und Ihrer Geschichte*, 2 vols (Tübingen: Mohr, 1915), 1, pp. 273–89; Heinrich Levy, *Die Hegel-Renaissance in der deutschen Philosophie* (Berlin: Pan-Verlag, 1927).

42. J. W. von Goethe, *Gespräche*, ed. Woldemar von Biedermann, 5 vols (Leipzig: Biedermann, 1909–11), 3, p. 426.

43. Karl Löwith, *From Hegel to Nietzsche: The Revolution in Nineteenth-Century Thought* (1941), trans. David E. Green (London: Constable, 1964), pp. 121ff.

44. Wilhelm Dilthey, *Die Jugendgeschichte Hegels* (1906), ed. Herman Nohl, in *Gesammelte Schriften*, 26 vols (Göttingen: Vandenhoeck & Ruprecht, 1914–2006), 4 (1959), pp. 141ff. The impact of Dilthey's interpretation can be seen alike in Richard Kroner, *Von Kant bis Hegel*, 2 vols (Tübingen: J.C.B. Mohr, 1921–24), 2, p. 145, and Herbert Marcuse, *Hegels Ontologie und die Theorie der Geschichtlichkeit* (Frankfurt am Main: Vittorio Klostermann Verlag, 1932), part 2, passim.

also in its new approach to scholarship in general.[45] As with his earlier work on Schleiermacher, Dilthey believed that he could illuminate the age by deepening his readers' appreciation of one of its leading figures. This was achieved by extensive use of available manuscript sources. The new material revealed less a rigidly fixed thinker than a developmental process that formed the basis for a 'cultural history' of Hegel.[46] Although Meinecke had studied at the University of Berlin while Dilthey held a professorship there, the elder historian was not a decisive force in his education. It was only later that Meinecke realised the value of the genetic method pioneered by his teacher. Before Dilthey, for instance in Ranke, ideas in history were treated as indeterminate entities whose influence on affairs was abstractly conceived.[47] With Dilthey and Meinecke, thought was traced to individual thinkers and contextualised with reference to their wider experiences.[48] Meinecke in particular combined this approach with the study of political events: he enriched 'intellectual history' with 'historico-political materials'.[49] In his first important contribution to *Ideengeschichte*, his subject was the role of Prussia in the pursuit of German unification. Hegel occupied a central place in the unfolding narrative.

45. Dilthey, *Die Jugendgeschichte Hegels*, pp. 36ff.

46. Ibid., p. 3.

47. Leopold von Ranke, *Epochen der neueren Geschichte: Vorträge dem Konige Maximilian II. von Bayern im Herbst 1854 zu Berchtesgaden Gehalten* (Leipzig: Duncker & Humblot, 1906).

48. Frederick Beiser, *The German Historicist Tradition* (Oxford: Oxford University Press, 2011), ch. 8.

49. Friedrich Meinecke, 'Preface to the Second Edition' (1911), in *Cosmopolitanism and the National State* (1907), trans. Robert B. Kimber (Princeton, NJ: Princeton University Press, 1970), p. 3.

Before the First World War, Meinecke had set out to justify the statesmanship of Bismarck in securing German unity thanks to Prussian power. In his classic work *Cosmopolitanism and the National State*, he traced the path towards this consummation from the more diffuse humanitarian ideals articulated by figures such as Humboldt in the 1790s.[50] On Meinecke's account, the aspiration to advance universal morality through the agency of culture had gradually been reconciled with power politics in the wake of 1848 and 1866 in Germany. By the turn of the century, his expectation was that the Prussian regime would be fully integrated with the German Reich and that, in the process, the forces of agrarianism and militarism could be reconciled with the social-democratic as well as liberal elements in society.[51] During the First World War, he continued to hope that his published research might offer inspiration in 'troubled times'.[52] The crushing defeat of 1918 prompted reflection on the path along which Germany had travelled, but not on the ideal of nationality itself, nor on the need for politics to promote its realisation.[53] Through all its editions, the main thrust of Meinecke's study remained a celebration of the vocation of the state as an instrument of national will. To the last, he saw the German 'cultural' nation as an essential part of European civilisation.[54] It preserved the features of humanity against rampant egotism. At the same time, it required executive means to ensure its preservation. In his later work, Meinecke emphasised how this resort to power stood in need of moral restraint, although he never

50. Meinecke, *Cosmopolitanism*, pp. 42–43.
51. Ibid., pp. 364 ff.
52. Meinecke, 'Preface to the Third Edition' (1915), in ibid., p. 4.
53. Meinecke, 'Preface to the Fifth Edition' (1918), in ibid., p. 5.
54. Friedrich Meinecke, *Die deutsche Katastrophe: Betrachtungen und Erinnerungen* (Wiesbaden: Eberhard Brockhaus Verlag, 1946).

abandoned the basic ingredients of his analysis.[55] Hegel played a pivotal role in the overarching argument: 'Hegel, Ranke, and Bismarck', Meinecke proposed, 'are the three great liberators of the state.'[56]

From Meinecke's point of view, Hegel contributed two main insights to the understanding of the modern state. The first was an appreciation of its central place in international conflict. The state, for Hegel, was 'the absolute power on *earth*'. He was sceptical about the plausibility of Kantian attempts to dissolve its agency in a federal structure that would guarantee perpetual peace. International obligations were a reality for Hegel, and clearly preferable to naked power. However, they could only ever be stipulated, never juridically enforced: there was, as Hegel put it, no 'praetor' in the international arena, only the reality of opposing 'independent units'.[57] Yet, for Meinecke, Hegel's argument still fell short of recognising the insuperable right of 'historical individualities', insofar as states remained subject to the vicissitudes of world spirit.[58]

Hegel's second insight, as Meinecke gleaned it, was his recognition of the dependence of public authority on the underlying support of national allegiance. The state was not an 'aggregate', but an 'organic' unity.[59] After the dissolution of the Holy Roman Empire, Hegel's idea of German political community encompassed the various entities that survived the

55. Meinecke, 'Preface to the Seventh Edition' (1927), in *Cosmopolitanism*, p. 6. See also Friedrich Meinecke, *Machiavellianism: The Doctrine of Raison d'État and Its Place in Modern History*, trans. Douglas Scott (1924) (New Brunswick, NJ: Transaction Publishers, 1998).

56. Meinecke, *Cosmopolitanism*, p. 197.

57. Hegel, *Philosophy of Right*, §§330A, 331, 333R, 339A.

58. Meinecke, *Cosmopolitanism*, p. 202.

59. Ibid., p. 199; Hegel, *Philosophy of Right*, §258.

process of mediatisation pursued during the Napoleonic period. In each case, Hegel believed, the state ought to be constituted by the 'substantial' will of a people. It could not be effectively based on the arbitrary choice of contracting parties, but only on a commitment that transcended personal interest. The state, for Hegel, was a political union, not an association for mutual protection. However, even though allegiance went beyond abstract agreement, it still involved an investment on the part of self-consciousness. Hegel intended this arrangement to contrast with classical antiquity. For the Greeks, patriotism excluded a developed sense of individuality. By comparison, with the modern state, the 'universal', or the common good, was linked with 'the complete freedom of particularity and the well-being of individuals'. In other words, modern liberty presupposed a regime of rights and personal prosperity.[60]

Meinecke followed Hegel in accepting that modern politics required a dependable alliance between particularity and universality. He was also aware of the forces that militated against that accord. Nonetheless, even during the Weimar era, he was confident that a balance could be preserved. This included collaboration across the branches of government, coordination between the *Länder* and the centre, and harmony among the components that made up society at large. Of course, in 1933, all this would come dramatically unstuck. However, for Meinecke's student Franz Rosenzweig, disintegration had already happened. The shock of fragmentation had registered by the end of the First World War. Originally inspired by the Hegelian renaissance, along with his faith in German Protestant culture, Rosenzweig had completed his dissertation on Hegel before the

---

60. Hegel, *Philosophy of Right*, §§258, 260, 260A.

outbreak of the war.[61] The experience of the next five years transformed his values and ideas. For him, the promise of spiritual renewal held out by the German national struggle terminated in sudden disappointment. Before the crisis, Rosenzweig confessed, it had been possible to look forward to the liberalisation of the German Reich. As first conceived, what became a two-volume study of Hegel was intended as a contribution to opening up the domestic scene to a freer and more cosmopolitan atmosphere via criticism of the rigidities of Hegelian doctrine. The project, however, was overtaken by events as Rosenzweig surveyed a 'field of rubble' where once the Reich had stood.[62] He then discarded political thought in pursuit of fulfilment of an extramundane kind. Instead of state-based nationalism, he held out for a more ethereal ideal of association, a spiritual *Heimat* for the Jewish people.[63]

Rosenzweig's rejection of the Hegelian tradition entailed the abandonment of political philosophy in favour of religious thought.[64] This left the issue of the pertinence of the idealist thinker hanging. It has been said that 'Left' and 'Right' Hegelianism finally confronted one another at the battle of Stalingrad.[65] However, the price of this depiction is extraordinary

---

61. Ferdinand Tönnies's review of Rosenzweig in *Zeitschrift für Politik*, 13: 2 (1923), pp. 172–76, picks up on his debt to Dilthey, but also on more recent editorial work by Hermann Nohl, Georg Lasson and Hermann Heller.

62. Franz Rosenzweig, *Hegel und der Staat* (1920), ed. Frank Lachmann (Frankfurt am Main: Suhrkamp, 2010), p. 18.

63. Peter Gordon, *Rosenzweig and Heidegger: Between Judaism and German Philosophy* (Berkeley, CA: University of California Press, 2003), pp. 115–16.

64. Axel Honneth, 'Das ambivalente Erbe Hegels: Franz Rosenzweig zu Beginn des Jahrhunderts', in *Vivisektionen eines Zeitalters: Porträts zur Ideengeschichte des 20. Jahrhunderts* (Frankfurt am Main: Suhrkamp, 2014).

65. Hajo Holborn, 'The Science of History', in Joseph R. Strayer, ed., *The Interpretation of History* (Princeton, NJ: Princeton University Press, 1943).

simplification. The relevance of past ideas to later circumstances is altogether a more intricate business. Hegel's commentary on the applicability of Plato can help us sharpen our approach to the question. Equally, as Hegel made plain in his own case, we should not rely on philosophers for abstract normative instruction. More generally, he denied that thinkers could offer practical direction. The idea of morality emerged as a disruptive moment in the history of Athenian politics, contributing to the dissolution of the polis. This change marked the ancient world off from modern life. A fateful, epochal revolution severed the universe of the Greeks from the principle of subjectivity that underpinned the modern state. Yet if, according to Hegel, the advent of morality separated ancient from modern conditions, he also believed that contemporary philosophy could not make progress armed with conscience alone. This, then, is the first lesson to be derived from Hegel's thought: although modern politics is grounded on the value of conscientious dissent, public life cannot be sustained by appeal to moral judgement alone.[66] As Hegel put it in the 'Preface' to the *Philosophy of Right*, the job of philosophy is not to issue guidance on how the world ought to be.[67]

IV

Ernst Cassirer claimed that no thinker exerted a greater influence on modern political life than Hegel. His ideas allegedly detonated with explosive force, finding their way from the mainstream into various ideological extremes.[68] This view,

66. Hegel, *Philosophy of Right*, §337R.

67. Ibid., 'Preface' pp. 21, 23.

68. Ernst Cassirer, *The Myth of the State* (New Haven, CT: Yale University Press, 1946), pp. 248, 253. For Cassirer's debt to Hegel, see the preface to his *The Philosophy*

however, was not universally accepted at the time. In the concluding remarks to *Hegel and the State*, Rosenzweig contended that Hegel's 'arc of flight' across the nineteenth century had been truncated. Luther and Goethe enjoyed enduring legacies, but the currency of Hegel did not last.[69] Rosenzweig pondered the relationship between 'thought' and 'deed' as explored in Hölderlin's 1799 ode 'To the Germans'.[70] Unlike Hölderlin's lightning 'flash' from the clouds, Rosenzweig insisted, the germinal Hegelian idea was not directly implemented. There was no clear path leading from the philosopher to unification in 1871. This was largely because—Rosenzweig thought—nation, state and individual were not reconciled in Hegel's work. While he certainly initiated a process, his philosophy was incapable of completing it. The baton had to pass to later thinkers and actors, consigning Hegel's 'state-ideal' to oblivion.[71] With this verdict, the significance of Hegel's theory of the state receded for a generation. By the time it attracted attention again, after the Second World War, it was largely subject to parodic treatment, most famously by Karl Popper. In the interim, the historical, anthropological and social dimensions of Hegel's thought loomed into focus, partly as a consequence of the impact of Marxism.

Highlighting this development, Carl Schmitt recalled in 1932 how Hegel had 'wandered to Moscow via Karl Marx and

---

of *Symbolic Forms*, vol. 2: *Mythical Thought* (New Haven, CT: Yale University Press, 1955). For comment, see Michael Friedman, *A Parting of the Ways: Carnap, Cassirer, and Heidegger* (Chicago: Open Court, 2000), p. 101.

69. Rosenzweig, *Hegel*, p. 526.

70. Friedrich Hölderlin, 'An die Deutschen', in *Sämtliche Werke und Briefe*, ed. Michael Knaupp, 3 vols (Munich: Carl Hanser Verlag, 1992–93), 1, p. 265, which formed an epigraph to the 1920 "Schlußbemerkungen" appended to Rosenzweig's work.

71. Rosenzweig, *Hegel*, p. 18.

Lenin.'[72] For his part, Lenin had turned to the study of Hegel's *Logic* after reading the newly edited Marx–Engels correspondence that appeared in Stuttgart in 1913, but this did not spark a general return to Hegel's writings.[73] Even so, six years before Schmitt's comment, Hermann Heller had made pretty much the same point when he outlined what he took to have been the impact of Hegel on German politics beyond the nineteenth century. While Heller accepted Meinecke's argument that Hegel's theory of the state had proved decisive in moving German nationalism from the age of cosmopolitanism to that of 'blood and steel', he also saw his influence behind the rise of the social democratic movement under the leadership of Ferdinand Lasalle.[74] The most sophisticated appropriation of Hegel following the Russian Revolution was spearheaded by Georg Lukács, who recruited him as an intellectual resource in combating unwanted strands of both orthodox and revisionist Marxism, represented by Bernstein, Kautsky and Mehring.[75] Lukács's recourse to Hegel served a dual purpose. First and foremost, he wanted to deepen the Marxist conception of social alienation. That objective was realised through the concept of

72. Carl Schmitt, *The Concept of the Political* (Chicago: University of Chicago Press, 2007), p. 63.

73. Lenin's 'Philosophical Notebooks' were not published in Russian until 1929–30 and would not appear in German until 1932. See James D. White, 'Lenin and Philosophy: The Historical Context', *Europe-Asia Studies*, 67: 1 (January 2015), pp. 123–42.

74. Hermann Heller, 'Hegel und die deutsche Politik', *Zeitschrift für Politik*, 13 (1924), pp. 132–43. See also Hermann Heller, *Hegel und der nationale Machstaatsgedanke in Deutschland: Ein Beitrag zur politischen Geistesgeschichte* (Leipzig : B. G. Teubner, 1921), and his 'Introduction' and annotations to GW. F. Hegel, *Die Verfassung Deutschlands* (Leipzig: Reclam, 1920).

75. Georg Lukács, *The Destruction of Reason*, trans. Peter R. Palmer (London: Merlin Press, 1980), pp. 548, 557.

reification presented in 1923 in *History and Class Consciousness*. But second, Lukács wished to advance that goal by a reappraisal of Hegel's thought, culminating in the publication of *The Young Hegel* after the Second World War. Although not appearing until 1948, the work had been completed in Moscow a decade earlier. It offered a fundamental reassessment, directed against what the author took to be the distortions that accompanied the Hegel revival, starting with Dilthey.

Up until that point, beginning around 1848, Hegel was commonly associated—in Britain, France and Germany—with what are roughly classed as epistemological questions. Among the British Idealists, this led to constructive philosophical engagement with his thought. This lasted until the generation of Russell and Moore dismissed his holism by attacking what they saw as bogus claims about the 'unreality of separateness'.[76] This filtered into the wider culture as a suspicion of pan-logicism, condemned under the name of 'monism'.[77] But at precisely the same time, Dilthey discovered in the young Hegel a spiritualised conception of 'life' that spoke to a generation of thinkers in search of existential meaning. For some, this brought Hegel into a kind of communion with Kierkegaard who, ironically, had spent his youth rebelling against Hegelian encyclopedism. Jean Wahl exemplified this resort to idealism as a spiritual remedy—as a source less of dialectical truths than of mental satisfaction.[78] At the centre of Wahl's treatment, much like that of Alexandre

76. Bertrand Russell, *A History of Western Philosophy* (New York, Simon and Schuster, 1945), pp. 731–46; Andrew Ushenko, 'The Logics of Hegel and Russell', *Philosophy and Phenomenological Research*, 10: 1 (September 1949), pp. 107–14.

77. W. J. Mander, *British Idealism: A History* (Oxford: Oxford University Press, 2011).

78. Jean Wahl, 'Hegel et Kierkegaard', *Revue philosophique de la France et d'étranger*, 112: 11–12 (November–December 1931), pp. 321–80.

Koyré, lay the travails of the unhappy consciousness, along with the promise of reparation.[79] However, Lukács's Hegel was not so remote from this edifying version, albeit applied to avowedly secular concerns. Appropriately enough, Lukács had been similarly attracted to Kierkegaard before the First World War.[80] Also, along with most participants in the revitalisation of Hegelianism between 1905 and 1945, his attention was largely concentrated on the *Phenomenology of Spirit*. To this extent he followed Marx, who claimed that the *Phenomenology* was 'the true point of origin and the secret of Hegelian philosophy'.[81] Finally, much like later existentialist Hegelians influenced by Koyré, Wahl and Kojève, Lukács saw in Hegel an antidote to the soullessness of modern conditions, variously depicted in the idioms of Weber and Simmel.[82]

By the time *The Young Hegel* was published, Lukács had streamlined his relationship to his subject matter, and separated himself from earlier French and German attempts at revival. French existentialist, no less than the German Idealist, appropriations of Hegel were deemed 'reactionary'. They were inspired by slogans that rose to prominence under the second Reich, which Lukács dubbed the 'age of imperialism'. It was a period, he argued, which fostered forms of 'irrationalism'. According to

---

79. Jean Wahl, *Le Malheur de la conscience dans la philosophie de Hegel* (Paris: Rieder, 1929); Alexandre Koyré, 'Hegel à Iena', *Revue d'histoire et de philosophie religieuses*, 15: 5 (September–October 1935), pp. 420–58.

80. Georg Lukács, 'The Foundering of Form against Life' (1910), in *Soul and Form*, trans. Anna Bostock (London: Merlin Press, 1971).

81. Marx, *Economic and Philosophical Manuscripts*, p. 329.

82. Georg Lukács, *The Theory of the Novel* (1916), trans. Anna Bostock (London: Merlin Press, 1978); Lukács, 'Reification and the Consciousness of the Proletariat', in *History and Class Consciousness* (1923), trans. Rodney Livingstone (London: Merlin Press, 1971).

Lukács, the problem with irrationalism was that it left the mal-
formations of capitalism unexamined and fed into the rise of
National Socialism. His study of Hegel was therefore a kind of
settling of accounts, a means of plotting a forward course for
scientific socialism by criticising pervasive attempts to align the
Phenomenology with conservative strands of romanticism.[83]
This critical endeavour was accompanied by a constructive enterprise. Where Plekhanov had scrapped the Idealist legacy,
Lukács would recuperate its Hegelian incarnation. He began by
contextualising German philosophy in the wake of 1789 in order
to account for its structural deficiencies. But he then proceeded
to extol the dialectical method as the only means of developing
a credible social theory. According to Lukács, Hegel had transcended the limits of his age by cultivating a holistic approach
to social understanding. He achieved this by yoking together
philosophy and economics, viewing each of them as forms of
historical knowledge. This yielded consequential insights: first,
that the individual was mediated by social relations, and second, that consciousness was a product of its own labour.[84] In
Lukács's mind, Marx's achievement derived from the fact that
he deepened and extended these discoveries.[85]

Lukács followed Hegel in categorically differentiating between the ancients and moderns. As a result, while Plato was
no longer an immediate source of instruction, Hegel remained

83. Georg Lukács, 'Preface to the New Edition of 1954', in *The Young Hegel: Studies
in the Relations between Dialectics and Economics*, trans. Rodney Livingstone (London:
Merlin Press, 1975).

84. The ascription of these views to Hegel was first made by Karl Marx in *Economic
and Philosophical Manuscripts*, pp. 332–33.

85. Lukács, *The Young Hegel*, p. 548. It was this thesis that Louis Althusser targeted
in 'Marx's Relation to Hegel', in *Politics and History: Montesquieu, Rousseau, Hegel and
Marx*, trans. Ben Brewster (London: New Left Books, 1972).

a vibrant intellectual presence.[86] This was also the conclusion drawn by Alexandre Kojève in his notorious and widely influential treatment of the struggle between master (*Herr*) and slave (*Knecht*) in Hegel's *Phenomenology*. Having taken over Koyré's teaching responsibilities after his departure for the University of Cairo, Kojève's arguments were first presented in a series of Friday evening seminars delivered between 1933 and 1939 at the École pratique des hautes études in Paris.[87] In one respect, Kojève went beyond Hegel himself: Plato, for him, had been completely surpassed rather than sublated (*aufgehoben*). Kojève grasped that Hegel's subject was universal history, yet he discounted the dynamic connections between its moments. As Hegel saw it, Plato was 'outmoded' but not entirely dissipated: his relevance persisted by virtue of the way in which he had been overcome. For Kojève, on the other hand, Plato had perished: he had been annulled without remainder.[88] In the larger, quasi-Hegelian narrative employed by Kojève to support this thesis, the eclipse of Plato was a consequence of the demise of a pagan-aristocratic ethic and its replacement by the post-Christian homogeneous state founded on the dignity of work. The *Phenomenology* was not, as commonly understood, an expression of Christianity; instead, it was devoted to explaining

86. Lukács, *Theory of the Novel*, p. 36.

87. Dominique Auffret, *Alexandre Kojève: La philosophie, l'état, la fin de l'histoire* (Paris: Grasset, 1990), p. 253; Ethan Kleinberg, *Generation Existentiul: Heidegger's Philosophy in France, 1927–1961* (Ithaca, NY: Cornell University Press, 2005), ch. 2; James H. Nichols, *Alexandre Kojève: Wisdom at he End of History* (Plymouth: Rowan and Littlefield, 2007), ch. 2; Marco Filoni, *Le Philosophe du dimanche: La vie et la pensée d'Alexandre Kojève* (Paris: Gallimard, 2008), p. 16.

88. Alexandre Kojève, *Essai d'une histoire raisonné de la philosophie paienne: Platon et Aristote* (Paris: Gallimard, 1972), pp. 17, 36, 143, 399; Kojève, *Introduction à la lecture de Hegel: Leçons sur la 'Phénoménologie de l'Esprit' professées à l'École des hautes études* (1947), ed. Raymond Queneau (Paris: Gallimard, 1968), p. 332.

religion by means of philosophical anthropology. It revealed the meaning of the Christ-God as the perfection of humanity.[89]

On Kojève's model, the shift from ancient to modern is characterised less by transition than by seismic rupture. At the same time, he presented the historical process in dramatically stylised terms, driven by an anthropological constant—the desire to be desired—and culminating in the post-Revolutionary Napoleonic regime.[90] According to Kojève, Napoleon marked the end of history, because he had successfully created a world in which all were free. The Napoleonic state was 'universal', in the sense that under its authority everyone was equal (*pairs*). But it was also 'homogeneous', insofar as the value pertaining to citizens derived from their intrinsic dignity instead of their particular attachments, whether in terms of class, nation or family. This condition amounted to the final 'satisfaction' of man.[91] However, Kojève's picture depleted the role of politics in Hegel's account. In actual fact, Napoleon was not some kind of climax for Hegel. His individualism approximated an empty world of rights, which the *Philosophy of Right* set out to indict. To this extent, the Kojèvean analysis encapsulated a wider trend. For both the religious and anthropological approaches which grew out of the Hegel renaissance, the actuality of politics played an ever-diminishing role.

In many ways, Kojève's reading of Hegel knowingly fostered a schematic approach. He sometimes described his forays into textual exegesis as deliberately propagandistic. Instead of trying

89. Ibid., pp. 57, 69; Alexandre Kojève, 'Hegel, Marx et le Christianisme', *Critique*, 3–4 (August–September 1946), pp. 339–66.

90. Kojève, *Introduction*, p. 168. For a critical assessment of Kojève's reading of 'desire' in Hegel, see Axel Honneth, *Recognition: A Chapter in the History of European Ideas* (Cambridge: Cambridge University Press, 2021), ch. 2.

91. Kojève, *Introduction*, p. 171.

faithfully to understand his subject, he wanted to put Hegelian philosophy 'to use'.[92] His enterprise, to that extent, was explicitly unhistorical. To achieve his goal, he set about constructing a portable account of Hegel to support a set of judgements about contemporary history. In pursuit of this, he laid aside the logical dimensions of Hegel's thought, consciously departing from the 'monism' of his great precursor.[93] But he also sacrificed the goal of historical depth. After the war, Kojève strove to connect his vision of the world to the structure of international politics. Famously, in 1945, he announced the end of the nation-state, marked by the rise of the Anglo-American and Slavo-Soviet empires along with a projected Franco-Latin alliance.[94] While Kojève expected these rival civilisations to form coherent blocs based on cultural kinship, he also envisaged a gradual ideological convergence that would bring Sino-Russian communism closer to the United States. As he wrote in 1962, 'the Russians and the Chinese are only Americans who are still poorer but are rapidly proceeding to get richer'.[95] This was a truly grandiose prediction—although, as it turned out, it was not demented. But it was not this strain of lofty world-historical projection that influenced the postwar understanding of Hegel. Kojève's lectures in the 1930s were attended by, among others, Raymond Aron, Georges Gurvitch, Jean Hyppolite, Georges

---

92. See his letter to a Vietnamese correspondent from 7 October 1948, reprinted in 'Exchange between Trân Duc Thao and Alexandre Kojève', *Graduate Faculty Philosophy Journal*, 30: 2 (2009), pp. 349–54.

93. Ibid.

94. Alexandre Kojève, 'L'Empire latin: Esquisse d'une doctrine de la politique française' (27 August 1945), translated as 'Outline of a Doctrine of French Policy' (1945), *Policy Review*, 126 (August–September 2004), pp. 3–40.

95. This comment appears as a footnote in the second (1962) edition of Kojève, *Introduction*, pp. 509–11n.

Bataille, Jacques Lacan, Raymond Queneau, Maurice Merleau-Ponty, Éric Weil and Georges Fessard.[96] An article by Kojève on 'Maîtrise et servitude' appeared in 1939, through which Jean-Paul Sartre and Simone de Beauvoir first encountered his work.[97] Under Kojève's influence, the idea that every social relationship could be analysed through the prism of the struggle between *Herr* and *Knecht* gained instant currency. Generalised typology supplanted contextual specificity. The return to Hegel energised existentialism and phenomenology, but it failed to create historically grounded political philosophy.

96. Raymond Aron, *Mémoires: 50 ans de reflexion politique* (Paris: Éditions Juillard, 1983), pp. 55–56.

97. Alexandre Kojève, 'Autonomie et dépendance de la conscience-de-soi: Maitrise et servitude', *Mesures*, 5: 1 (1939).

8

After the Hegel Renaissance

EVEN AS THE HEGEL renaissance blossomed, a strain of far-reaching criticism directed against the foundations of Hegelian Idealism surfaced in the thought of Martin Heidegger. It is true that Heidegger's target was far larger, comprehending the whole tradition of Western metaphysics. This much was plain from his 1927 masterpiece, *Being and Time*, where the 'destruction' of post-Platonic ontology was adopted as the goal of philosophical inquiry.[1] This 'negative' enterprise was billed by Heidegger as having 'positive' implications.[2] However, despite this assurance, all aspects of the intellectual inheritance extending from the Greeks to Descartes was to be surmounted. In practice, this entailed discarding rather than renovating its legacy. Heidegger claimed that a conceptual scheme transmitted from the ancients occluded a more primordial way of interacting with reality. This constituted a world-historical process of deterioration which was alleged to have culminated

1. Martin Heidegger, *Being and Time* (1927), trans. John Macquarrie and Edward Robinson (Eastford, CT: Martino Fine Books, 2019), pp. 41ff.
2. Ibid., p. 44.

in the work of Hegel.[3] Although Heidegger would become one of the most controversial figures in twentieth-century philosophy, his indictment proved highly influential. It helped to shape the character of Hegel's postwar reception. The rising tide of scepticism about Hegel was an intricate process. Somewhat ironically, it was given momentum by prominent neo-Hegelian figures, notably by Theodor Adorno and Max Horkheimer. Horkheimer, and more especially Adorno, were fierce critics of Heidegger.[4] Yet all three pursued a fundamental critique of occidental patterns of thought, notwithstanding important differences between them in point of detail. This gave rise to affinities between their mutually antagonistic endeavours.[5] Moreover, Frankfurt School Hegelianism was in practice post-Hegelian. Its representatives were attracted to the moment of 'negation' intrinsic to Hegel's dialectic.[6] In this they looked back to the 'critical criticism' of Bruno Bauer and his associates, mercilessly pilloried by Karl

3. Ibid., p. 43. For discussion of the merits of Heidegger's case, see Robert Pippin, 'Idealism and Anti-idealism in Modern European Thought', *The Journal of Speculative Philosophy*, 33: 3 (2019), pp. 349–67.

4. Theodor Adorno, *The Jargon of Authenticity* (1964), trans. Knut Tarnowski and Frederic Will (London: Routledge, 2003), passim.

5. Herman Mörchen, *Adorno und Heidegger: Untersuchung einer Philosophischen Kommunikationsverweigerung* (Stuttgart: Klett-Cotta, 1981); Rüdiger Bubner, 'Adornos Negative Dialektik', in Ludwig von Friedeburg and Jürgen Habermas, eds, *Adorno-Konferenz* (Frankfurt am Main: Suhrkamp, 1983); Brian O'Connor, 'Adorno, Heidegger and the Critique of Epistemology', *Philosophy and Social Criticism*, 24: 4 (1998), pp. 43–62.

6. Herbert Marcuse, *Reason and Revolution: Hegel and the Rise of Social Theory* (1941) (Boston, MA: Beacon Press, 1960), p. xv; Max Horkheimer, 'Traditional and Critical Theory' (1937), in *Critical Theory: Selected Essays*, trans. Matthew J. O'Connell (New York: Continuum, 2002), p. 210; Theodor Adorno, 'Aspects of Hegel's Philosophy' (1957), in *Hegel: Three Studies*, trans. Shierry Weber Nicholsen (Cambridge, MA; MIT Press, 1993), p. 30.

Marx.[7] However, negation prized just one dimension of a complex movement of thought. Excerpting a single element from the Hegelian system in this way distorted the larger intention animating the project. Hegel famously asserted that '[t]he true is the whole'.[8] Adorno responded by quipping that 'the whole is the untrue'.[9] For all its epigrammatic appeal, Adorno's riposte was in the end a superficial retort, and in any case a subversion of the Hegelian enterprise. Still, the intervention captured a mood of postwar melancholy. This gloom was understandable, and even inevitable. However, it capitalised on insights which are certainly questionable, and were originally articulated by Heidegger.

Since Heidegger was aiming to dismantle a tradition, textual exposition formed a core component of his approach. He offered interpretations that were certainly inventive, sometimes forcing the meaning of the works studied.[10] He famously applied this proactive style of reconstruction to Parmenides, Aristotle, Descartes, Kant and Nietzsche, among others. Yet Hegel was also a cardinal matter of concern. Already in 1915, when just a *Privatdozent* at the University of Freiburg, Heidegger emphasised the need to confront Hegel.[11] In due

7. Friedrich Engels and Karl Marx, *Die Heilige Familie, oder Kritik der kritischen Kritik: Gegen Bruno Bauer und Consorten* (Frankfurt am Main: Literarische Anstalt, 1845).

8. G.W.F. Hegel, *The Phenomenology of Spirit* (1807), ed. and trans. Michael Inwood (Oxford: Oxford University Press, 2018), §20.

9. Theodor Adorno, *Minima Moralia* (Frankurt am Main: Suhrkamp, 1969), p. 57.

10. On violently 'wringing' meaning from texts, see Martin Heidegger, *Kant and the Problem of Metaphysics* (1929), trans. Richard Taft (Bloomington, IN: Indiana University Press, 1997), p. 141.

11. Martin Heidegger, *Gesamtausgabe*, vol. 1: *Frühe Schriften*, ed. Friedrich-Wilhelm von Herrmann, (Frankfurt am Main: Vittorio Klostermann, 1978), pp. 410–11. Cf. Heidegger, 'Negativity' (1938–39, 1941), in *Hegel*, trans. Joseph Arel and Niels Feuerhahn (Bloomington, IN: Indiana University Press, 2015), p. 4.

course, Section 82 of *Being and Time* was given over to an examination of the relationship between time and spirit in Hegel's mature thought. Deepening this engagement, between the mid-1920s and the mid-1930s Heidegger repeatedly taught seminars on Hegel's *Logic, Phenomenology* and *Philosophy of Right*. But what was the encounter intended to achieve? Carl Schmitt claimed in his *Staat, Bewegung, Volk* that Hegel had in effect perished on 30 January 1933 when Hitler was sworn in as chancellor.[12] At that point, in Germany, liberal constitutionalism came to an end, yielding to the principles of the *Führer-Staat*. Heidegger concurred that, for this reason, there was no prospect of a Hegelian 'renewal' in politics.[13] Yet still there was a need to take the measure of Hegel's persistence at the most fundamental levels of thinking. In saying this, Heidegger was rejecting the very idea of a 'revival' of philosophers within the tradition of European metaphysics. As he explained in a 1927 lecture course on the basic problems of phenomenology, it was Hegel who, above all others, had to be 'overcome'. This involved appropriating but also moving beyond him. Hegel could not, in other words, be rehabilitated. He was, after all, the 'decisive terminus of the development of modern

12. Carl Schmitt, *Staat, Bewegung, Volk: Die Dreigliederung der politischen Einheit* (Hamburg: Hanseatische Verlagsanstalt, 1933), pp. 31–32. The wider National Socialist literature on Hegel was likewise dismissive: see Alfred Rosenberg, *Der Mythus des 20. Jahrhunderts: Eine Wertung der seelisch-geistigen Gestaltenkämpfe unserer Zeit* (Munich: Hoheneichen-Verlag, 1933), p. 525; Ernst Krieck, 'Der deutsche Idealismus zwischen den Zeitaltern', *Volk im Werden*, 1: 3 (May–June 1933), pp. 1–6; Franz Böhm, 'Hegel und Wir', in *Anti-Cartesianismus: Deutsche Philosophie im Widerstand* (Leipzig: Felix Meiner Verlag, 1938).

13. Martin Heidegger, *On Hegel's 'Philosophy of Right': The 1934–35 Seminar and Interpretative Essays*, trans. Andrew J. Mitchell (New York: Bloomsbury, 2014), pp. 119–20. Cf. Heidegger, 'Negativity', p. 7.

philosophy'.[14] On that basis he needed to be comprehended yet also supplanted.

Hegel had reformulated ancient metaphysics but, for Heidegger, he was still imprisoned by its underlying assumptions. Fundamental here was the framework in terms of which the category of 'substance' (*hypokeimenon* [ὑποκείμενον], *subiectum*) had been conceptualised by Plato, Aristotle and their successors. According to the Heideggerian narrative, this metaphysical support was rethought by Kant who, building on Descartes, made 'Being' dependent on self-consciousness.[15] This tradition culminated in the Hegelian claim that 'substance' was in fact 'subject'.[16] As Heidegger put it, Hegel was the 'completion' of the Greeks.[17] In response, the whole Graeco-Roman-Christian inheritance needed to be disassembled. This bequeathed to Heidegger the monumental task of 'tearing down' the products of the accumulated process that had led to the current state of mental 'deformation'.[19] The assignment should not be seen as a simple revision or amendment. Instead, Heidegger pledged a total overhaul. After all, for him, metaphysics was not just one factor among others in the order

14. Martin Heidegger, *The Basic Problems of Phenomenology* (1927 lectures), trans. Albert Hofstadter (Bloomington, IN: Indiana University Press, 1982), p. 125. Cf. ibid., pp. 100–101, 112, 178.

15. Ibid., pp. 127, 152.

16. Hegel, *Phenomenology*, §§17, 18, 25. For comment, see Heidegger, 'Negativity', p. 10. Cf. Martin Heidegger, 'Hegel's Concept of Experience' (1942–43), in *Off the Beaten Track*, trans. Julian Young and Kenneth Haynes (Cambridge: Cambridge University Press, 2002), p. 99.

17. Martin Heidegger, 'Hegel and the Greeks' (1958), in *Pathmarks*, ed. and trans. William McNeil (Cambridge: Cambridge University Press, 1998), p. 323.

18. Martin Heidegger, *Introduction to Metaphysics* (1935), trans. Gregory Fried and Richard Polt (New Haven, CT: Yale University Press, 2014), pp. 138, 15.

of things. On the contrary, *philosophia prima* 'grounds an age'; it constitutes 'the historical ground of the world history that is being determined by the West'.[19] This meant, ultimately, that metaphysics governs the decisions definitive of a given epoch. In the modern era, science and technology were an outgrowth of its metaphysics. Reality was thereby objectified, represented, pictured and calculated. Moreover, this 'will' to encapsulate was accompanied by disenchantment. In a Nietzschean vein, Heidegger lamented what he termed the 'loss of the gods' (*Entgötterung*). Resolve had fully atrophied in the midst of Christian belief. Religion could only thinly veil the desperate sense of void.[20]

Heidegger thus followed Hegel in taking the liberation of humanity to be the distinguishing feature of modernity. However, for Heidegger this newly discovered freedom was in truth a form of incarceration. Between Descartes and Hegel, Heidegger noted, man became 'the referential centre of beings as such'.[21] The conquered earth was placed at the disposal of humanity. To be human meant to deny the fact of finitude and reshape the world in the image of consciousness. This domineering brand of subjectivity amounted to a form of bondage. Ontology was made over into anthropology. All relations, including social relations, were comprehensively instrumentalised. Knowing the world was governed by its use. Humanism and individualism prospered, accompanied by a loss of community. In an idiom that would become generalised by the time of Derrida and Foucault, the self, as Heidegger put it, was now interpreted as

---

19. Martin Heidegger, 'The Age of the World Picture' (1938), in *Off the Beaten Track*, p. 57; Heidegger, 'Nietzsche's Word: "God is Dead"' (1943), in ibid., p. 197.

20. Heidegger, 'Age of the World Picture', p. 58.

21. Ibid., p. 67.

'subject'.[22] This, Heidegger argued, conditioned an attitude of mastery. The self took charge of its environment. The objective world was taken up into the immanence of subjectivity. In the end, the metaphysics of self-consciousness made technology the source of all value. Our surroundings, as well as our selves, were converted into a kind of 'standing-reserve'.[23] In the process, the coordinates of human life were devalued.[24] From this perspective, modern humanity was the cause of its own dehumanisation. Individuals had lost all sense of normative orientation.

In line with a number of postwar idioms, Heidegger saw the technological age as having precipitated a crisis.[25] In fact, in the 1930s it was widely thought that scientific reason bred an all-consuming impasse. Edmund Husserl declared in 1935 that there had occurred an *apparent failure of rationalism*.[26] He suggested that this began with the 'mathematization' of nature in early modern Europe, leading to the reduction of all phenomena to their physical coordinates. This attitude, he believed, brought dissatisfaction, distress and the impeding downfall of spiritual values. Yet, he went on, responsibility for this decline lay less with rationality as such than with a deficient understanding of reason popularised by the Enlightenment.[27] As the

22. Ibid., pp. 69–70. Cf. Martin Heidegger, 'Letter on Humanism' (1946), in *Basic Writings*, ed. David Farrell Krell, rev. edn (New York: Harper & Row, 1977), pp. 221, 228.

23. Martin Heidegger, 'The Question Concerning Technology' (1950), in *The Question Concerning Technology and Other Essays*, trans. William Lovitt (New York: Garland, 1977), pp. 17, 27.

24. Heidegger, 'Nietzsche's Word', p. 191.

25. Reinhart Koselleck, 'Crisis', *Journal of the History of Ideas*, 67: 2 (April 2006), pp. 357–400, pp. 397ff.

26. Edmund Husserl, 'Philosophy and the Crisis of European Humanity' (1935), in *The Crisis of European Sciences and Transcendental Phenomenology*, trans. David Carr (Evanston, IL: Northwestern University Press, 1970), p. 299.

27. Ibid., p. 290.

atmosphere of crisis reached a crescendo, the criticism of instrumental reason spread. Horkheimer and Adorno epitomised the feeling of despair. In a series of lectures delivered in the United States in 1944, Horkheimer traced the travails of industrial society to a dangerously narrow conception of rationality.[28] In collaboration with Adorno, he further pursued an all-encompassing indictment of prevailing values by resort to the Hegelian activity of 'critique'. However, the result had nothing in common with Hegel's conception of modernity. The epic struggles of world history seemed to have produced only depravity. The means of life were made complicit with a spiral of destruction. In their bleakest moments, Horkheimer and Adorno came close to denouncing the conditions of existence.

II

This spirit of renunciation is most conspicuous in *Dialectic of Enlightenment*, a collaborative work first circulated in 1944 and published in a revised format three years later. The book was intended to build on Hegel's treatment of enlightenment presented, as we saw, in chapter 6 of the *Phenomenology*.[29] Despite this, instead of capitalising on Hegel's argument, Horkheimer and Adorno circumvented his claims. In dramatising the eighteenth-century confrontation between faith and reason, Hegel sought to expose the destructiveness of critical thought. However, the *Dialectic of Enlightenment* simply recharged the

28. Max Horkheimer, *Eclipse of Reason* (London: Bloomsbury, 2013), p. vii.

29. Jay M. Bernstein, 'Dialectic as Fate: Adorno and Hegel', in Tom Huhn, ed., *The Cambridge Companion to Adorno* (Cambridge: Cambridge University Press, 2004), pp. 19–50.

programme of negative critique. As Hegel presented the contest between 'insight' and 'belief', religion was ultimately shattered because it tacitly conceded the norms of rational inquiry. As Diderot foresaw, the idol of superstition came crashing to the ground. However, in Hegel's account, by operating as a purely critical force, reason failed to appreciate the value of the world it deposed. It functioned exclusively as an engine of disavowal. It could therefore see no virtue in the objectives that faith pursued. This deprived rational criticism of any constructive purpose. Lacking positivity, it became self-devouring. Yet the same verdict can be applied to the *Dialectic of Enlightenment* itself. The work was originally intended to 'prepare a positive concept of enlightenment'.[30] Nonetheless, it never succeeded in distilling what its affirmative message was. Freedom, humanity and progress were extolled, but deprived of tangible content. In place of positive commitments, the *Dialectic of Enlightenment* offered unsubstantiated hope.

The immediate context for the book was the contemporary European scene. For many at the time, the rise of fascism could be explained in terms of the defeat of reason by resort to myth. Tackling this argument, Horkheimer and Adorno in the 1944 'Preface' to their work took issue with the idea that modern barbarism, epitomised by National Socialism, was a species of atavism. It was Ernst Cassirer who first argued, in April 1944, that totalitarian politics reverted to the use of myth to indoctrinate populations deranged by the current state of society.[31]

---

30. Max Horkheimer and Theodor Adorno, *Dialectic of Enlightenment: Philosophical Fragments* (1947), trans. Edmund Jephcott (Stanford, CA: Stanford University Press, 2002), p. xviii.

31. Ernst Cassirer, 'Judaism and the Modern Political Myths', *Contemporary Jewish Record*, 7: 2 (April 1944), pp. 115–27.

Two years later, Cassirer explicitly censured Heidegger for facilitating the relapse by insisting that human beings were condemned to permanent bewilderment (*Geworfenheit*).[32] In tune with Cassirer, the *Dialectic of Enlightenment* railed against the 'fascist' doctrine of 'the self-destruction of enlightenment'.[33]

At the same time, however, the leading argument of the book was that the advent of enlightenment plunged the world into calamity. The implication was that human development had been subject to an abysmal fate. The *Dialectic of Enlightenment* treated this process at a level of high-flown abstraction. This included awarding enlightenment a transhistorical significance stretching from Homer to the twentieth century. The resulting account of the course of affairs bordered on fatalism. Its narrative resembled the popular image of the Hegelian march of *Geist*, except that spirit's course in the *Dialectic of Enlightenment* was guided by a malevolent force. Deterioration beset the advance of history: 'The curse of irresistible progress is irresistible regression.'[34]

Having rebutted Heidegger's view that reason is intrinsically beleaguered, Horkheimer and Adorno also rejected Cassirer's contention that enlightenment presaged an escape from myth.[35] First, they claimed that myth itself was already a form of enlightenment. After all, even the story of the wily Odysseus promoted the virtues of rational calculation. Second, they tried to establish that enlightenment was ensnared in the forms

32. Cassirer, *Myth of the State*, p. 293. For discussion, see Peter E. Gordon, *Continental Divide: Heidegger, Cassirer, Davos* (Cambridge, MA: Harvard University Press, 2010), pp. 300–306.

33. Horkheimer and Adorno, *Dialectic of Enlightenment*, p. xiv.

34. Ibid., p. 28.

35. For Cassirer's account of human progress out of myth, see his *The Philosophy of Symbolic Forms*, 4 vols (New Haven, CT: Yale University Press, 1965–96).

of oppression from which it promised liberation. Socialisation, they argued, imposed self-control along with the repression of individuality. For this reason, the putatively rational society was exposed as the most irrational of institutions. So, unlike in Heidegger, reason was not ineluctably debauched for Hork-heimer and Adorno, but it was 'implicated' in successive stages of domination. However, the way in which it was implicated was under-specified. Inchoate notions like 'entanglement' and 'intertwinement' were offered instead of lucid explana-tion.[36] The means of emancipation were deemed complicit with despotism: 'Enlightenment', the authors concluded, 'is totalitarian.'[37]

One problem with this conclusion was that the stages of co-ercion were not clearly differentiated, and the causes of the abuse were not precisely determined. Instead, each situation was explained by resort to analogy. Intellectual classification was seen as 'like' social regulation. Alternatively, values were incriminated by alleged collusion with their opposites. As a re-sult, in general, the basic ingredients of social life were chided. Accordingly, the division of labour was disparaged. The 'compul-sive character' of self-preservation was roundly blamed. Subjec-tivity was conflated with subjection. Technology was identified with social manipulation. Categorisation, regularisation and standardisation were condemned, and connected with regi-mentation. Exchange itself was reprimanded, while functional-ity and fungibility were castigated. Even the basic requirement of justice—namely, the equalisation of differences—was dis-trusted: 'Bourgeois society is ruled by equivalence. It makes dissimilar things comparable by reducing them to abstract

36. Horkheimer and Adorno, *Dialectic of Enlightenment,* pp. xviii, 25.
37. Ibid., p. 4.

quantities.'[38] However, without at least some kind of 'equivalence', no society or economy can function.

In this way, Horkheimer and Adorno impeached the dynamics of civilisation, which they believed began with rationalisation and ended in exploitation.[39] This contention, as we know, has its roots in an eighteenth-century debate. Kant associated this sort of critique with Rousseau's first and second *Discourses*, branding his castigation of reason as an exercise in 'misology'.[40] There was, Kant thought, a misanthropic strain in Rousseau which encouraged him to formulate paradoxical pronouncements about the detrimental effects of progress from crudeness to culture.[41] Yet beneath Rousseau's arraignment of the arts, the sciences, society and the state lay a more constructive purpose, which included a defence of the moral faculty alongside the possibility of its corruption.[42] Kant himself drew from this the conclusion that culture (*Bildung*) was not inexorably in conflict with nature, even though it generated a plethora of social ills. He conceded that cultivation, education and civilisation brought costs and damage in tow, but they also fostered the only means of moral and political improvement. For Kant— unlike Heidegger, Horkheimer and Adorno—the negative impact of civilisation was a consequence of social betterment. As a result, he considered the rhetoric of Rousseau's hostility to

38. Ibid., pp. 2–4, 8, 16, 20, 23–26.

39. Ibid., p. 29.

40. Kant, *Groundwork*, AA 4: 395.

41. Immanuel Kant, 'Anthropology Mrongovius' (Mongrovius MS; 1784–85), trans. Robert C. Clewis, in *Lectures on Anthropology*, ed. Allen W. Wood and Robert B. Louden (Cambridge: Cambridge University Press, 2012), AA 25: 1420.

42. Immanuel Kant, 'Conjectural Beginning of Human History' (1786), in *Anthropology, History, and Education*, ed. and trans. Robert B. Louden and Günter Zöller (Cambridge: Cambridge University Press, 2007), AA 8: 116.

Bildung to be fundamentally retrograde. In Kant's mind, it seemed little better than a reprise of the reactionary asceticism of Diogenes the Cynic.[43]

Hegel later accepted this comparison and the implied criticism. In the end, he thought, the posture of *contemptus mundi* struck by Diogenes was a creation of the very society he rejected: 'Diogenes in his barrel is conditioned by the world.'[44] He similarly deemed Juvenal, Perseus and Quakerism to be reactive products of their culture.[45] Moreover, the mental attitude which discovered only perversity in its environment was itself a product of selfishness and vanity. As Hegel saw things, instead of inveighing against the structure of existence, it made better sense to investigate the means of renovation. Negation, for Hegel, could never be a sufficient end in itself. Instead, it was a method for examining past failures. This procedure also revealed relative successes. For Horkheimer and Adorno, however, it seemed as though every historical advance led only to its own bankruptcy. For this reason, they scolded the 'idolization' of the existing order.[46] Moreover, they ultimately linked Hegel with this 'positivist' submission to power.

The *Dialectic of Enlightenment* celebrated the Hegelian technique of 'determinate negation'.[47] According to Horkheimer and Adorno, it conferred leverage against prevailing values, especially in an age of repression where authoritarianism

---

43. Immanuel Kant, 'Lectures on Moral Philosophy' (Collins MS; 1784–85, in *Lectures on Ethics*, ed. Peter Heath and J. B. Schneewind, trans. Heath (Cambridge: Cambridge University Press, 1997), AA 27: 249.

44. Hegel, *Phenomenology*, §524. Cf. Hegel, *Philosophy of Right*, §195A.

45. Hegel, *First Philosophy of Right*, §90A.

46. Horkheimer and Adorno, *Dialectic of Enlightenment*, p. xix.

47. Ibid., p. 18.

reigned.[48] Yet Hegel himself, they concluded, betrayed his own ideals and ultimately 'succumbed to mythology'.[49] This was, they alleged, because he mixed criticism with blind capitulation. The main symptom of this was his apparent endorsement of the 'absolute' as the final upshot of his sceptical 'way of despair'.[50] The 'known result', the *Dialectic of Enlightenment* argued, determined the shape of the inquiry. This account of Hegel persisted through Adorno's later renditions of his thought. It reappeared in 1966 in *Negative Dialectics*, as well as in his mature essays on Hegel and his late lectures on the philosophy of history. One of the final sections of *Negative Dialectics* argued that Hegel had in effect mythologised history. By way of response, Adorno advocated a 'decisive break' with his predecessor.[51] Hegelian philosophy was alleged to be 'one-sided'; it was apparently the victim of its own 'blind spot'. It failed to recognise its dependence on prevailing norms, which Adorno described as adding up to an 'odious totality'.[52] Hegel's thought was seen as an extension of his conformism, which shackled him to the existing condition of the world. For Adorno, such a limited horizon in practice disregarded the dissenting voice of conscience.[53]

48. Theodor Adorno, 'Remarks on the Authoritarian Personality' (1950), in T. W. Adorno et al., *The Authoritarian Personality* (London: Verso, 2019).

49. Horkheimer and Adorno, *Dialectic of Enlightenment,* p. 18.

50. Hegel, *Phenomenology*, §78.

51. Theodor Adorno, *Negative Dialectics* (1966), trans. E. B. Ashton (London: Routledge & Kegan Paul, 1973), pp. 357, 160.

52. Theodor Adorno, *History and Freedom: Lectures 1964–1965*, trans. Rodney Livingstone (Cambridge: Polity, 2008), pp. 17, 41, 47.

53. Ibid., p. 63. For Adorno's revision of Hegelian dialectics, see Michael Rosen, *Hegel's Dialectic and Its Criticism* (Cambridge: Cambridge University Press, 1982), ch. 7.

Notwithstanding these profound reservations about Hegel, Adorno was keen to resuscitate one element of his thought. In 1957 he wrote that 'Hegel's philosophy is [. . .] essentially negative'. It thrived on 'critique'.[54] By this he meant that negativity was its only enduring virtue. From this perspective, Lukács's efforts to co-opt Hegel in the service of really existing socialism seemed to Adorno to be a betrayal of the dialectic.[55] At the same time, Adorno detected in Hegel himself a complacency about the status quo. With this conclusion, he was rehashing the picture of Hegel first popularised in the 1850s by Rudolf Haym, which depicted the one-time radical as having sold out to the authorities. The notorious assertion in the 'Preface' to the *Philosophy of Right* that the 'actual' was 'rational' was taken by Adorno to confirm this assessment.[56] Hegel was condemned as having sided with the 'big guns'.[57] For this reason, in Adorno's mind, Hegel could be rescued but not rejuvenated. However, few scholars today would accept Adorno's reading of the equation between actuality and rationality in the *Philosophy of Right*. The misinterpretation stemmed from a sharp divergence in goals. Hegel had been keen to spurn what Adorno hoped to revive: the use of philosophy as a form of moral protest against politics. It was Kant who appealed to conscience to convict existing conditions. Hegel, for that reason, had been his foremost critic. Adorno missed the force of Hegel's case against Kantian moralism.

54. Theodor Adorno, 'Aspects of Hegel's Philosophy' (1957), in *Hegel: Three Studies*, p. 30.

55. Theodor Adorno, 'The Experiential Content of Hegel's Philosophy' (1959), in *Hegel*, p. 82.

56. Hegel, *Philosophy of Right*, p. 20.

57. Adorno, 'Experiential Content', p. 83.

III

Given the neo-Hegelian animus against Hegel exemplified by Horkheimer and Adorno, there were few resources for defending his ideas when explicit attacks began to appear at the end of the Second World War. Perhaps the most flagrant onslaught came from Karl Popper. It is well known that Popper's *The Open Society and Its Enemies* was written during the early 1940s, and that Hegel was one of its principal targets, along with Plato and Marx.[58] While based at the University of Canterbury, Popper lacked access to a wealth of primary materials. Presumably on account of this, his references to Hegel were largely to a selected edition of texts compiled in 1929 for the US student market.[59] As a result, the treatment is replete with mistranslations. Possibly for the same reason, it recycles remarkably crude misinterpretations. Almost all the major scholarship from the period is ignored. Dilthey, Meinecke, Rosenzweig, Kroner, Wahl and Marcuse are never mentioned. Given this generally slipshod approach, it must have seemed to Popper that he could depend on a readership already hostile to Hegel.

At that point in the anglophone world, scepticism about Hegel's system had been widely disseminated—by Bertrand Russell, G. E. Moore, William James, Paul Tillich and Reinhold Niebuhr. Popper's intervention was the *coup de grâce*. Thereafter it became fashionable to parody Hegel's thought, and then to convict the belittled remnant for the crimes of modern history.

58. Karl Popper, *The Open Society and Its Enemies* (1945), 2 vols (London: Routledge & Kegan Paul, 1984).

59. G.W.F Hegel, *Hegel Selections*, ed. J. Loewenberg (New York: Charles Scribner's Sons, 1929). In an earlier article covering Hegel, Popper cites the *Logic*, but only in passing. See Karl Popper, 'What is Dialectic?', *Mind*, 49: 196 (October 1940), pp. 403–26.

The pattern after the Second World War gained momentum in the 1960s. Already by 1955, Jean Hyppolite was registering the influence of Heidegger across France and a corresponding move away from Sartre, humanism and Hegel.[60] A decade later, Louis Althusser set about expunging all vestiges of Hegel from what he saw as the workable tenets of Marxism.[61] For a generation of French philosophers who followed, Hegel came to stand for 'totalising' methods—the enemy of 'indeterminacy' and 'otherness'.[62] Nietzsche, Freud and Heidegger were co-opted to serve a 'hermeneutics of suspicion', substantially directed against German Idealism.[63] 'Micro-politics' supplanted 'metanarratives' of emancipation; 'différance' replaced the dialectic.[64] But it was Popper who most loudly equated

60. Jean Hyppolite, 'A Chronology of French Existentialism', Yale French Studies, 16 (1955), pp. 100–102.

61. Louis Althusser, For Marx (1965), trans. Ben Brewster (London: Verso, 2005).

62. Relevant figures include Michel Foucault, Jacques Derrida, Jean-François Lyotard, Gilles Deleuze, Julia Kristeva, Jean-Luc Nancy, Luce Irigaray and Alan Badiou. For an overview of the period, see Vincent Descombes, Modern French Philosophy (Cambridge: Cambridge University Press, 1979). See also Michael Kelly, 'Hegel in France Today: A Bibliographical Essay', Journal of European Studies, 16 (1986), pp. 249–70; Michael S. Roth, Knowing and History: Appropriations of Hegel in Twentieth-Century France (Ithaca, NY: Cornell University Press, 1988); Alison Stone, 'Hegel and Twentieth-Century French Philosophy', in Dean Moyar, ed., The Oxford Handbook of Hegel (Oxford: Oxford University Press, 2017).

63. Paul Ricœur identified a 'school of suspicion' with Marx, Nietzsche and Freud in his Freud and Philosophy: An Essay on Interpretation (1965), trans. David Savage (New Haven, CT: Yale University Press, 1970), p. 32. The phrase was later associated with poststructuralist and postmodern criticisms of humanistic values. The original idea of a 'school of suspicion' (Schule des Verdachts) comes from Nietzsche's self-description in the preface to his Human, All Too Human: A Book for Free Spirits (1878), trans Marion Faber and Stephen Lehmann (Lincoln, NE: Nebraska University Press, 1984), p. 4.

64. On the 'micro-physics of power', see Michel Foucault, Discipline and Punish: The Birth of the Prison (1975), trans. Alan Sheridan (London: Allen Lane, 1977), p. 26;

Hegel with totalitarianism. Heidegger, Horkheimer and Adorno prepared the philosophical ground. But Popper reached the widest audience, and had an impact on English-speaking political science departments, especially where the history of political thought was taught. Partly under Popper's influence, it became standard to oppose schools of thought to each other and categorise them as either malevolent or sound.[65]

When the study of the history of political ideas was placed on a new footing in the late 1960s, the principal fallacies challenged were associated with the preceding generation. These included anachronism, especially in the form of prolepsis; the metaphysical hypostatisation of 'ideas'; the construction of bogus traditions; and the itemisation of spurious transhistorical doctrines.[66] These were seen as elementary errors in historical reasoning, and each of them is to be found in Popper's book. This is not because Popper was incompetent, but because he had an overriding purpose. That objective became a standard one among Cold War political thinkers. He wanted to pinpoint the philosophical antecedents to totalitarian ideologies. This fostered the notion that there existed a benign liberal heritage

On 'différance' as the 'destruction' of Hegel's *Aufhebung*, see Jacques Derrida, 'Interview with Jean-Louis Houdebine and Guy Scarpetta' (1971), in *Positions*, trans. Alan Bass (Chicago: Chicago University Pres, 1981), pp. 40–41; on postmodernism as a challenge to enlightenment and Hegelian grand narratives of freedom, see Jean-François Lyotard, *The Postmodern Condition: A Report on Knowledge* (1979), trans. Geoff Bennington and Brian Massumi (Minneapolis: University of Minnesota Press, 1984).

65. See, for example, Jacob L. Talmon, *The Origins of Totalitarian Democracy* (London: Secker & Warburg, 1952).

66. See John Dunn, 'The Identity of the History of Ideas', *Philosophy*, 63: 164 (April 1968), pp. 85–104; Quentin Skinner, 'Meaning and Understanding in the History of Ideas', *History and Theory*, 8: 1 (1969), pp. 3–53.

alongside a rival scheme of autocratic ideas. Popper viewed these Manichean alternatives through an Austro-Hungarian lens. The basic problem that had confronted modern Europe, he believed, was Prussian-led German nationalism.[67] This had been the target of the Austrian School of economics, with which Popper was familiar, not least through Friedrich Hayek. For the leading Austrian economist Carl Menger, and followers like Hayek, there was a problem that underlay German politics as well as its supporting social science. This was the sin of 'historicism', which facilitated nationalism in all its forms—including state-based socialist planning and race-based National Socialism.[68] Beside these, the cosmopolitan achievements of the Austro-Hungarian Empire were a beacon of civility. As far as Hayek and Popper were concerned, a particular style of thought had enabled nationalist tendencies.[69]

Popper traced the offending creed back to the Platonic revolt against the rise of critical rationalism among the 'Great Generation' of sophists in fifth-century BCE Athens, which included Protagoras, Gorgias, Herodotus and Socrates.[70] The notion that an abrupt change in attitude divided pre-Socratic Greece from subsequent world history was, ironically, a quasi-Hegelian construction. However, in recycling the thesis, Popper added dimensions of oversimplification. He dramatically divided one moral universe from another, pitting 'tribal' collectivism against

---

67. Popper, *Open Society*, 2, pp. 49–50, 58.

68. Karl Popper, *The Poverty of Historicism* (1944–45) (London: Routledge, 2007). For the original context of the work, see Malachi Haim Hacohen, *Karl Popper: The Formative Years, 1902–1945* (Cambridge: Cambridge University Press, 2000), pp. 353–82.

69. See, for example, F. A. Hayek, 'Introduction' to Wilhelm Röpke, *The German Question*, trans. E. W. Dickes (London: The Blackfriars Press, 1946).

70. Popper, *Open Society*, 1, p. 185.

an opposing culture of personal responsibility. The process of civilisation drove this confrontation. In the face of the 'strain' of a society based on rational obligations, Popper argued, reactionary thinkers channelled a longing for the old simplicities represented by 'closed' societies struggling against their 'open' counterparts.[71] The 'ideas of 1789', Popper thought, brought about an equivalent modern reaction against the forces of progress. Allegedly, Hegel invented a 'spirit'-oriented nationalism to spearhead a conservative backlash.[72] Popper charged his approach with trading unapologetically in essentialism and historicism, both together causing the corruption of post-Kantian thought. Popper drew repeatedly on the polemical work of Aurel Kolnai, a Hungarian émigré who had studied under Moritz Schlick and Ludwig von Mises. In 1938 Kolnai published *The War against the West*, a sustained broadside against National Socialist ideas about race, mythology and nation.[73] Kolnai explored the uses of these concepts by an assortment of National Socialist ideologues from Alfred Rosenberg to Ernst Krieck. For Popper, Hegel was the original source of these abhorrent products of the German mind.

The Austrian critique of historicism stemmed from a rejection of various organicist ideas that were regarded as fundamental to German jurisprudence and economics, both of which depended on the idea of national community.[74] Against this Menger, and fellow travellers like Popper, defended a species of

71. Ibid., 1, pp. 171, 173.

72. Ibid., 2, p. 30.

73. Aurel Kolnai, *The War against the West* (New York: The Viking Press, 1938).

74. On the identification of organicism with nationalism in German historical thought, see Max Weber, 'Roscher and Knies and the Logical Problems of Historical Economics' (1903), in *Max Weber: Collected Methodological Writings*, ed. Hans Henrik Bruun and Sam Whimster, trans. Bruun (London: Routledge, 2012), pp. 8–9

methodological individualism.[75] Yet in the same period there emerged a distinctly German debate about historicism which shaped a generation of thinkers who followed in the wake of Nietzsche.[76] Leo Strauss came to maturity in the shadow of this controversy, which would preoccupy him for the remainder of his career.[77] However, in this context, historicism stood for cultural relativism instead of organicism. Strauss considered Popper to be a commonplace philosopher, out of his depth in any serious discussion of politics. He agreed with Eric Voegelin that Popper was an 'ideological brawler' rather than a substantial thinker in his own right.[78] In line with this, Strauss believed that the 'open society' did not solve the problem of modern despotism. In Strauss's lexicon, an 'open' society connoted liberal cosmopolitanism, precisely the scheme of values that he felt had failed after the First World War.[79] After all, as Strauss emphasised, it was liberalism that gave way to totalitarianism. The passage from the one to the other called for an urgent

75. Carl Menger, *Untersuchungen über die Methode der Sozialwissenschaften* (Leipzig: Duncker & Humblot, 1883).

76. Ernst Troeltsch, *Der Historismus und seine Probleme: Das logische Problem der Geschichtsphilosophie* (1922), ed. F. W. Graf and M. Schloßberger (Berlin: De Gruyter, 2008); Charles Bambach, *Heidegger, Dilthey, and the Crisis of Historicism* (Ithaca, NY: Cornell University Press, 1995); Frederick Beiser, *The German Historicist Tradition* (Oxford: Oxford University Press, 2011).

77. Liisi Keedus, *The Crisis of German Historicism: The Early Political Thought of Hannah Arendt and Leo Strauss* (Cambridge: Cambridge University Press, 2015).

78. Eric Voegelin to Leo Strauss, 18 April 1950, in *Faith and Political Philosophy: The Correspondence between Leo Strauss and Eric Voegelin, 1934–1964*, ed. Peter Emberly and Barry Cooper (University Park, PA: Pennsylvania State University Press, 1993), p. 68.

79. Leo Strauss, 'German Nihilism' (1941), *Interpretation*, 26: 3 (Spring 1999), pp. 353–78. Strauss took the distinction between open and closed societies not from Popper but from Henri Bergson, *Les Deux Sources de la morale et de la religion* (Paris: Félix Alcan, 1932).

explanation. For Strauss, historicism in particular had facilitated the transition.

Strauss associated historicism with the thought of Heidegger, although he assumed its roots lay deeper in the culture of the modern West. In ascertaining these origins, Strauss focused on the passage from Machiavelli to Hobbes, culminating in the loss of objective rational norms as criteria for judging the institutions of justice.[80] According to this narrative, the increase in human mastery over nature since the seventeenth century was accompanied by a corresponding decline in the availability of moral standards.[81] By relativising all criteria of judgement to specific historical horizons, Strauss argued, figures like Heidegger deprived society of a standpoint from which to condemn the rise of National Socialism.[82] Because Weimar liberalism had grown to accept a rampant historicist perspective, it prized the toleration of diversity over the defence of absolute values. In Strauss's mind, this assisted the forces of nihilism in the 1930s. As a consequence, civilisation became an object of widespread contempt. Strauss regarded these developments as part of a general pattern leading from the decline of classical ideas of right to the rise of modern relativism in the guise of liberal historicism. The United States in the 1950s was exposed to the same corrosive pattern. In response, Strauss called for political philosophy to turn to the insights of the

---

80. Leo Strauss, *The Political Philosophy of Hobbes: Its Basis and Its Genesis* (Oxford: Clarendon Press, 1936); Leo Strauss, *Thoughts on Machiavelli* (Glencoe, IL: Free Press, 1958).

81. Leo Strauss, 'Introduction' to *Natural Right and History* (Chicago: University of Chicago Press, 1953), passim.

82. Leo Strauss, 'What is Political Philosophy?' (1954–55), in *What is Political Philosophy? And Other Studies* (Chicago: University of Chicago Press, 1988), p. 27.

ancients as a means of criticising the deficiencies of prevailing approaches to politics.[83]

Hegel's role in Strauss's story was strangely unresolved. On the one hand, he presented Hegel as the fulfilment of a tradition that began with Rousseau which identified freedom as the locus of basic value.[84] This claim might be expected to distinguish German Idealism from utilitarian precepts insofar as the latter took their bearings from the place of the passions in moral life.[85] Despite this, Strauss followed Kojève in regarding Hegel's account of the struggle between 'master and slave' as a contest for 'prestige' driven by 'vanity'.[86] As Strauss recognised, this was to ground the foundations of Hegelianism in Hobbesian anthropology. Regarding this equation, Kojève himself wrote, 'Hegel undoubtedly takes Hobbes as his point of departure.'[87] However, the problem with this formulation is not just that it misses the meaning of freedom in Hegel, but more generally that it collapses idealism into empiricism. In the end, this blurs the specific character of Hegel's thought. Strauss clearly wanted to move away from what he regarded as Popper's distortions. For instance, in a course on the philosophy of history delivered in 1965 he insisted that Hegel was not a

83. Leo Strauss, *The City and Man* (Chicago: University of Chicago Press, 1964), pp. 11–12.

84. Strauss, *Natural Right*, p. 279; Leo Strauss, 'The Three Waves of Modernity', in *Political Philosophy: Six Essays*, ed. Hilail Gildin (New York: Bobbs-Merrill, 1975), p. 92.

85. This is implied in Leo Strauss, 'Preface' (1962) to *Spinoza's Critique of Religion* (1930) (Chicago: University of Chicago Press, 1997), p. 2.

86. Alexandre Kojève, 'Tyranny and Wisdom' (1954), in Leo Strauss, *On Tyranny* (Chicago: University of Chicago Press, 2000), pp. 142, 146; Leo Strauss, 'Restatement on Xenophon's *Hiero*' (1954), in ibid., p. 192.

87. Alexandre Kojève to Leo Strauss, 2 November 1936, reprinted in *On Tyranny*, p. 231.

'precursor of totalitarianism'.[88] Nonetheless, a decade earlier, he
had described the 'delusions' of communism as having been
anticipated by Hegel.[89] This pointed to a deeply ambivalent attitude to Hegel's view of history.

It seems that Strauss never managed to settle this ambivalence.
He recognised that Hegel had tried to combine philosophy with
history in a bid to circumvent relativism.[90] Nonetheless, already
committed to a vision of the West's decline, Strauss never probed
the depths of what this combination entailed.[91] Truth, Hegel argued, was a child of its time.[92] However, for Strauss, this conclusion left all ideals at the mercy of mutability. For his part, Hegel
solved this problem by privileging his own era as providing the
benchmark against which previous epochs could be assessed. In
opposition to this, Strauss resorted to ancient Athens as offering
a superior measure. Modernity, he contended, respected comfort
above excellence. As a consequence, it compromised higher values in the name of security and ease. This diagnosis led Strauss to
align Hegel with Oswald Spengler.[93] Since Hegel had depicted
modern history as a consummation, Strauss construed this climax as a kind of enervation.[94] In his mind, the very idea of an

88. Leo Strauss, *On Hegel* (1965 lectures), ed. Paul Franco (Chicago: University
of Chicago Press, 2019), p. 192.

89. Strauss, 'What is Political Philosophy?', p. 54.

90. Leo Strauss, 'Political Philosophy and History' (1949), in *What is Political
Philosophy?*, p. 58.

91. On Strauss as a diagnostician of decline indebted to the philosophy of history,
see Robert Pippin, 'The Unavailability of the Ordinary: Strauss on the Philosophical
Fate of Modernity', *Political Theory*, 31: 3 (June 2003), pp. 335–58.

92. Hegel, *Philosophy of Right*, p. 21.

93. Strauss, *On Hegel*, p. 28.

94. Leo Strauss, 'Relativism' (1961), in *The Rebirth of Classical Political Rationalism: Essays by Leo Strauss*, ed. Thomas L. Pangle (Chicago: University of Chicago
Press, 1989), pp. 19–20.

historical terminus implied the satiety of Nietzsche's 'last man'.[95] From this perspective, Hegel seemed to have conceded what Spengler would conclude: that the West now faced its final point of exhaustion. Strauss's project was dedicated to arresting this decline. That could not be achieved by a simple 'return' to the ancient world. Nonetheless, Strauss maintained there was promise in seeking guidance from the classics.[96]

IV

From Heidegger to Strauss, the experience of decline inspired attempts to revive the ancients. The idea that the West had been subject to degeneration was a thesis originally developed by fatalistic philosophies of history. Most often, these were inversions of progressive narratives whose warrant rested upon faith alone. Notwithstanding his postwar reputation, Hegel had sought to discount both alternatives as teleological. As he argued in the 'Preface' to the *Phenomenology*, the purpose of a temporal process can be found exclusively in its 'result': its meaning is only apparent 'at the *end*'.[97] Hegel's goal was to liberate historical narratives from superstition. For him, the direction of history could not be left to blind credulity. Instead, he aimed to justify claims to improvement by studying past failures. His argument was that previous breakdowns had led to rational outcomes in the absence of a providential plan.[98] However, the sense of foreboding that surrounded the First

95. Strauss, *On Tyranny*, p. 208, referring to Friedrich Nietzsche's 'letzter Mensch' in *Thus Spake Zarathustra*.

96. Strauss, *The City and Man*, p. 11.

97. Hegel, *Phenomenology*, §20.

98. Terry Pinkard, *Does History Make Sense? Hegel on the Historical Shapes of Justice* (Cambridge, MA: Harvard University Press, 2017), pp. 103, 140ff.

World War convinced many that what Hegel had regarded as advances were merely fragments of a larger pattern of deterioration. Belief in the degradation of civilisation had taken hold. Given the incidence of evil since 1914, virtually every manifestation of modernity was disparaged by one commentator or another. Accordingly, figures like Strauss turned to earlier periods to uncover material for instruction. The ancients became a resource for indicting the failures of the moderns. In this vein, Eric Voegelin, Hannah Arendt and Sheldon Wolin turned to classical thought for moral capital.

This remedy was based on a paradoxical approach to philosophical history. Strauss, Voegelin and Arendt were openly critical of the philosophies of history that flourished between Kant and Marx.[99] However, they reproached this 'historicist' trend not by an appeal to empirical fact, but by relying on their own rival philosophies of history. At the centre of Voegelin's attention was the turn to 'labour' as a source of value. He pointed to Marx's 1844 *Manuscripts* as exemplifying the problem: world history, Marx wrote, was nothing but the 'self-creation of man'.[100] As Marx recognised, his pronouncement was a distillation of Hegel's *Phenomenology of Spirit*.[101] For Voegelin, this very conception was a latter-day expression of Gnosticism. The suggestion here was an elaboration of the popular idea that modern extremism was a species of 'political religion' or a brand

---

99. See, for example, Hannah Arendt, 'The Concept of History: Ancient and Modern', in *Between Past and Future: Eight Exercises in Political Thought* (New York: Viking, 1961).

100. Eric Voegelin, *Science, Politics and Gnosticism* (Chicago: Henry Regnery Company, 1968), p. 24, citing Marx, *Economic and Philosophical Manuscripts*, p. 332.

101. Marx, *Economic and Philosophical Manuscripts*, p. 333.

of secularised theology.[102] In advancing the more specific thesis that the Enlightenment along with German Idealism were indebted to resurgent Gnostic values, Voegelin made use of various accounts of heterodoxy to convict post-classical thought of subordinating divinity to the mind of man.[103] Voegelin contended in Heideggerian language that mankind was 'thrown' or forlorn. The difficulty, in Voegelin's mind, was that humanity responded to this abandonment by becoming its own means of redemption: 'gnostic man must carry on the work of salvation himself'.[104]

The problem with this for Voegelin was twofold. First, politics had become a sort of ersatz religion. Second, religion itself had lost any sense of transcendence. This was a consequence of man's rebellion against the objective order of nature. Voegelin argued that defiance came about with the decline of classical philosophical culture. That culture reached its perfection in the philosophies of Plato and Aristotle and above all in the ideal of

102. The argument rose to prominence between the 1920s and 1950s. See Carl Schmitt, *Political Theology: Four Chapters on the Concept of Sovereignty* (1922, 1934), trans. George D. Schwab (Chicago: University of Chicago Press, 2005); Jacob Taubes, *Abendländische Eschatologie* (Bern: Francke, 1947); Karl Löwith, *Meaning and History: The Theological Implications of the Philosophy of History* (Chicago: University of Chicago Press, 1949); Raymond Aron, *The Opium of the Intellectuals* (1955), trans. Terence Kilmartin (London: Secker & Warburg, 1957); Jacob Talmon, *Political Messianism: The Romantic Phase* (London: Secker & Warburg, 1960); Norman Cohn, *The Pursuit of the Millennium: Revolutionary Millenarians and Mystical Anarchists of the Middle Ages* (London: Secker & Warburg, 1957). A critical treatment of the view was developed at length in Hans Blumenberg, *The Legitimacy of the Modern Age* (1966), trans. Robert M. Wallace (Cambridge, MA: MIT Press, 1983).

103. Christian Baur, *Die christliche Gnosis, oder die Religionsphilosophie in ihrer geschichtlichen Entwicklung* (Tübingen: Osiander, 1835); Hans Jonas, *Gnosis und spätantiker Geist: Die mythologische Gnosis* (Göttingen: Vandenhoeck & Ruprecht, 1934); Henri Lubac, *Le Drame de l'humanisme athée* (Paris: Éditions Spes, 1944).

104. Voegelin, *Science, Politics and Gnosticism*, p. 11.

a standard of rational ethics. As this achievement receded with the advance of secular worldviews, Christianity stood firm against a canon of man-made values. In Voegelin's scheme, Greek philosophy supported Christian orthodoxy. As with Heidegger and Arendt, both of whom he ultimately rejected, Voegelin disdained the main currents of modern thought. While Arendt similarly turned to Hellenic civilisation in the hope of arresting epochal decline, she nonetheless concluded that its philosophical tradition lacked the means of aiding the recovery. Hegel saw that every age would 'eternally feel drawn to Greece'.[105] Yet, unlike Strauss, Voegelin and Arendt, he insisted that the limits of the attraction should be maintained. The beauty of Athenian society would forever be apparent, but aesthetic appeal fell short of guaranteeing the 'truth' of its values. Nonetheless, Arendt ignored Hegel's message of caution. For her, even though philosophy had failed to capture the virtues of Athens, activity on the ground presented a model of political conduct.[106]

What drew Arendt to the Athenian conception of politics was its separation between practical affairs and the domain of family existence. In accordance with the common Greek understanding, these corresponded to spheres of freedom and necessity. In the familiar typology laid out in Aristotle's *Politics*, the arena of independent action characteristic of political life (*bios politikos*) was counterposed to the realm of household (*oikos*) exigency associated with the satisfaction of needs.[107] Whereas

---

105. Hegel, *Vorlesungen Weltgeschichte* (Lasson), 3, p. 640.

106. The limitations of the model for Arendt herself are set out in Roy T. Tsao, 'Arendt against Athens: Rereading *The Human Condition*', *Political Theory*, 30: 1 (February 2002), pp. 97–123.

107. Aristotle, *Politics*, 1252a10–15, 1252a25–30, 1252b10–15, 1277b1–8, 1332b1–5, 1333a30–35.

the citizen occupied the autonomous world of praxis, the slave was confined to consumption, labour and want. Hegel developed the most sophisticated post-classical interpretation of these relations in the sections on self-consciousness and spirit in the *Phenomenology*. The cultivation of freedom within the context of necessity forms the subject matter of the master–slave dialectic, followed by an analysis of the Stoic withdrawal from public affairs and the rise of early Christian consciousness.[108] The ancient Greek antithesis between *polis* and *oikos* is explored in perhaps the richest example of exegesis in the *Phenomenology*, the interpretation of Sophocles's *Antigone*.[109] While for Arendt the ancient family was the negation of the city, for Hegel they formed a dynamic interrelationship. In Hegel's rendition, after these relations had re-formed—first under the Roman principate and Christianity, and later under European feudalism—the system of needs as it emerged in modern civil society proved compatible with constitutional liberty. Since necessity and freedom were not antithetical in Hegel, they could be dialectically reconciled.

Hegel's reconstruction of ancient and modern history makes no appearance in Arendt's treatment of the same terrain in *The Human Condition*. Instead, studies by Fustel de Coulanges and Werner Jaeger shaped her account.[110] Citizenship and domesticity were normatively polarised. This antithesis proved

108. Hegel, *Phenomenology*, §§178–230.

109. Ibid., §§ 444–76.

110. Hannah Arendt, *The Human Condition* (Chicago: University of Chicago Press, 1958), pp. 24n5, 24n6, 30n19, 61n56, 62n60, referencing Werner Jaeger, *Paideia: The Ideals of Greek Culture* (1934), trans. Gilbert Highet, vol. 3: *The Conflict of Cultural Ideals in the Age of Plato*, (Oxford: Blackwell, 1945) and Numa Denis Fustel de Coulanges, *The Ancient City: A Study of Religion, Laws and Institutions of Greece and Rome* (1864), trans. Willard Small (New York: Doubleday, 1956).

decisive for Arendt's narrative, since developments in the aftermath of ancient city-states led to the domestication of social life
in general. According to Arendt, economics corrupted the integrity of politics; rote behaviour supplanted the initiative of
free action; and 'labor' dictated the terms of human relationships.[111] From Arendt's perspective, public life had collapsed
into purely social relations, and society was reduced to a cycle
of production and consumption.[112] This outcome seemed a
perfect manifestation of futility. Modern existence had been
compressed into little more than 'making a living'. Arendt's
overall verdict was bleak: 'we have almost succeeded in levelling
all human activities to the common denominator of securing
the necessities of life and providing for their abundance'.[113]
Higher ideals and activities had perished or were disappearing. The only respite from the circle of biological survival was
the mindless consumption of mass culture.[114] In light of this
trajectory, the modern world represented a downturn from
antiquity.

Despite the stark division between the ancients and us, the
opposition was not a purely aesthetic one for Arendt. There
was a substantive point to her appeal to the Greeks. Even though
her account of the Athenian polis was perfunctory, with the
features of the Homeric and Periclean agora blended into a
single type, Arendt foregrounded the distinction between the
'common' world of politics, and kinship relations based on the
model of the family. In Roman terms, the *res publica* was pitted

111. Arendt, *The Human Condition*, pp. 28ff., 43–45, 96ff.
112. Ibid., p. 98.
113. Ibid., pp. 126–27. Cf. Hannah Arendt, 'On Violence' (1970), in *Crises of the
Republic* (New York: Harcourt, 1972), pp. 179–80.
114. Arendt, *The Human Condition*, pp. 134–35.

against the *gens*.[115] Implicit in this comparison was the difference between 'national' belonging and the 'civic' allegiance of republican politics. This juxtaposition built on interwar condemnations of nationalism as a form of 'enlarged tribal consciousness'.[116] It enabled Arendt to differentiate between the city-state and the nation. The distinction served to highlight the descent from political man to the 'herdlike' existence of modern mass society.[117] Since dignity was the chief characteristic of the receding life of the polis, the past became a repository of value in Arendt's thought—an archive, in her words, of 'lost treasure'.[118] In the same spirit, a version of the classical ideal of the *vita activa* lent critical purchase to the early Jürgen Habermas and Wolin. Like Arendt, both celebrated truly civic engagement in opposition at once to Stoic withdrawal and private consumption.[119]

Wolin grew sceptical about what he saw as Arendt's predilection for the aristocratic ideal of excellence at the cost of

115. Ibid., pp. 24, 24 n. 6, 28–29.

116. The phrase comes from Emil Deckert, *Panlatinismus, Panslawismus und Panteutonismus in ihrer Bedeutung für die politische Weltlage* (Frankfurt am Main: H. Keller, 1914), p. 4, cited in Hannah Arendt, *The Origins of Totalitarianism* (1951) (London: André Deutsch, 1973), p. 223. For the related antithesis between civic and ethnic nationalism, see Hans Kohn, *The Idea of Nationalism: A Study in Its Origins and Background* (New York: Macmillan, 1944). The contrast reappears in John Plamenatz, 'Two Types of Nationalism', in Eugene Kamenka, ed., *Nationalism: The Nature and Evolution of an Idea* (Canberra: Australian National University Press, 1973).

117. Arendt, *The Human Condition*, p. 160.

118. Hannah Arendt, *On Revolution* (1963) (London: Pelican, 1986), p. 280.

119. Sheldon Wolin, *Politics and Vision: Continuity and Innovation in Western Political Thought* (1960) (Princeton, NJ: Princeton University Press, 2004), pp. 4–5, 10–11, 63–65, 69, 71–75, 85, 257–60, 314, 315–17; Jürgen Habermas, 'The Classical Doctrine of Politics in Relation to Social Philosophy' (1963), in *Theory and Practice*, trans. John Viertel (London: Heinemann, 1974).

democratic standards.[120] Nonetheless, he continued to cherish the way she practised political theory as an act of 'recovery'.[121] On this understanding, Arendt's method amounted to a kind of archaeology in which the excavated materials breathed new life. The ongoing relevance of past examples nonetheless remained unclear. It seemed that, on the one hand, ancient politics was a privileged moment to which the historian could bear witness. In that case, the act of remembering paid homage to a definitively departed world. On the other hand, the study of past political ideas could be presented as an attempt to reacquire lost meanings. This implied that the retrieval of historical worldviews could still illuminate and apply to our situation. However, the ambiguity inherent in these recuperative strategies left the historian of political thought facing in two directions. They could either savour the things of the past, or directly seek to use them. Fearing the charge of antiquarianism, most historians since Wolin have striven to adopt the more practical approach. Yet this has left them trying to explain how an older currency could lose its value and later have it restored.

120. Sheldon Wolin, 'Hannah Arendt: Democracy and The Political', *Salmagundi*, 60 (Spring–Summer 1983), pp. 3–19.

121. Sheldon Wolin, 'Hannah Arendt and the Ordinance of Time Wolin', *Social Research*, 44: 1 (Spring 1977), pp. 91–105, p. 96.

9

Political Thought and
Its Discontents

THE 1960S IS GENERALLY associated with an historical turn in the study of political thought. For most commentators, the change can be traced to research connected to the University of Cambridge.[1] The new approach was signalled by a number of manifesto pieces published by J.G.A. Pocock, Quentin Skinner and John Dunn.[2] According to Germanic jargon, the outcome was the establishment of neither a 'school' of disciples (*Schule*) nor a 'circle' of participants (*Kreis*). In the 1950s and 1960s there

1. Richard Tuck, 'History', in Robert E. Goodin, Philip Pettit and Thomas Pogge, eds, *A Companion to Contemporary Political Philosophy* (Oxford: Blackwell, 2017); David Runciman, 'History of Political Thought: The State of the Discipline', *British Journal of Politics and International Relations*, 3: 1 (April 2001), pp. 84–104; Annabel Brett, 'What is Intellectual History Now?', in David Cannadine, ed., *What is History Now* (London: Palgrave Macmillan, 2002); Samuel James, 'The "Cambridge School"' in 'The History of Political Thought, 1948–1979', PhD thesis, University of Cambridge, 2012.

2. J.G.A. Pocock, 'The History of Political Thought: A Methodological Inquiry' (1962), in *Political Thought and History: Essays on Theory and Method* (Cambridge: Cambridge University Press, 2009); Dunn, 'History of Ideas'; Skinner, 'Meaning and Understanding'.

was no British equivalent to the Austro-German 'seminar' devoted to the production of trained pupils. Equally, our protagonists did not engineer interdisciplinary 'meetings' in pursuit of a common goal after the fashion of the Vienna Circle. What arose instead was more like a competitive collaboration. On a banal level, what each of these founding figures had in common was that they studied at the same History Faculty and, more significantly, applied historicising methods to the interpretation of texts.

It is possible to overstate the novelty of the shift announced by the emergence of a Cambridge School. For one thing, Pocock himself drew attention to earlier exemplars of historical interpretation, which he associated with the work of Peter Laslett in particular.[3] In addition, Pocock has emphasised the impact upon him of the historian Herbert Butterfield, as well as that of the historian-turned-political-philosopher Michael Oakeshott. Both of these then influenced Maurice Cowling, Duncan Forbes and John Burrow. Besides Pocock, other scholars have unearthed a longer Cambridge pedigree stretching back to John Seeley, Henry Sidgwick, John Dahlberg-Acton, Frederic Maitland and John Figgis.[4] A pedigree, however, does not make a history. While Pocock was conscious of his influences from the 1950s, he did not identify his own activity with a lineage going back to the nineteenth century. Even more conspicuously, with Dunn and Skinner the assumption prevailed that their approach marked a departure. Both were taught by Forbes and Walter Ullmann, and influenced by Moses

---

3. J.G.A. Pocock, 'Present at the Creation: With Laslett to the Lost Worlds', *International Journal of Public Affairs*, 2 (2006), pp. 7–17.

4. James Alexander, 'The Cambridge School, c. 1875–c. 1978', *Journal of the History of Political Thought*, 37: 2 (2016), pp. 360–86.

Finley, but nonetheless they exuded the sense that they were breaking new ground. When Pocock summarised their collective efforts in 1971, he described their work as amounting to a 'transformation' of the field.[5]

Even so, as we have seen, Strauss, Voegelin, Arendt and Wolin also took historical texts as their primary subject matter. In dealing with this material, they employed exegetical techniques long established as fundamental to historical inquiry. This kind of work had already flourished among ancient historians, biblical scholars and classical philologists in the nineteenth century. We therefore associate its methods with, among others, Barthold Niebuhr, David Strauss and Ulrich von Wilamowitz-Moellendorff.[6] It was the paralysing burden of this historical consciousness that roused Nietzsche in 1874 to impeach its consequences.[7] As a product of this culture, even Leo Strauss self-consciously wrote within the tradition of historical scholarship. As he himself observed, after the decline of classical philosophy, modern conditions demanded the 'recollection' of past ideas. Given the situation as it now stood, Strauss concluded, 'concern with the various phases of earlier thought becomes an integral part of philosophy'.[8] Philosophy, he was arguing,

5. J.G.A. Pocock, 'Languages and their Implications: The Transformation of the Study of Political Thought' (1971), in *Politics, Language, and Time: Essays on Political Thought and History* (Chicago: University of Chicago Press, 1989), p. 3.

6. See Georg Iggers, *The German Idea of History: The National Tradition of Historical Thought from Herder to the Present* ((Middletown, CT: Wesleyan University Press, 1988); Frederick C. Beiser, *The German Historicist Tradition* (Oxford: Oxford University Press, 2011).

7. Friedrich Nietzsche, 'On the Uses and Disadvantages of History for Life' (1874), in *Untimely Meditations*, ed. Daniel Breazeale, trans. R. J. Hollingdale (Cambridge: Cambridge University Press, 1997).

8. Leo Strauss, *Persecution and the Art of Writing* (1952) (Chicago: University of Chicago Press, 1988), p. 158.

needed history to revitalise itself. Pocock, Dunn and Skinner, however, adopted a different tack. For them, at least initially, history was not the servant of philosophical inquiry. It was valuable, they argued, in its own right.

George Sabine's *History of Political Theory*, published in 1937, survived as an authoritative textbook down to the 1960s.[9] Its aim was to reconstruct past systems of ideas with the ultimate goal of evaluating their truth. The political philosopher was not an 'antiquarian', Sabine insisted, but someone who sought to test the veracity of theories.[10] The Cambridge approach was first and foremost a rejection of this conception. 'Sabine's book is obsolete,' Pocock declared in 1971.[11] In repudiating his work, the Cantabrigians implicitly separated themselves from Strauss and Arendt as well. In general terms, they contrasted the philosopher with the historian. As Pocock saw things in 1962, while philosophers examined the rational coherence of political theories, historians simply studied their occurrence.[12] This last activity pointed to two distinct procedures. First, it involved reconstructing the original character of ideas as distinct from later attempts at systematisation. Second, it entailed ascertaining their role in the world of social and political action. The former procedure necessitated discriminating among 'languages' of political thought, which Pocock also labelled 'traditions of discourse.'[13] Later, for a time, and

9. George H. Sabine, *The History of Political Theory* (London: George G. Harrap, 1937).

10. George H. Sabine, 'What is a Political Theory?', *The Journal of Politics*, 1: 1 (February 1939), pp. 1–16.

11. J.G.A. Pocock, 'Working on Ideas in Time' (1971), in *Political Thought and History*, p. 21.

12. Pocock, 'A Methodological Inquiry', pp. 9–10. Cf. Dunn, 'History of Ideas', pp. 90, 93.

13. Pocock, 'A Methodological Inquiry', p. 18.

with some reluctance, he designated these idioms by the Kuhnian term 'paradigms'.[14] Such idioms, he noted, came in disparate shapes, whose differences philosophers tended not to notice. Their distinctness was partly a function of their institutional setting, as they emerged in governments, law courts, churches or universities. Pocock distinguished the types of argument which might be employed in these divergent contexts.[15]

Each of these preoccupations generated further debate and analysis. This led, for a period, to a parting of the ways between philosophical and historical analyses of texts. As noted above, in his teaching at Harvard, Rawls brought forward and developed what he identified as the Kantian approach: the philosopher improved upon the canon of inherited texts. On this model, which still prevails among philosophers interested in past thinkers, understanding is followed in the last instance by criticism.[16] However, before a description of Rawlsian pedagogy was in print, Pocock, Dunn and Skinner rejected the critical stance which had characterised the work of Popper, Talmon, Voegelin, Strauss, Arendt and Wolin. Instead, they strove to refine the business of historical reconstruction.

This gave rise to a number of methodological clarifications. As is generally known, insights were collected from anglophone

14. Pocock, 'Languages and their Implications', pp. 13–15.

15. As illustrated in J.G.A. Pocock, *The Ancient Constitution and the Feudal Law: A Study of English Historical Thought in the Seventeenth Century* (Cambridge: Cambridge University Press, 1957).

16. See, for example, Robert Brandom, *Tales of the Mighty Dead: Historical Essays in the Metaphysics of Intentionality* (Cambridge, MA: Harvard University Press, 2002); Robert Pippin, *Interanimations: Receiving Modern German Philosophy* (Chicago: University of Chicago Press, 2015). Scepticism about the viewpoint is registered in Susan James, 'The Relationship between Philosophy and Its History', in Richard Bourke and Quentin Skinner, eds, *History in the Humanities and Social Sciences* (Cambridge: Cambridge University Press, 2023).

philosophy, notably from the work of Ludwig Wittgenstein, W.V.O. Quine, Elizabeth Anscombe, J. L. Austin and Donald Davidson.[17] Equally, hypotheses were adopted from the social sciences as well as the philosophy of history, not least from Collingwood, William Dray, Arthur Danto, Peter Winch, Alasdair MacIntyre and Charles Taylor.[18] Cumulatively, this led to a tidying-up operation, which entailed closely identifying meaning with intention; distinguishing between propositions and performances in language; elucidating the relationship between utterances and their contexts; and delineating the character of historical explanation. In Pocock's mind, the rise of linguistic philosophy had caused the decline of political theory while unintentionally boosting the history of political thought. This advance came with a peremptory repudiation of alternative styles of intellectual history and political theory. Partly because of the focus among Cambridge scholars on the seventeenth century, figures such as George Mosse, H. Stuart Hughes and Peter Gay were ignored. Equally, the preferred emphasis on the role of ideas in the justification of political events meant that the concerns with enduring *mentalitées* characteristic of *Annales* historians were overlooked. Skinner was forthright about work that

17. James Tully, ed., *Meaning and Context: Quentin Skinner and His Critics* (Cambridge: Polity Press, 1988); Danielle Charette and Max Skjönsberg, 'State of the Field: The History of Political Thought', *History*, 105: 366 (July 2020), pp. 470–83; Richard Whatmore, *The History of Political Thought: A Very Short Introduction* (Oxford: Oxford University Press, 2021), ch. 5.

18. Quentin Skinner, 'The Limits of Historical Explanations,' *Philosophy*, 41: 157 (July 1966), pp. 199–215; Skinner, '"Social Meaning" and the Explanation of Social Action', in Peter Laslett, W. G. Runciman and Quentin Skinner, eds, *Philosophy, Politics and Society*, Fourth Series (Oxford: Blackwell, 1972); John Dunn, 'Practising History and Social Science on "Realist" Assumptions', in Christopher Hookway and Philip Pettit, eds, *Action and Interpretation: Studies in the Philosophy of the Social Sciences* (Cambridge: Cambridge University Press, 1978).

did not pass muster. The views of J. B. Bury, Karl Jaspers, Ernst Cassirer, Carl Friedrich, Carl Becker, John Higham, John Passmore, C. B. Macpherson, John Plamenatz and Arthur Lovejoy were reprimanded.[19] Curiously enough, at this early stage, the writings of Isaiah Berlin went unmentioned.

The new approach signalled by Pocock, Skinner and Dunn brought with it both immediate and long-term dividends. Contextualism was firmly established as an essential facet of interpretation. At the same time, the historical method led to a massive accumulation of detail. This was matched by an increase in subtlety of exposition and an obvious extension of historical knowledge. The opportunity was also seized to build on existing historiography. As a result, perceptions of the origins of liberalism, the impact of the Renaissance, the character of the Reformation and the roots of the American Revolution were dramatically revised. The diffuse insights of earlier scholarship were marshalled with a sense of purpose. The sheer weight of the addition to learning represented by Hans Baron, Felix Gilbert, Julian Franklin, Caroline Robbins, Zera Fink, Bernard Bailyn and Gordon Wood, as well as the writings of Pocock, Dunn and Skinner themselves, was overwhelming.

Within a generation, understanding of the history of political economy and the ideological origins of the French Revolution would likewise be overhauled.[20] In due course, the history of rights, international relations and imperial ideologies were

---

19. Skinner, 'Meaning and Understanding'.

20. Istvan Hont, *Jealousy of Trade: International Competition and the Nation-State in Historical Perspective* (Cambridge, MA: Harvard University Press, 2005); Michael Sonenscher, *Before the Deluge: Public Debt, Inequality, and the Intellectual Origins of the French Revolution* (Princeton, NJ: Princeton University Press, 2007).

fundamentally re-examined.[21] However, two outstanding issues remained unresolved. To begin with, the question of the historical significance of ideas was still unanswered. In other words, the role played by theories in effecting change had yet to be clarified. In addition, the reason for studying political thought continued to be controversial. If canonical texts could not be studied for their capacity to deliver instruction, it seemed as though their importance was confined to their place in the past. Since their causal significance had also still to be determined, this left the intellectual historian looking like a collector: amassing data without much sense of what the enterprise was supposed to achieve. For Pocock, the charge of antiquarianism was easily dismissed. Investigating the past, including changes in its leading intellectual assumptions, enjoyed for him a self-evident importance. But, over time, Skinner and Dunn were afflicted by doubts about their original recommendations. Ultimately, this led to an about-turn.

II

Scepticism about the social significance of ideas had two principal sources at the time. One derived from the revisionist style of political history pioneered by Lewis Namier, the other from the influence of Marxist thought on mid-century historians. For the former, ideas were belated rationalisations; for the latter, they were superstructural reflections of material causes. Yet

---

21. Richard Tuck, *Natural Rights Theories: Their Origin and Development* (Cambridge: Cambridge University Press, 1979); Tuck, *The Rights of War and Peace: Political Thought and the International Order from Grotius to Kant* (Oxford: Oxford University Press, 1999); David Armitage, *The Ideological Origins of the British Empire* (Cambridge: Cambridge University Press, 2000).

ultimately these conclusions were half-hearted. Namier himself had contributed to intellectual history and basically conceded the relevance of precepts to politics. In many ways his corpus registered the concession by dividing eighteenth-century Britain from nineteenth-century Europe: to the former he ascribed the good sense of sacrificing principles to tactics, while he blasted the latter for succumbing periodically to idealism.[22] Marxist historians, including Christopher Hill, E. P. Thompson and Eric Hobsbawm, were in practice drawn more forcefully to the study of intellectual culture.[23] In fact, maintaining the priority of material forces over ideas proved difficult for these historians, just as it had done for Marx. After all, Marx himself was a follower of Hegel. Whatever his criticisms of the master, he therefore accepted that political economy involved the study of the history of consciousness in its cultivation of nature. Illustrating this insight, Hegel remarked around 1802 that even a physical tool (*Werkzeug*) is 'ideally determined by labour', since it was fabricated with a view to serving an intended purpose.[24]

Notwithstanding this complicated picture, which involved the Hegel-style recognition that matter itself (*hyle*, ὕλη) was a concept, the Cambridge School was keen to resist any charge of idealism. Accordingly, Dunn lambasted the notion that

22. Lewis Namier, *The Structure of Politics at the Accession of George III* (London: Macmillan, 1929); Lewis Namier, *1848: The Revolution of the Intellectuals* (London: Oxford University Press, 1946).

23. See, for example, E. P. Thompson, *William Morris: Romantic to Revolutionary* (London: Lawrence and Wishart, 1955); Christopher Hill, *Intellectual Origins of the English Revolution* (Oxford: Clarendon Press, 1965); Eric Hobsbawm and Terence Ranger, eds, *The Invention of Tradition* (Cambridge: Cambridge University Press, 1983).

24. G.W.F. Hegel, *System der Sittlichkeit* (1802/3), ed. Horst D. Brandt (Hamburg: Felix Meiner Verlag, 2002), p. 9.

doctrines had historical agency, while Skinner came close to accepting that although principles might justify a course of action after the fact they rarely motivated its adoption.[25] Suspicion about the determining role of thought stemmed from confusing the ineffectiveness of moral principles with the ideal character of intentionality.[26] Of course, the claim that ideals operated as mere pretexts in human conduct was a longstanding theme in the history of ethics. As shown in chapter 2 above, Kant himself had demonstrated the extent to which moral maxims were habitually rationalised (*vernünftelt*).[27] Yet this was not to deny that ideas guided conduct. Indeed, it is inconceivable that they do not shape behaviour. Scepticism on this score led to the strange result that intellectual historians grew hesitant about the term 'idea', preferring words such as 'practice', 'intervention', 'language', 'parole', 'idiom', 'strategy' and 'event' to depict their subject matter.[28] Consciousness, it seemed, was only a metaphysical construct. Accordingly, conceptual schemes were deemed to lack actual traction in politics. This unforeseen fallout made pressing cultural realities such as liberalism, communism and totalitarianism difficult to explain. Having anatomised so minutely the character of ideologies, the Cantabrigians inadvertently denied their potency.

25. Dunn, 'History of Ideas', p. 85; Quentin Skinner, 'Some Problems in the Analysis of Political Thought and Action', *Political Theory*, 2: 3 (August 1974), pp. 277–303.

26. For discussion, see Richard Bourke, 'Max Weber and Anglophone Historiograph,', *CAS Blog: Max Weber Today*, 17 December 2020, https://www.blog.cas.uni-muenchen.de/topics/max-weber-today (accessed 14 February 2023).

27. Kant, *Groundwork*, AA 4: 407.

28. These taxonomic preferences relate to developments in epistemology from the 'way of ideas' (Locke) to the age of the 'sentence' (Quine) and beyond. For an overview, see Ian Hacking, *Why Does Language Matter to Philosophy?* (Cambridge: Cambridge University Press, 1975).

Reservations about the role of doctrines and the reality of concepts followed misgivings about the persona of the philosopher. These doubts were a bequest of the 1950s. In the face of the enormous challenges of the epoch, philosophy seemed to many to have precious little to offer. Even Wittgenstein appeared to diminish what the enterprise could achieve, demoting it to little more than a description of usages.[29] In deliberately programmatic interventions, its limits were articulated by Peter Laslett, and its shortcomings by David Easton.[30] The same deflationary attitude characterised T. D. Weldon's influential *Vocabulary of Politics*, which discarded as 'metaphysical lumber' the notion that philosophy could discover political truths.[31] Against this background, the history of ideology promised more substantive insights. Its conclusions, however, were exclusively about the character of the past. The past mattered, the Cambridge historians contended, but they struggled to demonstrate how. Their difficulties were compounded by the rise of political science. As the importance of political philosophy appeared to decline in anglophone philosophy departments, political theory maintained its position in politics and government. In the end, this was the institutional setting in which the careers of Carl Friedrich, Michael Oakeshott, Hannah Arendt, Leo Strauss, Isaiah Berlin, Judith Shklar and Sheldon Wolin flourished. Cambridge historians might charge

29. Ludwig Wittgenstein, *Philosophische Untersuchungen/Philosophical Investigations* (1953), ed. P.M.S. Hacker and Joachim Schulte (Oxford: Wiley-Blackwell, 2009), §124.

30. Peter Laslett, 'The Face-to-Face Society', in Laslett, ed., *Philosophy, Politics and Society*, First Series (Oxford: Basil Blackwell, 1956); David Easton, 'The Decline of Modern Political Theory', *The Journal of Politics*, 13: 1 (February 1951), pp. 36–58.

31. T. D. Weldon, *The Vocabulary of Politics* (London: Penguin, 1953), p. 15.

theorists with a lack of historical sense, but they were soon up-braided in return with accusations of irrelevance.

Dunn defended the 'moral seriousness' of the historian.[32] Yet this largely entailed restoring the character of bygone thought to its original significance. This archaeological activity showed that the history of ideas was not a record of seamless continuity. The viewpoint had been forcefully stated a decade earlier by Anscombe: the decline of a moral framework based on divine command, she argued, separated modern ethical thought from the more uniformly Christian ages.[33] For Dunn, the trajectory of what he called 'liberalism' illustrated the point. He argued that an epochal break disconnected Locke's vision of a rational life from the outlook promoted by modern capitalist economies. Dunn recognised that contemporary societies still clung to residual elements of the doctrine of toleration formulated by Locke, but nonetheless our world was separated from his by the rise of the moral legitimacy of acquisitiveness and the decline of the appeal of the Calvinist calling on which Lockean philosophy was based.[34] For this reason, Dunn concluded, current political philosophy had nothing to learn from Locke.[35]

However, as Dunn was writing, a 'renaissance' was under way in the fortunes of liberal theory.[36] Much of this revitalisation

---

32. John Dunn, 'Preface' (1968) to *The Political Thought of John Locke: An Historical Account of the Argument of the 'Two Treatises of Government'* (Cambridge: Cambridge University Press, 1969), p. xiii.

33. G.E.M. Anscombe, 'Modern Moral Philosophy', *Philosophy*, 33: 124 (January 1958), pp. 1–19, singled out by Dunn in *Political Thought of John Locke*, p. 24n.

34. Dunn, *Political Thought of John Locke*, pp. 262–67.

35. Ibid., p. x.

36. Nancy Rosenblum, 'Introduction', in Rosenblum, ed., *Liberalism and the Moral Life* (Cambridge, MA: Harvard University Press, 1989), p. 1.

took place in Massachusetts, with Judith Shklar, John Rawls, Michael Walzer, Ronald Dworkin and Robert Nozick contributing to new developments. For all of them, past philosophy was a resource rather than an inapplicable remnant. From this perspective, it made no sense to consign great thinkers to a redundant past. From the first, Shklar regarded political theory as a dialogue with predecessors. Her first book, *After Utopia*, reflected on the nature and limitations of our inheritance.[37] Her subsequent work on Rousseau, Hegel and Montesquieu was intended to treat these luminaries as aids to understanding.[38] She advised that, to carry this off, we ought to approach them constructively rather than passively, 'criticizing and rethinking their own and our words and thoughts'.[39] Shklar once saluted Arendt's conviction that we could not think without the ancients.[40] This contrasts explicitly with Skinner's injunction that we ought to do our thinking 'for ourselves'.[41] The problem for Skinner was that thought was immersed in an inherited body of reflection. We are the heirs of Platonism, Marxism and liberalism and cannot simply extract ourselves from the history they have made. But if thinking is inevitably 'rethinking', in Shklar's sense, where does this leave the relationship between the philosopher and the past?

37. Judith Shklar, *After Utopia: The Decline of Political Faith* (Princeton, NJ: Princeton University Press, 1957).

38. Judith Shklar, *Men and Citizens: A Study of Rousseau's Social Theory* (Cambridge: Cambridge University Press, 1969); Shklar, *Freedom and Independence: A Study of the Political Ideas of Hegel's 'Phenomenology of Mind'* (Cambridge: Cambridge University Press, 1976); Shklar, *Montesquieu* (Oxford: Oxford University Press, 1987).

39. Shklar, *Freedom and Independence*, p. xv.

40. Judith Shklar, 'Between Past and Future by Hannah Arendt', *History and Theory*, 2: 3 (1963), pp. 286–92.

41. Skinner, 'Meaning and Understanding', p. 52.

Skinner approached historic texts armed with the principle of anthropological charity.[42] Historians should regard themselves as 'set down' in alien territory where they have to learn to see things as their ancestors did.[43] Keith Thomas's work on the history of magic encouraged the analogy with anthropology.[44] For the early Skinner, what interpreters needed was essentially 'less philosophy, and more history'.[45] However, in the process of entering the world of the past, the exegete left their immediate surroundings behind. Skinner's insistence on the 'unimportance' of canonical works led him to settle for the local character of knowledge.[46] Each era was defined by its own contingent body of beliefs. All history could do was recover the plurality of values and encourage toleration between forms of life.[47] A gap opened up between current imperatives and antiquated conditions. By comparison, Shklar and Rawls engaged their authors by employing the axioms of philosophical charity. This decreed that venerated thinkers ought to be read with a view to amending their incoherence when all else failed.[48] Even Alasdair

42. Quentin Skinner, 'Conventions and the Understanding of Speech Acts', *The Philosophical Quarterly*, 20: 79 (April 1970), pp. 118–38.

43. The famous phrase 'set down' comes from Bronislaw Malinowski, *Argonauts of the Western Pacific* (London: Routledge & Kegan Paul, 1922), p. 4. Skinner's access to the anthropological literature was facilitated by Peter Winch's critique of Edward Evans-Pritchard in 'Understanding a Primitive Society', *American Philosophical Quarterly*, 1: 4 (October 1964), pp. 307–24.

44. Keith Thomas, *Religion and the Decline of Magic: Studies in Popular Beliefs in Sixteenth- and Seventeenth Century England* (London: Weidenfeld and Nicolson, 1971).

45. Quentin Skinner, 'Hobbes's *Leviathan*', *The Historical Journal*, 7: 2 (1964), pp. 321–33, at p. 333.

46. For Skinner's view of their unimportance, see James, 'The "Cambridge School"', p. 90.

47. Skinner, 'Meaning and Understanding', pp. 52–53.

48. For discussion, see Michael Rosen, 'The History of Ideas as Philosophy and History', *The History of Political Thought*, 32: 4 (Winter 2011), pp. 691–720.

MacIntyre and Charles Taylor, notwithstanding their historicist sensibilities, turned to the philosophical past to think about
the present.[49] After all, critical engagement with written docu-
ments was a feature of every literate society.[50] It was in this
spirit that Plato took on the Homeric epics, just as Kant corrected the traditions of metaphysics that preceded him.

The advance of political theory forced a rethink among the
Cambridge historians. Against Oakeshott, Pocock came to un-
derline the political relevance of historical reflection.[51] Professional reorientation also prompted a reassessment. Dunn was
appointed visiting lecturer in political science at the University
of Ghana in 1968–69, and then a lecturer in politics in Cambridge in 1972. His work in Ghana self-consciously combined
history, anthropology and political science.[52] He then turned
to research in the history of revolutions.[53] Returning from
Princeton in 1979, Skinner took up the chair in political science at Cambridge. Although the position was based in the
Faculty of History, it became impractical to ignore the current
state of political theory. Denials, subtle revisions and recanta-
tions followed. In a lecture delivered at Harvard in 1986, Dunn

49. Alasdair MacIntyre, *A Short History of Ethics* (London: Macmillan, 1966);
Charles Taylor, *Hegel* (Cambridge: Cambridge University Press, 1975).

50. Jack Goody, *The Domestication of the Savage Mind* (Cambridge: Cambridge
University Press, 1977), ch. 3.

51. J.G.A. Pocock, 'Time, Institutions and Action: An Essay on Traditions and
their Understanding', in Preston King and B. C. Parekh, eds, *Politics and Experience:
Essays Presented to Michael Oakeshott*, (Cambridge: Cambridge University Press,
1968); Pocock, 'The Historian as Political Actor in Polity, Society and Academy'
(1996), in *Political Thought and History*.

52. John Dunn and A. F. Robertson, *Dependence and Opportunity: Political Change
in Ahafo* (Cambridge: Cambridge University Press, 1973).

53. John Dunn, *Modern Revolutions: An Introduction to the Analysis of a Political
Phenomenon* (Cambridge: Cambridge University Press, 1972).

repudiated his youthful perceptions of the incongruity of Locke.[54] Skinner's journey was complete by 1997 when he delivered his inaugural lecture as Regius Professor of History at Cambridge. The past began to appear less as foreign terrain than as an archive of values that could stimulate a reappraisal of our beliefs. Skinner was now trawling for 'buried intellectual treasure.'[55] But, as with Arendt and Wolin, the problem was that if earlier norms were to inspire this revaluation, their applicability out of context would inevitably be called into doubt. In fact, it was precisely this translation from the old into the new that Skinner had been questioning throughout his early work.

III

Notwithstanding their sense that the great philosophical landmarks inhabited a remote past, the Cambridge historians appreciated the intellectual power of the materials to which their research exposed them. Accordingly, despite their strictures, they inevitably drew on insights they had culled from their primary sources. For example, while Pocock was extolling the virtues of historicist interpretation, he also urged an historical approach to politics. This chimed with the material on which he had laboured most in the 1950s: above all, the precedent-based arguments characteristic of the seventeenth-century common lawyers covered in his first book and the reappearance of their assumptions in the thought of Edmund Burke.[56] Pocock's belief

54. John Dunn, 'What Is Living and What Is Dead in the Political Theory of John Locke?', in *Interpreting Political Responsibility* (Cambridge: Polity Press, 1990).

55. Quentin Skinner, *Liberty before Liberalism* (Cambridge: Cambridge University Press, 1998), p. 112.

56. J.G.A. Pocock, 'Burke and the Ancient Constitution' (1960), in *Politics, Language, and Time.*

in inherited norms and institutions as preconditions for any sustainable scheme of political criticism made him sceptical of the pretensions of revolutionary rhetoric, notably as this caught on in the 1960s. The contents of a teach-in conducted by Pocock in 1965, published in a student newspaper the following year, signalled his antipathy to revolutionary consciousness.[57] He acknowledged the earnestness of 'alienated' protesters, along with their attraction to the rhetoric of civilisational repression popularised by Herbert Marcuse, but he had little sympathy with what he saw as their 'Romantic' conception of politics as an arena for creative self-expression.[58] He agreed with Burke: the world could not be made anew without power and violence.[59] For this reason he concluded, in Hegelian language, that the lurch towards absolute freedom brought terror.[60] This intuition enabled Pocock to integrate his political preferences with his methodological injunctions. The combined force of these commitments sustained a career-long fascination with the varieties of historical awareness. This took him from his engagement with mutability in Machiavelli to an extended account of the uses of philosophical history in Gibbon.[61]

57. J.G.A. Pocock, 'U.S. Strategy in Vietnam', *Salient: Victorian University Students' Paper*, 29: 1 (1966).

58. J.G.A. Pocock, 'On the Non-Revolutionary Character of Paradigms: A Self-Criticism and Afterpiece', in *Politics, Language, and Time*, p. 275. See also 'Preface', in ibid., p. xi.

59. J.G.A. Pocock, 'Edmund Burke and the Redefinition of Enthusiasm: The Context as Counter-Revolution', in François Furet and Mona Ozouf, eds, *The French Revolution and the Creation of Modern Political Culture*, vol. 3: *The Transformation of Political Culture, 1789–1848* (Oxford: Pergamon Press, 1989).

60. Pocock, 'Non-Revolutionary Character,' p. 278.

61. J.G.A. Pocock, *The Machiavellian Moment: Florentine Political Thought and the Atlantic Republican Tradition* (Princeton, NJ: Princeton University Press, 1975);

Dunn was also quick to combine his historical concerns with his political preoccupations. After 1969, all his writing on Locke included reflection on his legacy and the pertinence of his claims.[62] Other topics that Dunn addressed were more immediately attuned to issues of contemporary relevance: revolutions, socialism, liberalism and democracy.[63] Already by the early 1970s, Dunn had transitioned from the history of political thought to political theory. He followed Shklar in finding the available traditions of analysis inadequate in the face of current dilemmas.[64] This implied a lack of fit between past philosophical systems and the practical demands of the present. Despite this divergence, Dunn evaluated modern democracy against its ancient incarnation and found the former wanting. Democracy constituted a common theme in the writings of senior members of the Cambridge School, which came to include Richard Tuck and Istvan Hont. Hont had originally arrived in Cambridge to work on relations between historical reasoning and the

Pocock, *Barbarism and Religion*, 6 vols (Cambridge: Cambridge University Press, 1999–2015).

62. For example, John Dunn, 'The Concept of "Trust" in the Politics of Locke', in Richard Rorty, J. B. Schneewind and Quentin Skinner, eds, *Philosophy in History* (Cambridge: Cambridge University Press, 1984); Dunn, 'The Dilemma of Humanitarian Intervention: The Executive Power of the Law of Nature, after God', in *The History of Political Theory and Other Essays* (Cambridge: Cambridge University Press, 1996).

63. John Dunn, 'Understanding Revolutions', *Ethics*, 42 (January 1982), pp. 229–315; Dunn, *The Politics of Socialism: An Essay in Political Theory* (Cambridge: Cambridge University Press, 1984); Dunn, 'The Future of Liberalism', in *Rethinking Modern Political Theory: Essays, 1979–1983* (Cambridge: Cambridge University Press, 1985); Dunn, *Setting the People Free: The Story of Democracy* (London: Atlantic Books, 2005).

64. John Dunn, *Western Political Theory in the Face of the Future* (Cambridge: Cambridge University Press, 1979; 1993).

development of political economy.[65] But, along with his peers, he too became absorbed by the place of democracy in the modern state.[66]

While democracy afforded a shared topic, it also engendered conflict. Accordingly, the Cambridge School became an arena of contestation. Dunn's core claim was that the contemporary understanding of democracy was a product of two rival theories, one indebted to the utopian appeal of Athenian democracy, the other to the analytical frameworks cultivated by American political science. In Dunn's mind, the Greek archetype had been rendered impractical by the rise of the modern state. At the same time, he alleged that American portrayals of current reality were ideologically inflected.[67] This, he argued, was a conspicuous feature of accounts of democracy advanced by Joseph Schumpeter, Robert Dahl and Seymour Martin Lipset.[68] These commentators believed that the pluralism of the US system justified the extent of the political division of labour and with it the concentration of decision-making in select hands. At this stage, Dunn agreed with Skinner: allegedly empirical studies of US political practice masked underlying normative commitments.[69] They served to vindicate an oligarchical distribution

65. Istvan Hont, application letter to King's College, Cambridge, Political Economy Project, 29 September 1977, Hont Papers, Intellectual History Archive, Institute of Intellectual History, University of St. Andrews.

66. Istvan Hont, 'The Permanent Crisis of a Divided Mankind: "Contemporary Crisis of the Nation State" in Historical Perspective' (1994), in *Jealousy of Trade*.

67. John Dunn, 'Democracy', in *Western Political Theory*, pp. 27–28.

68. Joseph Schumpeter, *Socialism, Capitalism and Democracy* (London: Routledge, 1943); Robert Dahl, *A Preface to Democratic Theory* (Chicago: University of Chicago Press, 1956); Seymour Martin Lipset, *Political Man: The Social Bases of Politics* (New York: Doubleday, 1960).

69. Quentin Skinner, 'The Empirical Theorists of Democracy and Their Critics: A Plague on Both Their Houses', *Political Theory*, 1: 3 (August 1973), pp. 287–306.

of power in the name of popular rule. In other words, a show of neutrality legitimised unequal subordination. With this conclusion, Dunn and Skinner aligned themselves with the argument of Moses Finley to the effect that modern bureaucratic government betrayed the ancient Greek ideal.[70] Citizen self-rule had succumbed to the apparatus of centralised power.

Dunn's case turned on the gap between the standard set by Athenian practice and the monopolistic design of contemporary politics. This involved accepting the moral authority of Greek precedent without explaining how an outdated model could retain its normative charm. In any case, as Dunn saw it, the norm lacked traction, though not charisma. Patently, modern citizenship did not entail eligibility to rule. Given this fact, Dunn came over time to acknowledge the accuracy of the Schumpeterian picture.[71] Since it now looked plausible, it could no longer be represented as just an ideologically determined portrait. The modern bourgeois constitutional republic carried conviction, Dunn believed, because it lacked any credible rival. Even so, the Greek paradigm continued to be imaginatively seductive for those subject to the discipline of the modern state. In this way, Dunn recognised the moral allure of ancient liberty while he denied its pragmatic cogency. At this point he parted company from Skinner. In recovering Renaissance ideals of civic participation, Skinner came to see classical accounts of

70. M. I. Finley, *Democracy Ancient and Modern* (New Brunswick, NJ: Rutgers University Press, 1973).

71. John Dunn, 'Conclusion', in *Democracy: The Unfinished Journey, 508 BC to AD 1993* (Oxford: Oxford University Press, 1992), p. 260; Dunn, 'Situating Democratic Political Accountability', in Bernard Manin, Adam Przeworski and Susan C. Stokes, eds, *Democracy, Accountability and Representation*, (Cambridge: Cambridge University Press, 1999); Dunn, *Setting the People Free*, p. 165; Dunn, *Breaking Democracy's Spell* (New Haven, CT: Yale University Press, 2014), p. 137.

citizenship as offering a viable scheme of politics. He first developed his analysis in dialogue with Pocock. Where *The Machiavellian Moment* had unearthed a conception of public virtue extending from the Greeks to the American Revolution, Skinner focused his attention on a more narrowly Roman lineage.[72] His point was not that archaic arrangements should be materially revived, but that values intrinsic to Roman republicanism continued to have purchase.

Between 1980 and 1985, Skinner refined his thesis through a critique of Isaiah Berlin. Whereas Berlin had distinguished personal from public liberty, Skinner sought to demonstrate their interdependence: 'No democracy, no liberty,' as he later proclaimed.[73] The path to this conclusion was halting and circuitous, partly shaped by input from Philip Pettit in the 1990s.[74] At one point Machiavelli enjoyed exemplary status for Skinner; later the law of persons in the Roman *Digest* assumed this role.[75] Scholars have questioned Skinner's interpretation of the Roman

72. Quentin Skinner, 'The Paradoxes of Political Liberty', in Sterling M. McMurrin, ed., *The Tanner Lectures on Human Values*, vol. 7 (Cambridge: Cambridge University Press, 1986).

73. Quentin Skinner, 'On Neo-Roman Liberty: A Response and Reassessment' in Hannah Dawson and Annelien de Dijn, eds, *Rethinking Liberty Before Liberalism* (Cambridge: Cambridge University Press, 2022), p. 264. The criticism was directed against Isaiah Berlin, *Two Concepts of Liberty* (Oxford: Oxford University Press, 1958).

74. See Philip Pettit, *Republicanism: A Theory of Freedom and Government* (Oxford: Clarendon Press, 1997). Cf. Pettit, 'Negative Liberty, Liberal and Republican', *European Journal of Philosophy*, 1 (1993), pp. 15–38. Skinner acknowledges Pettit in *Liberty before Liberalism*, p. xi.

75. The shift in emphasis is evident between Quentin Skinner, 'The Idea of Negative Liberty: Philosophical and Historical Perspectives', in Rorty, Schneewind and Skinner, eds, *Philosophy in History* and Skinner, 'A Third Concept of Liberty', *Proceedings of the British Academy*, 117 (2002), pp. 237–68.

precedents.[76] But my concern is with the adoption of historical templates per se as a source for moral judgement in political theory. Hont advocated Adam Smith as an appropriate framework for political analysis.[77] Tuck approved the Girondins as a model of representative government.[78] In effect, the contextual relativity of historical judgement lost its significance. In place of this, to invoke Laslett's phrase, the 'world we have lost' was assumed to hold the key to modern conditions of existence.[79] Skinner proposed that supposedly 'better' values had disappeared while continuing to enjoy normative authority in a new context. He claimed that a 'neo-Roman' conception of liberty had been eclipsed by a Hobbesian vision of freedom. Somewhat brusquely, he equated this newly ascendent theory with liberalism. Morally and intellectually, it seems, history had suffered a decline.

This verdict fits a pattern of postwar political argument, itself indebted to narratives popularised by Nietzsche and Heidegger. The values of the classical or pre-classical past were invoked to sit in judgement on the present. As a result, normative and historical forms of evaluation were misaligned. This is not to deny the validity of rational reconstruction in the interpretation of canonical thinkers. The unmediated study of past texts has long been an integral part of philosophical inquiry.[80]

76. Clifford Ando, "A Dwelling beyond Violence: On the Uses and Disadvantages of History for Contemporary Republicans', *The History of Political Thought*, 31: 2 (Summer 2010), pp. 183–220.

77. Istvan Hont, *Politics in Commercial Society: Jean-Jacques Rousseau and Adam Smith* (Cambridge, MA: Harvard University Press, 2015).

78. Richard Tuck, *The Sleeping Sovereign: The Invention of Modern Democracy* (Cambridge: Cambridge University Press, 2016).

79. Peter Laslett, *The World We Have Lost: Further Explored* (London: Routledge, 1983).

80. Richard Rorty, 'The Historiography of Philosophy: Four Genres', in Rorty, Schneewind and Skinner, eds, *Philosophy in History*.

Plato presumed to correct both Homer and the tragedians, just as Hume exposed what he saw as faulty assumptions in Malebranche. As noted at the start of this chapter, for Kant philosophy can only proceed by interrogating previous efforts in the subject. Applying this principle to Kant himself, modern commentators from Rawls to Korsgaard tried to exorcise theological components from Kantian ethics.[81] This leaves us with the question of the relationship between Kant and neo-Kantianism. But it also forces us to ask which alternative works best for us.

In the end, rational reconstruction should be reconciled with historical judgement. That is, analysis ought to be supplemented by contextual investigation. For historical judgement of the kind to serve a practical purpose, it is necessary to explore the relationship between divergent contexts. We will inevitably try to make sense of antique virtues by our standards, but we also need to appreciate when these values cannot be carried forward. From Marx and Engels's perspective, Saint Just made the mistake of translating ancient principles into an incompatible modern setting.[82] This serves as a reminder that, in addition to the virtue of timeliness (*kairos*) in politics as celebrated from Aristotle to Machiavelli, we also need a sense of historicity, whose relevance was developed between Herder and Hegel.

Skinner has come to describe himself as a moralist in political theory, seeking to 'make explicit' a set of norms already 'implicit'

---

81. John Rawls, 'Kant', in *Lectures on the History of Moral Philosophy* (Cambridge, MA: Harvard University Press, 2000); Christine M. Korsgaard, *Creating the Kingdom of Ends* (Cambridge: Cambridge University Press, 1996).

82. On this, see Bernard Williams, 'Saint-Just's Illusion', in *Making Sense of Humanity and Other Philosophical Papers* (Cambridge: Cambridge University Press, 1995), referring to a discussion of the topic in *The Holy Family*.

in the history of Roman jurisprudence and its reception.[83] During the Renaissance, he went on, these ideals had broad appeal. But they were subsequently displaced by a rising orthodoxy articulated by Hobbes and then taken up by utilitarians in the eighteenth and nineteenth centuries. Against this trend, Skinner has argued for the abandonment of the newly established hegemony by resort to counter-hegemonic values. He has presented this move as a replay of the Renaissance strategy, conjuring the living from the dead. Having started with a contextualist method of interpretation, Skinner embraced an anti-contextualist understanding of politics. Moreover, insofar as historical precedent was invoked to serve a normative agenda, Skinner's hermeneutic practice risked compromising his historicist principles. In the face of this development, I suggest that Hegel's apprehensions about this kind of approach should still hold. Instead of inviting the ancients to speak for us, we need to understand why their patterns of thought became impossible. Hegel recognised that we live with the residues of Platonism whilst also insisting that we no longer inhabit Plato's universe. Since philosophy was concerned with what we had become, it had to work with what remained of the useable past. But it should not in the process forget the pastness of the historical past by employing discarded worldviews out of season.

IV

As Skinner embraced moralism, many of his colleagues switched to realism. This last commitment was formulated in the early 1980s, particularly in the work of Dunn. American liberalism and the prevailing forms of socialism were his principal

83. Skinner, 'Response and Reassessment', p. 262.

targets.[84] Dunn's plea was for an approach to politics attentive to the limitations of the moral capacities of the species and conscious of the social and economic preconditions for any scheme of values to be realised. The demand for realism achieved more prominence in the early twenty-first century, not least under the influence of Raymond Geuss and Bernard Williams. Both men were in a loose sense part of Cambridge debates about the relationship between history and philosophy.[85] They rejected a decontextualised view of politics under which ideal arrangements were justified in abstraction from practical affairs.[86]

Williams regularly assailed two leading schools of moral philosophy: utilitarianism and neo-Kantianism.[87] According to the first, as Williams described it, philosophy prescribed norms with a view to their enactment. According to the second, ethical theory worked out principles which would place constraints on power.[88] Geuss was particularly focused on Rawls as a paragon of neo-Kantian thought. In opposition to both, he challenged the notion that political philosophy should begin with ideal

84. John Dunn, 'Introduction', in Rethinking; Dunn, 'The Future of Liberalism', in ibid.

85. Bernard Williams was Knightsbridge Professor of Philosophy and then provost of King's College, Cambridge, from 1967 to 1987. Raymond Geuss took up a post at Cambridge in 1993 and became Professor of Philosophy there in 2007.

86. David Runciman, 'What Is Realistic Political Philosophy?', Metaphilosophy, 43: 1–2 (January 2012), pp. 58–70; Paul Sagar, 'From Scepticism to Liberalism: Bernard Williams, the Foundations of Liberalism and Political Realism', Political Studies, 64: 2 (2016), pp. 368–84; Katrina Forrester, 'Judith Shklar, Bernard Williams and Political Realism', European Journal of Political Theory, 11: 3 (2012), pp. 247–72.

87. J. C. Smart and Bernard Williams, Utilitarianism: For and Against (Cambridge: Cambridge University Press, 1973); Bernard Williams, Ethics and the Limits of Philosophy (London: Harper Collins,1985).

88. Bernard Williams, 'Realism and Moralism in Political Theory', in In the Beginning Was the Deed: Realism and Moralism in Political Argument (Princeton, NJ: Princeton University Press, 2005), pp. 1–2.

standards and then move to have them implemented in the real world. In this way, Geuss and Williams alike took issue with an 'ethics first' approach.[89] In short, they insisted that political theory was not 'applied morality'.[90] By this they meant that there were no universal norms that could be taken and applied in any circumstance whatsoever with a view to generating a model of a just polity.

Despite this overlap, there is a key difference separating Geuss from Williams. At least on the face of it, Geuss sought to undermine the legitimacy of liberalism, while Williams strove to develop a defence.[91] From this angle, Williams's project was different from the aims of Dunn and Skinner as well, both of whom have underlined their doubts about dominant liberal values. However, since none of these protagonists offered a developed account of liberalism, disagreements between them are not easily specified. For Williams, liberalism was roughly synonymous with Weber's account of modernity, although he neglected to identify the content of the Weberian vision.[92] For Dunn, liberalism covered the new wave of political philosophy that rose to prominence in America in the 1970s, encompassing all positions from Rawls and Dworkin to Nozick.[93] Meanwhile, Geuss associated liberal theory with the Kantian doctrine of autonomy.[94] By comparison, Skinner's conception included a

89. Raymond Geuss, *Philosophy and Real Politics* (Princeton, NJ: Princeton University Press, 2008), p. 6.

90. Williams, 'Realism and Moralism,' p. 2.

91. Raymond Geuss, 'Did Williams Do Ethics?', in *A World without Why* (Princeton, NJ: Princeton University Press, 2014), p. 184; Geuss, *Not Thinking like a Liberal* (Cambridge, MA: Harvard University Press, 2022).

92. Williams, 'Realism and Moralism', p. 9.

93. Dunn, 'Future of Liberalism', p. 159.

94. Geuss, *Philosophy and Real Politics*, pp. 7–8.

wider frame of reference: based on the commitment to non-interference, it extended from Hobbes to Berlin.[95] This cate-gorisation included Rawls, whose ideas, as we have noted, were the focus of Geuss's critique. In all this, there is an element of fetishising minor differences. The political preferences ex-pressed by Geuss, Williams, Skinner and Dunn uniformly pre-suppose core principles of liberalism. In the end, each of them is offering refinements on the theme. In this spirit, Williams and Geuss are united in their equation of Rawls with Kant. To that extent they share the purpose of rejecting Kantianism.

In criticising Rawls, Dunn and Skinner implicitly also rebuffed Kantianism, but without seriously studying Kant. Classifying positions gets even more difficult, since Geuss and Williams have tended to distort aspects of Kant or, worse, fundamentally mis-understand him. Debunking Kant, a realistic political theory for Dunn, Geuss and Williams should instead begin with the Hobbesian conception of legitimacy.[96] On the other hand, for Skinner, Hobbes failed to deliver a sufficiently rich understand-ing of freedom as a basis for political justice. From this perspec-tive, politics should not only be about securing rights and pro-tecting liberties, but equally about the promotion of duties, and thus the establishment of a more public-spirited idea of free-dom. Freedom in this sense means the absence of arbitrary de-pendence. In the later Skinner, the principle of non-dependent freedom supplies something like a generalised imperative. Not-withstanding his avowed suspicion of Rawls, this brings Skin-ner close to the popular image of Kant as developing a moral

95. Skinner, 'Idea of Negative Liberty', pp. 194–95.

96. John Dunn, *The Cunning of Unreason: Making Sense of Politics* (London: Harper Collins, 2000), pp. 86–88; Williams, 'Realism and Moralism', p. 3; Geuss, *Philosophy and Real Politics*, pp. 21–22.

philosophy on which to base a political theory. Skinner's stance here neatly captures what Geuss and Williams meant by an 'ethics first' approach. However, this standpoint was never actually advocated by Kant.

Kant's moral theory was folded into a philosophy of history.[97] Within this larger framework, whilst ideally morality ought to give the law to politics, in practice it failed to do so.[98] This analysis fundamentally distinguishes Kant's position from the conception of justice advanced by Rawls. For Kant, while rational norms set a standard for human conduct, self-interest, self-regard and self-deception perpetually thwart their application. There is certainly no lack of realism in this depiction. The moral life is not an easily available mode of behaviour but a struggle in which selfishness wrestles with pure intentions. The possibility of virtuous action is forever overwhelmed by the actuality of self-serving individuals.[99] Given the precariousness of moral judgement, ethics stands in need of favourable conditions to prosper. In Kant's eyes, security was a precondition for its development. Consequently, the effectiveness of the moral will presupposed the enjoyment of basic rights. Rudimentary justice in this sense depended on the existence of the state. For the state to prioritise rights, Kant thought, it had first to acquire a conducive constitutional shape. In turn, establishing a legitimate form of government meant first creating concert among warring nations. However, according to Kant, this would be brought about not by moral enlightenment, but by the

97. Allen W. Wood, *Kant's Ethical Thought* (Cambridge: Cambridge University Press, 1999).

98. Immanuel Kant, 'On the Common Saying: That May Be Correct in Theory, but Is of No Use in Practice' (1793), in *Practical Philosophy*, ed. and trans. Mary J. Gregor (Cambridge: Cambridge University Press, 1996).

99. Kant, *Groundwork*, AA 4: 407.

dynamics of commerce and the play of interests.[100] So much for the picture of Kantianism as a system based on 'ethics first', or the application of an ideal benchmark to the contingencies of power politics. What Geuss and Williams miss in their delineation of Kant is his scepticism about the influence of ethical principles on behaviour. It is fair to say that neo-Kantians, too, underplay this aspect of his philosophy. Rawls is perhaps the most prominent culprit in this regard.

What is striking about Kant is not his lack of interest in 'heteronomous' motivation, or the impact of desires on moral choices. He examined this subject throughout his career in his lectures on anthropology. Equally, Kant was never complacent about the transparency of moral evaluation, or the dependability of impartial judgement. Instead, what is notable about Kant's approach is his categorical distinction between normative and prudential reasoning. According to Geuss, Williams tried to overcome this separation by challenging its terms. To achieve this, he sought to privilege politics over morals: 'What should replace philosophical ethics, in Williams's view, was politics.'[101] If Geuss is right, there is a problem with his reversal of priorities. Geuss proposed that Williams was following Aristotle's lead, since ethics for him was a department of political science. However, the ancient understanding of political life had expired, and for good reasons. In his 1802–3 essay on 'Natural Law', Hegel claimed that the 'absolute ethical life' of the Greeks was centred on the activity of *politeúein*, which meant to live as

---

100. Immanuel Kant, 'Idea for a Universal History with a Cosmopolitan Aim' (1784), in *Anthropology, History, and Education*, ed. and trans. Robert B. Louden and Günter Zöller (Cambridge: Cambridge University Press, 2007); Kant, 'Toward Perpetual Peace', in *Practical Philosophy*.

101. Geuss, 'Did Williams Do Ethics?', p. 177.

a citizen under a free regime.[102] In Hegel's words, this entailed 'living in and with and for one's people, leading a general life wholly devoted to the public interest'.[103] As we have seen, it followed from this that Plato was a child of his time. Like Aristotle, he had internalised the idea of living for one's city. Public sentiment, for the Athenians, governed individual judgement. But the important point is that this arrangement had disappeared. Citing the authority of Gibbon, Hegel noted how the culture of city-state regimes was replaced by the 'languid indifference of private life' that came to characterise the Roman Empire.[104]

Hegel's difficulties with Kant have been broadly covered in the literature.[105] Much of this has centred on his critique of Kant's moral theory.[106] Williams himself saluted the cogency of his challenge.[107] In fact, many of Williams's broadsides are based on Hegel's objections. Nonetheless, an important feature differentiates their respective conclusions. For Hegel, duty and right ought to overlap in modern constitutional monarchies. By

102. G.W.F. Hegel, *Natural Law: The Scientific Ways of Treating Natural Law, Its Place in Moral Philosophy, and Its Relation to the Positive Science of Law (1802–3)*, trans T. M. Knox (Philadelphia: University of Pennsylvania Press, 1975), p. 100. For typical usage, see Thucydides, 1.9; Xenophon, *Anabasis*, 3.2.26; Polybius, 4.76.2.

103. Hegel, *Natural Law*, p. 100.

104. Ibid., p. 102, citing Edward Gibbon, *The Decline and Fall of the Roman Empire*, ed. J. B. Bury, 7 vols (London: Methuen 1909), 1, pp. 63–64.

105. Sally Sedgwick, *Hegel's Critique of Kant: From Dichotomy to Identity* (Oxford: Oxford University Press, 2012); Stephen Houlgate, 'Hegel's Critique of Kant', *Proceedings of the Aristotelian Society*, 89: 1 (2015), pp. 21–41.

106. Karl Ameriks, 'The Hegelian Critique of Kantian Morality,' in *Kant and the Fate of Autonomy: Problems in the Appropriation of Critical Philosophy* (Cambridge: Cambridge University Press, 2000); Allen W. Wood, 'Hegel on Morality', in David James, ed., *Hegel's 'Elements of the Philosophy of Right': A Critical Guide* (Cambridge: Cambridge University Press, 2017).

107. Williams, *Ethics*, p. 104.

comparison, in ancient democracies duty submerged right. In the *Philosophy of Right*, Hegel cited the famous saying attributed to Pythagoras, that right conduct could be instilled in the individual by making him 'the citizen of a state with good laws'.[108] One aspect of this injunction remained relevant in Hegel's time: no one was independent of their socialisation. The 'breath of the spiritual world', as Hegel put it, will eventually find its way into each person's solitude.[109] Yet in another respect Pythagoras's admonition was inapplicable. Modern attitudes were not educated simply through good laws. They were also a product of conscientious self-interrogation. As emphasised already in this book, 'free infinite personality' had become an intrinsic part of European culture. Kant was both a symptom and a cause of that transformation. Consequently, for Hegel, unlike for Geuss and Williams, there was no credible prospect of simply supplanting Kantianism. It could only, strictly speaking, be sublated.

The moral point of view that culminated in Kant was a product of a sequence of world revolutions that formed the subject of Hegel's historical and political philosophy. As we have seen, Christianity succeeded the demise of the ancient republics, having already revolutionised the principles of Judaism. Modern subjectivity resulted from this shift as modified by the Reformation and the Enlightenment. The overall process was neither seamless nor predetermined. But it did insert a gap between our world and the ancients. Williams believed we were closer to the Greeks than is sometimes thought.[110] And it is of course true

108. Hegel, *Philosophy of Right*, §153R. Cf. Hegel, *Phenomenology*, §352.

109. Hegel, *Philosophy of Right*, §153A.

110. Bernard Williams, *Shame and Necessity* (Berkeley, CA: University of California Press, 1993), ch. 1.

that we have inherited vital elements of their civilisation. However, as Hegel saw, their legacy was mediated, and so their input was transformed. The rise of critical consciousness was one result of this transfiguration. It has become an ineliminable part of our heritage. Under modern conditions, justice must be vindicated by our own lights. Nonetheless, subjecting objective norms to individual standards of judgement is a fraught and potentially hazardous activity. It breeds the raging attitudes of disaffected conscience evident during the French Revolution and since. Hegel sought to reconcile such dissidence with actuality. The alternative was a dizzying leap into the void.

Conclusion

ONLY TWO POSTWAR PHILOSOPHERS have made serious attempts to revive Hegel as a focal point for thinking about politics. These are Joachim Ritter and Charles Taylor respectively. Of course, Jürgen Habermas is also a relevant figure in this context. Since early in his career, he has repeatedly engaged with Hegel's work in an effort to develop a political philosophy of his own. However, although he has turned intermittently to Hegel, Habermas has for the most part set out to reject his insights. Naturally, he has acknowledged the scale of Hegel's contribution. Moreover, commentators have often noted his debt to Hegelian patterns of thought.[1] Nonetheless, Habermas has from the start been keen to signal the distance between him and his predecessor. He first adopted this attitude in the early 1960s, when he published a number of essays on Hegel's

---

1. Fred Dallmayr, 'The Discourse of Modernity: Hegel and Habermas', *The Journal of Philosophy*, 84: 11 (November 1987), pp. 682–92; Kenneth Baynes, 'Freedom and Recognition in Hegel and Habermas', *Philosophy and Social Criticism*, 28: 1 (2002), pp. 1–17; Robert Brandom, 'Towards Reconciling Two Heroes: Habermas and Hegel', *Argumenta*, 1: 1 (2015), pp. 29–42.

political writings.[2] There he approved some aspects of the youthful Hegel's approach, but this was intended to contrast with what he regarded as his apostasy. It goes without saying that the charge of defection is a familiar one, originally rehearsed in the 1850s. Repeating essentially the same accusation, Habermas claimed that Hegel, from around 1807, began to adopt a bogus theory of consciousness, a metaphysical conception of absolute spirit and a posture of resignation towards established power. Although most scholars contest the accuracy of this account, Habermas has stuck by his central contention that Hegel subscribed to a grandiose metaphysical world picture which encouraged reconciliation with established authority.[3]

Habermas extended his line of reproach in *Knowledge and Human Interests*. He recognised Hegel's indebtedness to the traditions of scepticism, but concluded that his doubts led him to dogmatism. From this perspective, the arguments of the *Phenomenology* were ultimately 'half-hearted'. Habermas's challenge followed directly in the footsteps of Adorno: 'from the beginning,' as Habermas put it, 'Hegel presumes as given a knowledge of the Absolute'.[4] Two decades later, in *The Philosophical Discourse of Modernity*, Habermas returned once more to Hegel as an intellectual resource. He remarked that Hegel

2. These have been collected in Jürgen Habermas, *Theory and Practice* (1963), trans. John Viertel (London: Heinemann, 1974).

3. For criticism of the Habermasian account, see Robert Pippin, 'Hegel, Modernity and Habermas' (1991), in *Idealism as Modernism: Hegelian Variations* (Cambridge: Cambridge University Press, 1997); Douglas Moggach, 'Hegel and Habermas', *The European Legacy*, 2: 3 (1997), pp. 550–56.

4. Jürgen Habermas, *Knowledge and Human Interests* (1968), trans. Jeremy J. Shapiro (Cambridge: Polity Press, 1987), p. 10.

stood out among his contemporaries in making modernity a pivotal concern of philosophy. Yet, having taken this positive step, Habermas alleged that Hegel squandered his advance by sacrificing the critical import of political theory. Hegel is supposed to have done this by concocting a spurious solution to the antagonistic character of modern commercial society. As Habermas construed Hegel, the rampant selfishness of civil society is overcome by the subordination of the individual to the state. On this reading, the competing aims of self-interested agents in society are coordinated by means of subjection to the institutions of a rational state.[5]

According to Habermas, everything hangs on the justification for the rationality of Hegel's state. It is precisely here that he took the credibility of Hegel's strategy to break down. As he argued in 1992, Hegel developed a model that set 'unattainable standards for us'.[6] According to this verdict, Hegelian values were unreachable, because they could not be vindicated, except when judged 'from the viewpoint of absolute spirit'.[7] Since it appeared that modern sensibilities could no longer credit this perspective, the implementation of Hegel's vision was assumed to depend on coercion. For Habermas, this recourse was an affront to the very idea of valid norms. It was on this objection that he sought to ground his own political theory. What

5. Jürgen Habermas, 'Hegel's Concept of Modernity', in *The Philosophical Discourse of Modernity* (1985), trans. Frederick Lawrence (Cambridge: Polity Press, 1987), p. 40.

6. Jürgen Habermas, *Between Facts and Norms* (1992), trans. William Rehg (Cambridge: Cambridge University Press, 1996), p. xxxix.

7. Jürgen Habermas, 'From Kant to Hegel and Back Again: The Move towards Detranscendentalization' (1999), in *Truth and Justification*, ed. and trans. Barbara Fultner (Cambridge: Polity Press, 2003), p. 206.

mattered to him was 'uncoerced will formation'.[8] In a sense, this is what really mattered to Hegel as well. However, on Hegelian principles, freedom is not a function of some ideal form of association. It is based on self-subjection to structures of authority. Hegel's argument therefore turned on the legitimacy of forms authority whose soundness Habermas took to be unfounded. This was not a marginal uncertainty about Hegel's system; it registered an opposition to his whole approach.

Ritter, on the other hand, had no such antipathy. He positively embraced what he regarded as Hegel's concept of freedom. In fact, it was largely on the back of readings of Aristotle and Hegel that Ritter built his postwar political philosophy.[9] Having worked under Cassirer in the 1920s, he became a *Privatdozent* in Hamburg in the 1930s, and then moved to Münster after the war. At that point he joined the general search for a convincing explanation of National Socialism. This required a philosophical inquiry into the inherited shape of politics, amounting to a 'hermeneutics of historical actuality'.[10] According to various strands of German opinion after 1945, the Nazi state had not simply been a domestic aberration. Instead, it was seen as a symptom of a deeper European malaise.[11] Among such analysts, its original cause was often traced to the 'pathologies'

8. Habermas, *Philosophical Discourse*, p. 40.

9. Joachim Ritter, *Metaphysik und Politik: Studien zu Aristoteles und Hegel* (Frankfurt am Main: Suhrkamp, 1969).

10. On this theme in Ritter, see Mark Schweda, 'Metaphysik und Politik: Joachim Ritters Philosophie als "Hermeneutik der geschichtlichen Wirklichkeit"', in Schweda and Ulrich von Bülow, eds, *Entzweite Moderne: Zur Actualität Joachim Ritters und seiner Schüler* (Göttingen: Wallstein Verlag, 2017).

11. Gerhard Ritter, *Europa und die deutsche Frage: Betrachtungen über die geschichtliche Eigenart des Deutschen Staatsdenkens* (Munich: F. Bruckmann Verlag, 1948); Hans Rothfels, *The German Opposition to Hitler* (Hinsdale, IL: Henry Regnery Company, 1948).

of modernity, most usually to the watershed of 1789.[12] According to this framing, the doctrine of the 'rights of man' had displaced the traditions of Christian natural law. It was claimed that this shift in priorities led to a loss of value and ultimately to the collapse of the Weimar Republic. In opposition to this reactionary-style reconstruction, Ritter drew on Hegel as an advocate of reconciliation (*Versöhnung*). The idea was to foster rapprochement with modernity. This set an example for disciples who followed in his wake, among them Odo Marquand, Hermann Lübbe and Ernst-Wolfgang Böckenförde.[13]

Ritter drew inspiration from his interpretation of Hegel's understanding of the French Revolution. His grasp of the relevant events was abstract and generalised, and in point of fact remote from Hegel's more complex and sceptical assessment. Nonetheless, the idea was to welcome 1789 as the gateway to the present. This implied a rejection of regressive forms of nostalgia, and an acceptance of the prevailing forms of subjectivity. There could be no restoration of the world before the deluge. The value of autonomy and the principle of individualism were acknowledged to be ineliminable. Unlike Arnold Gehlen and Helmut Schelsky, Ritter renounced the habit of blind submission to institutions and deplored the prospect of generalised political apathy. At the same time, emerging out of the widespread disruption of the 1930s, and the comprehensive dictatorship that followed, Ritter prized the achievement of stability.[14] For him,

12. This diagnosis was apparent in the subtitle of Reinhart Koselleck, *Kritik und Krise: Ein Beitrag zur Pathogenese der bürgerlichen Welt* (Munich: Alber Verlag, 1959).

13. Jens Hacke, *Philosophie der Bürgerlichkeit: Die liberalkonservative Begründung der Bundesrepublik* (Göttingen: Vandenhoeck & Ruprecht, 2006).

14. Aline-Florence Manent, '"In der Bundesrepublik zu Hause sein". Joachim Ritter und die politische Philosophie der Stabilität', in Schweda and von Bülow, eds, *Entzweite Moderne*.

this meant that politics ought to redress the disaggregating effects that beset modern civil society. It also implied that 'negation' could not be a value in itself. There was a need for national cohesion alongside aimless critique. He agreed with Hegel that the era of unreflective trust was over, but there still remained a requirement for social confidence.

In drawing on the wisdom of Hegel in this way, there was a tendency on Ritter's part to minimise the divergence between the values of the nineteenth and twentieth centuries. Mass democracy, communism and fascism only emerged after the death of Hegel, and so it is prima facie clumsy to treat both situations as symmetrical. Charles Taylor has likewise been inclined to diminish the gap between the two eras. In the 'Preface' to *Hegel and Modern Society*, he claimed that Hegel provided the means of confronting present-day problems.[15] His relevance, it seems, was taken to lie in his conception of a shared predicament, rather than in specific solutions he might have offered. The idea was that we still face an array of circumstances that first appeared in the 1790s. Taylor thought that Hegel furnished the most cogent representation of the situation. He submitted that his own epoch, much like Hegel's, was endeavouring to come to terms with the Enlightenment. To him, this meant that we still live under the yoke of utilitarian values. He suggested that a combination of atomism and instrumentalism constituted the main characteristics of capitalist society. However, he also contended that a yearning for alternative values persisted. These included the longing for community and freedom as expressed in the eighteenth century by Herder and Kant.[16] For Taylor, Hegel grasped this condition of plural

15. Charles Taylor, *Hegel and Modern Society* (Cambridge: Cambridge University Press, 1979, 2015), p. xiii.

16. Ibid., pp. 9, 67, 69, 132.

aspirations, and undertook to bring about their mutual accommodation.

Taylor believed that the specific form of Hegel's solution was non-viable. According to what most readers now see as a far-fetched portrait of the *Phenomenology*, he assumed that Hegel saw nature as an 'emanation of Spirit' and history in turn as the 'unfolding' of this radiating *Geist*.[17] But while Hegel's metaphysics were dismissed as defective, at the same time his social theory was applauded for its bite. Not least, in Taylor's opinion, Hegel's understanding of freedom exposed the dangerous frivolity which he himself associated with the politics of May 1968, and perhaps more generally with the posture of the New Left at that time.[18] Specifically, Taylor objected to the absence of a positive agenda: values like pleasure, creativity, spontaneity and immediacy were not just vague, but also abstract. They were predicated on the absence of opposition as well as pre-existing structural limitations.

By extension, Taylor took the general rage for *décloisonnement* (breaking down barriers) to be vacuous. In his judgement, it equated freedom with the state of being 'untrammelled'.[19] This fostered opposition to every kind of division—including, *in extremis*, all forms of representation, and functional distinctions between work and leisure. It likewise bred hostility to every species of hierarchy. On this model, virtually any institution could be regarded as repressive. Yet, after the layers of imperfection had been swept away, it was unclear what kinds of establishment might be introduced. Following Hegel, Taylor construed these hankerings as a desire for contentless freedom. They

17. Ibid., p. 135.
18. Ibid., p. 69.
19. Ibid., pp. 151, 162.

amounted to a recurrence of the impulse to 'leap' in a single bound into a new world order. What was missing was any attempt to contextualise the inclination, along with a failure to examine the preconditions for its realisation.

The application of this Hegelian insight to the late 1960s might be strained, but the effort is surely not absurd. After all, Hegel had himself reflected on student unrest in the context of the disturbances leading to the Carlsbad Decrees. When he wrote the 'Preface' to the *Philosophy of Right*, he was delicately treading between the authority of the government and the ideological ambitions of student associations (*Burschenschaften*) which at that time were being stoked by enthusiastic professors.[20] On the one hand, student aims around 1819 ought not to be confused with the agitation unleashed in 1968. The *Burschenschaften* embodied their own curious mix of patriotism, Christian piety and liberal reformism, little of which can be mapped onto modern campus protests. On the other hand, Hegel was trying to determine the precise character of moral outrage and its source in modern disaffected conscience. There are evident continuities between the mindset he uncovered and the subsequent history of what he taught us to call the 'moral point of view'. However, the same does not apply to Taylor's larger analysis bearing on the character of modern social conflict. Central here is the value of 'identity' in Taylor's framework, linked in his mind to the 'politics of recognition'.[21] Once again, Hegel for him is the pre-eminent student of this phenomenon.

20. Adriaan Th. Peperzak, *Philosophy and Politics: A Commentary on the Preface to Hegel's 'Philosophy of Right'* (Dordrecht: Martinus Nijhoff, 1987).

21. Charles Taylor, 'The Politics of Recognition', in Amy Gutmann, ed., *Multiculturalism: Examining the Politics of Recognition*, (Princeton, NJ: Princeton University Press, 1994), p. 25.

Yet there are two immediate problems with Taylor's approach: first, he misrepresented Hegel's take on the dynamics of recognition; and second, he projected onto Hegel his own conception of social reality.

Taylor claimed that the passion for recognition can only be satisfied by reciprocity between equals.[22] However, despite his doubts about Hegel's presumed metaphysics, Taylor's model is more teleological than the original. The figures of master and slave in the Hegelian paradigm only discover what they are seeking as their struggle proceeds.[23] But here, by Taylor's lights, the endpoint is evident from the start. Furthermore, while Hegel's protagonists in the first instance are struggling for survival, Taylor's are battling to gratify their identities. This last perspective was meant to supply an outline of 'multicultural' society—as found in the United States, France or Quebec.[24] However, the rudimentary concept of identity in play is not adequate for decoding the totality of relations, either in Hegel's time or our own. Hegel himself was certainly alive to the insufficiency. In his draft essay on the German Constitution from around 1800, he set out his view that identity, though once the fulcrum of allegiance, had been supplanted by a more complex set of arrangements. Modern citizens, for Hegel, lacked the kind of uniform culture that underwrote the patriotism of ancient Greece and Rome. 'In our times,' he wrote, politics was not grounded on an integrated structure of 'customs, education, and language.'[25]

22. Ibid., p. 50.

23. G.W.F. Hegel, *The Phenomenology of Spirit* (1807), ed. and trans. Michael Inwood (Oxford: Oxford University Press, 2018), §§178ff.

24. See Taylor, 'Politics of Recognition', p. 60.

25. G.W.F. Hegel, 'The German Constitution', in *Hegel: Political Writings*, ed. Laurence Dickey and H. B. Nisbet, trans. Nisbet (Cambridge: Cambridge University Press, 1999), p. 19.

Taylor interpreted Hegel in the light of Rousseau. As a consequence, he elevated the desire for 'esteem' (*amour-propre*) as the defining feature of social interaction.[26] There can be no doubting the significance of this craving to be appreciated as a feature of interpersonal and intercultural relations. But, in isolation, it scarcely provides a nuanced account of modern society in all its complexity. As a blanket term it encourages indiscriminate amalgamation, blending one distinct historical moment into another: a problem of identity in the eighteenth century becomes a problem of identity in the twenty-first, with concrete realities which make all the difference rendered immaterial. However, compelling political analysis should achieve the opposite result, locating different experiences within their appropriate temporal registers. After all, to understand an occurrence means to appreciate its historical background. As I have tried to show throughout this book, this applies with equal force to the values of distinct periods. It is this insight that defines the Hegelian approach to philosophy as it strives to combine historical reconstruction with conceptual discrimination. As Hegel summarised the point in his *Encyclopedia*, it is a mistake to view the business of thought as a mode of static inquiry. The implications of a scheme of value formulated in one age do not necessarily follow from the principles developed in another.[27]

Based on my assumptions, the history of political thought is diagnostic rather than prescriptive. It helps us understand the character of political structures as products of earlier

26. Taylor, 'Politics of Recognition', pp. 45ff. By contrast, for crucial differences between Rousseau and Hegel, see Axel Honneth, *Recognition: A Chapter in the History of European Ideas* (Cambridge: Cambridge University Press, 2021).

27. G.W.F. Hegel, *Encyclopedia of the Philosophical Sciences in Basic Outline*, Part 1: *Science of Logic* (1817), trans. Klaus Brinkmann and Daniel O. Dahlstrom (Cambridge: Cambridge University Press, 2010), pp. 14–15.

constellations of forces. It spurs us to pick apart distinct formations as well as to identify continuities across time. Its first duty is to avoid confusion between these dimensions. Viewed from this angle, the most important task of contextualisation is to highlight the diversity of contexts, not least their lack of homogeneous synchronicity. We do not study Hegel to confound his circumstances with our own, but precisely to evaluate discrepancies between past and present. The process might reveal correlations and affinities, or equally it might bring out significant disparities. As Hegel argued near the beginning of the *Science of Logic*, there is no merit in cleaving 'to the forms on an earlier culture': 'They are like withered leaves pushed aside by the new buds already being generated at their roots.'[28] However, the dialectic was equally a process of preservation, which demanded that we take account of persistence through change. As Hegel emphasised, it is imperative to recognise the distance between ourselves and Plato, just as it is vital to acknowledge the common ground between Rousseau and the French Revolution.

28. G.W.F. Hegel, *The Science of Logic* (1812–16), ed. and trans. George di Giovanni (Cambridge: Cambridge University Press, 2010), p. 8.

INDEX

Abraham, 92–93, 97

absolute, the, 238, 290–91

Absolute Knowing, 131

absolutism, 15

Adorno, Theodor, xvi, 194, 226–27, 232–39, 242

Aeschylus, 160

After Utopia (Shklar), 269

d'Alembert, Jean-Baptiste le Rond, 136

Alexander the Great, 105

alienation, 13, 23, 42, 139, 140, 146, 155, 180, 217, 273. *See also* estrangement; social alienation

Altenstein, Karl von, 98

Althusser, Louis, 5, 241

America, xi, 3, 44, 75, 223, 275. *See also* American Revolution; United States

American Revolution, 263, 277, 280, 282

amour-propre, 39, 298. *See also* self-conceit; self-love

Anaxagoras, 116

Ancient Greece, xi, 13, 14, 15, 22–23, 26, 42–43, 55, 62, 82, 89, 92, 187, 192, 213, 215, 229, 243, 285–87, 297; Arendt on, 252–56; Cambridge School on, 276–77; Hegel on decline of city-state(s) in, 37–39; Hegel on ethical

life (*Sittlichkeit*) in, 132–33, 151, 202–8, 285–86; Hegel on religion in, 89–90; Hegel on revolution and, 26; Voegelin on, 251–52. *See also* *Antigone* (Sophocles); Antiquity; Aristotle; Athenians; Athens; city-state(s); Homer; Lycurgus; Oedipus; *Oresteia* (Aeschylus); Plato; polis; Solon; Sparta

Ancient Rome, ix, xi–xii, 14–15, 26, 37–39, 42–43, 63, 82, 84, 89–90, 133, 144, 158–59, 171, 177–78, 180–81, 192, 203, 229, 253, 254–55, 277, 279–80, 286, 297. *See also* Antiquity; Roman jurisprudence and law

Annales School, 262

annulment, 95. *See also* critique; dialectic; negation

'An Old Question Raised Again: Is the Human Race Constantly Progressing?' (Kant), 76–77

Anscombe, Elizabeth, 261–62, 268

Antigone (Sophocles), 132, 253

anti-humanism, 3. *See also* humanism; postmodernism

antiquarianism, 260, 264

Antiquities of the Jews (Josephus), 92

Antiquity, 192, 213, 254. *See also* Ancient Greece; Ancient Rome

A NOTE ON THE TYPE

This book has been composed in Arno, an Old-style serif typeface in the
classic Venetian tradition, designed by Robert Slimbach at Adobe.

Printed in the USA
CPSIA information can be obtained
at www.ICGtesting.com
JSHW082129230923
48331JS00002B/3/J